The Ionian Islands

Corfu, Cephalonia,
Ithaka and Beyond

CANCELLED

John Freely

CANCELLED

I.B. TAURIS

LONDON · NEW YORK

Published in 2008 by I.B.Tauris & Co. Ltd
6 Salem Road, London W2 4BU
175 Fifth Avenue, New York NY 10010
www.ibtauris.com

In the United States and Canada distributed by Palgrave Macmillan,
a division of St. Martin's Press, 175 Fifth Avenue, New York NY 10010

ISBN 978 1 84511 696 5

A full CIP record for this book is available from the British Library
A full CIP record for this book is available from the Library of Congress
Library of Congress catalog card: available

Typeset in Minion by Dexter Haven Associates Ltd, London
Printed and bound in India by Replika Press Pvt. Ltd

Contents

Introduction   1

1   The Ionian Islands   7
2   Corfu I: The Town   27
3   Corfu II: The Kanoni Peninsula   55
4   Corfu III: Around the Island   67
5   Paxos   89
6   Lefkas   103
7   Ithaka   127
8   Cephalonia   149
9   Zakynthos   179
10 Kythera   207

Appendices

1   Chronology   233
2   Festivals (*Paneyeria*)   235
3   Bibliography   239
4   Glossary   243

Index   245

Introduction

This is a book about the Ionian Islands: Corfu, Paxos, Ithaka, Lefkas, Cephalonia, Zakynthos and Kythera. These are the westernmost of the Greek isles, the first six of them rising from the Ionian Sea between Greece and Italy, the seventh lying off the south-eastern cape of the Peloponnesos. Corfu and the other Ionian Islands have been renowned since antiquity for their beauty, part of the attraction that has now made them internationally famous as summer resorts. Anthony Sherley was the first English traveller to sing the praises of Corfu, writing of it nostalgically in his *Persian Adventure*, published in 1601.

> A Greekish isle, and the most pleasant place that ever our
> eyes beheld for the exercise of a solitary and contemplative
> life… In our travels many times, falling into dangers and
> unpleasant places, this only island would be the place where
> we would wish ourselves to end our lives.

My book is a guide to the historic monuments and other places of interest on the Ionian isles as well as to the way of life of the islanders, past and present, which I first came to know half a lifetime ago, before the tide of tourism engulfed the Greek world, changing it beyond recognition.

Greek island civilisation is as old as that of mainland Greece but with a greater continuity because of the remoteness of the isles. The Ionian Islands, as stepping stones between Greece and Italy, as well as between the Greek mainland and Crete, have been involved in every act of the unending historical drama that has been played out in the eastern Mediterranean since settlers first made their way out to the isles in the night of time. The tides of history that have washed over the Ionian Islands have left not only monuments but also patterns of culture that span the whole timeline of Greek civilisation, extending back even to the pre-Hellenic dawn of human existence in what is now Greece.

One aspect of Greek life that keeps it in touch with its past is its religious calendar. This revolves around the religious festivals known as *paneyeria*, which mark the passing seasons of the agricultural year, whose cycles were established in antiquity, adapted by the succession of peoples and religions that took root in the archipelago – Greek and Italian, pagan and Christian – and celebrated in songs and dances that have not changed since time immemorial. The Ionian Islands celebrate all these *paneyeria*, the high points in the life of every community in the archipelago, and the traveller fortunate enough to come upon them is always welcome.

The first chapter is a brief history of the Ionian Islands from antiquity to the present. This is followed by chapters on the individual islands of the archipelago, along with their satellite isles, describing their topography, history, monuments and customs in itineraries that take one to all their distinctive villages, churches, monasteries, medieval fortresses, archaeological sites and other places of interest. There are also appendices with information that might help in exploring the islands, such as the dates and location of their *paneyeria*, where the famous folk dances and songs of the islands are still performed in church courtyards and village squares as they were in times past.

Despite the commercialism of modern tourism the Ionian Islands still have an air of romance, partly because of their location on the seaways between Greece and Italy, which adds an Italianate element to their Hellenic character, and also because of their association with the wanderings of Odysseus. The Greek poet Kostis Palamas catches this enchantment on the wing in these lines from his *Song of the Seven Islands*, translated by Ian Scott-Kilvert:

> Your waters dazzle like a floor of diamonds
> Westward your tides
> Grope and caress the shores of Italy.
> In a circumference of blue the seven islands
> Foam-chiselled, rise, dissolve,
> Join hands and dance upon the waves
>
> Zakynthos drowned in flowers
> Cephalonia seamed with toil
> Kythera and Paxoi
> Corfu the enchantress of the mind and heart
> Ithaka a mariner's rhyme in stone
> Levkas the watch-tower of the Armatoli.
>
> From the Ionian shore
> From the Ionian shore
> Since Homer, since Solomos,
> The poet's song, the statesman's art
> Haunted these islands like sea-birds,
>
> As if here lay the fields of Elysium
> And the heroes of myth and of history
> The shades of Odysseus, the spirit of Capodistrias
> Walked together under a Greek sky.

GREECE

one
The Ionian Islands

T he Ionian Islands are the westernmost of the Greek archipelagos that are scattered like marine constellations across the eastern Mediterranean. All but one of the Ionian isles lie off the western coast of Greece in the Ionian Sea, south of the Adriatic Sea, with the high-heeled shoe of Italy off to the north-west.

There are seven principal Ionian Islands: Corfu, Paxos, Lefkas, Ithaka, Cephalonia, Zakynthos and Kythera, with the first six in the Ionian Sea and the seventh far removed from the others south of Cape Malea in the Peloponnesos, the southern part of the Greek mainland. (Kythera was added to the Ionian Islands in 1669 by the Venetians, who had previously administered the island from Crete, which had fallen to the Turks earlier that year.)

The Ionian Islands are the peaks of a submerged mountain range that extends from the north-western corner of the Balkans through the seas bounding Greece to its west, curving from there in a great arc around to Crete. The islands in the southern part of the Ionian Sea are close to two separate geologic faults extending out from the Greek mainland; one of these runs south from the mountains of Epirus, the north-westernmost region of mainland Greece, and ends at Lefkas; the second, which is the more severe flaw, stretches from the western end of the Corinthian Gulf to the seismic epicentre in the bottom of the sea between Cephalonia and Zakynthos. These faults have given rise to numerous earthquakes, the two most recent occurring in 1948 and 1953, with the first centred on Lefkas and the second hitting Ithaka, Cephalonia and Zakynthos. The two quakes destroyed more than 70 per cent of the buildings on the four islands, sparing few of their historic monuments.

The high rainfall of the islands in the Ionian Sea has made them unusually rich in wild flowers and flowering fruit trees, bushes, herbs and weeds, particularly in Corfu and Zakynthos, known to the Venetians as Zante, which they called *Fior de Levante*, or Flower of the East. Zakynthos is famous for its sultana grapes, the basis for the currant trade that in times past made it the wealthiest of the Ionian isles. Zakynthos is also celebrated for its *verdea* wine, which led Sir Richard Torkington to write after his visit to the island in 1517: 'There is the greatest wines and strongest that ever I drank in my life.'

The landscapes of the Ionian isles are dominated by the olive tree, covering the islands in vast groves that look like silvered green seas as their leaves quiver in the breeze. Another ubiquitous Greek tree is the pine, whose resin has since antiquity been used to caulk ships and to flavour retsina wine. The most beautiful variety is the Aleppo pine, which usually graces country chapels and the courtyards of old Venetian mansions. Still another is the tamarisk, whose wind-swept groves often shade remote beaches on the islands, forming a pale green frieze between the blues of sea and sky. Less common is the palm tree, which one sees occasionally in the neglected gardens of old Venetian estates in the interior of the islands.

A small tree with interesting mythological associations is the bay or laurel (in Greek, *daphne*), which in ancient Greece was sacred to Apollo, because the mountain nymph he pursued turned into that form to elude him. Laurel trees have since classical Greek times been associated with catharsis, or ritual cleansing; hand-brooms made from its branches were (and still are) used to sweep the floors of holy places, and its leaves were affixed to houses as talismans, carried in procession and used to crown the victors in athletic games, and even today at religious festivals are scattered on the floors of churches.

Another tree with mythological connections is the fragrant myrtle, which was used at weddings because of its association with Aphrodite, and whose leaves were used to weave crowns for initiates in the Eleusinian Mysteries. In Christianity it became associated with the Panagia Myrtidiotissa, Our Lady of the Myrtles, whose miraculous icons are always found enveloped in myrtle leaves, as was the fragment of the True Cross discovered in Jerusalem by St Helena, mother of the Emperor Constantine the Great.

The Ionian isles have an abundance of fruit in season. A catalogue of some of the fruits in the Greek cornucopia, all of which grow on the Ionian isles, is found in these verses from the *Palatine Anthology*, a collection of ancient Greek poetry:

> Lamon, the gardener, to Priapos prays,
> Grant that his limbs keep strong and all his trees,
> And this sweet gift before him lays:
> This golden pomegranate, this apple, these
> Elfin-faced figs, new grapes, a walnut green
> Within its skin, cucumber's leafy sheen,
>
> And dusky olives, gold with gleaming oil –
> To you, oh friend of travellers, this spoil.

Homer does not mention the Ionian Islands as such, and there is some confusion about the names that he uses for the various isles of the group. Homer's first mention of these islands in the *Iliad* is in the 'Catalogue of Ships', in which the only isles that can be identified definitely are Zakynthos, Cephalonia and Ithaka, whose combined contingent of twelve ships was commanded by Odysseus, son of Laertes. This contingent is mentioned directly after one from 'Doulichion and the sacred Echinai islands', a flotilla of forty ships led by Meges, son of Phyleus. The Echinaia are obviously the Echinades, a tiny archipelago off the mainland east of Ithaka, but the identification of Doulichion is uncertain, though some have suggested that it is the ancient city of Pale on Cephalonia. Corfu, known in Greek as Kerkyra, is not mentioned in either of the Homeric epics, but it is generally identified with the island of

Scheria, which in the *Odyssey* is the land of the Phaiakians, who had first settled there under the leadership of 'godlike Nausithoos', father of King Alkinoos. Homer describes Scheria as being 'at the extreme ends of the Earth', which is to say that in his time it was on the outer limits of the *oecumenos*, the 'inhabited world', particularly for a poet from the eastern Aegean.

According to mythology, Corfu took its Greek name from the nymph Kerkyra, but there are two different versions of her origins. One version has it that she was a daughter of the river god Asopus by the Arcadian maiden Netope. The second version says that she was the daughter of the sea god Oceanus and the goddess Tethys, the personification of the feminine fecundity of the sea. Both versions agree that Kerkyra was kidnapped by Poseidon, who married her on the northernmost of the Ionian isles, which was thereafter named for her. They also agree in saying that Kerkyra bore Poseidon a son, Phaeax, who gave his name to the Phaiakians.

The earliest reference to the Ionian Sea is by Aeschylus in his *Prometheus Bound*, written ca 463 BC. There Prometheus identifies Io as 'the child of Inachus, the sting-vexed virgin, for whom the heart of Zeus is hot with love, but Hera hates her and drives her far asea, travelling perforce in unexampled ways'. Telling Io of her wanderings, Prometheus describes how she crossed the lower Adriatic (literally 'the Gulf of Rhea'), 'wherefore that gulf and corner of the main shall bear the name Ionian for all time'.

Corfu is also associated with the mythical voyage of the Argonauts, one version of which has Jason and Medea marrying on the island at the end of their long journey from the Land of Colchis.

One version of the myth of Aphrodite has it that the goddess of love was born on the island of Kythera. Hesiod writes that she was the daughter of the sky god Uranus, whose sperm spilled into the sea after he was castrated by his son Cronus, giving birth to Aphrodite, the 'foam-born goddess'.

The Ionian Islands were first inhabited in the early Palaeolithic period (ca 70,000–40,000 BC), as evidenced by stone tools found in a cave at Agios Mattheos on Corfu. Archaeologists have found flint works on the beaches of Cephalonia and Zakynthos dating from the Mesolithic period (ca 10,000–6000 BC), as well as a settlement at Sidari on Corfu dating from early in the Neolithic period (ca 6000–3000 BC). Bronze Age (ca 3000–1150 BC) settlements have also been found on Corfu at Kephali, Aphionas and Ermones. During the Bronze Age there was an influx of settlers from Asia Minor on Lefkas, Ithaka, Cephalonia, Zakynthos and Kythera.

Excavations on Kythera have found the remains of a trading colony established by Minoans from Crete dating from the period ca 2000–1500 BC. The first Greek-speaking people arrived on the islands in the Ionian Sea during the Mycenaean period (ca 1500–1150 BC), probably crossing from Epiros, in what is now north-western Greece and southern Albania. During the Dark Ages of the ancient world (1150–750 BC) the Phoenicians seem to have had a trading post on Kythera, and perhaps also on Corfu.

The islands in the Ionian Sea have always been stepping stones between the Greek mainland and southern Italy. The Corinthians, for example, founded a colony on Kerkyra in 733 BC, using it as a port on their trading expeditions to southern Italy and Sicily. The Corinthians also founded a colony on Lefkas ca 625 BC.

Lefkas was the only one of the Ionian Islands to contribute a contingent to the Greek fleet that defeated the Persian navy of King Xerxes at the Battle of Salamis in 480 BC, sending three ships. The Lefkadians and Cephalonians were the only Ionian islanders who fought at the Battle of Plataea the following year, when the Greeks defeated the army of Xerxes and forced him to give up his invasion of Greece, ending the Persian Wars.

During the fourth year of the Peloponnesian War, in 427 BC, a civil war erupted on Kerkyra between the supporters of Sparta and those who sided with Athens. Thucydides writes: 'There were fathers who killed their sons; men were dragged from the temples or butchered on the very altars; some were walled up in the temple of Dionysos and died there.'

During the early Hellenistic period, which began with the accession of Alexander the Great in 336 BC, the Ionian Islands were part of Macedonia. In 229 BC Kerykra was captured by Queen Teuta of the Illyrians, whose corsairs had been ravaging the Adriatic. The Romans soon recaptured the island in their successful campaign to put down the Illyrian pirates, after which Kerkyra was in effect a Roman colony. The other Ionian Islands fell to the Romans during their war with Philip V of Macedon in the years 200–188 BC. Then in 146 BC the whole of Greece and its islands was annexed by Rome.

A new era began in AD 330, when Constantine the Great shifted his capital to Constantinople. This gave rise to what came to be called the Byzantine Empire, the Christian Greek realm that developed from the pagan Latin empire of Rome. According to tradition, Christianity had already come to the Ionian Islands by then through the missionary work of SS Jason and Sosipator, two disciples of St Paul who preached on Kerkyra. In 876 Kerkyra became a *metropolis*, or archbishopric, under the direct jurisdiction of the Patriarch of Constantinople.

The Greek islands were cut off from the capital in Constantinople throughout much of the Byzantine period, as waves of corsairs and conquerors swept though the Aegean and Ionian Seas. Kerkyra was raided by the Goths under Totila in 562, which led to the building of the first fortress in what is now Corfu town. During the ninth and tenth centuries the islands were on several occasions attacked by the Saracens, whose raids forced the islanders to abandon most of their coastal towns to settle in remote mountain villages, where they could take refuge in towers called *pyrgoi* or in fortified monasteries.

In 1081 the Normans under Robert Guiscard captured Kerkyra at the beginning of the first of their three invasions of Greece, taking all the other islands in the Ionian Sea during their subsequent raids in 1148 and 1182. The Byzantines managed to recapture the Ionian Islands after the first two of these invasions, but in the peace treaty that ended the third one, in 1187, the empire lost Ithaka, Cephalonia and Zakynthos (known to the Latins as Zante), which were ruled as a personal fief by the Norman Admiral Margaritone. When Margaritone died in 1194 he was succeeded by his son-in-law Matthew Orsini, the scion of a noble Roman family, who thus founded what came to be known as the County Palatine of Cephalonia.

Another chapter in Greek history began in 1204, when Constantinople was captured by the Latin knights of the Fourth Crusade and the Venetians under Doge Enrico Dandolo. The Latins divided up the former territories of the Byzantine Empire, with Crete and most of the other islands falling to the share of the Venetians, who then set out to conquer their new possessions. The Cyclades, the islands in the central Aegean, were taken in 1207 by Marco Sanudo, Dandolo's nephew, who thus founded the Latin Duchy of the Archipelago. That same year the Venetians took Corfu, as Kerkyra was known to the Latins, and five years later they conquered Crete.

The Greeks reconquered Constantinople from the Latins in 1261, restoring the Byzantine Empire in its ancient capital on the Bosphorus, but of their former island possessions they were able to recapture only some of the northern Aegean isles.

The first Venetian occupation of Corfu lasted only until 1214, when the island became part of the Despotate of Epiros, one of the fragments of the Byzantine Empire that had survived the Latin conquest. In 1267 Corfu and the County Palatine of Cephalonia passed to Charles of Anjou, King of the Two Sicilies (i.e. Sicily and southern Italy), founder of the Angevin dynasty.

Angevin rule lasted until 1368 on Corfu and until 1404 on the other Greek islands in the Ionian Sea. Prince Robert of Taranto deposed the last Orsini as Count of Cephalonia in 1324, and 33 years later he awarded the principality to William Tocco of Benevento. Thus began the dynasty of the Toccos, who broke their feudal ties to the Angevins in 1404 and went on to rule the County of Cephalonia until the beginning of the last quarter of the fifteenth century.

Meanwhile, the Venetians re-established themselves on the Ionian Islands, taking Kythera (known to the Latins as Cerigo) in 1309, Corfu in 1386, Zante in 1482, Cephalonia in 1500, Lefkas (then known as Santa Maura) in 1502 and Ithaka in 1503.

The revived Byzantine Empire lasted until 1453, when the Turks under Sultan Mehmet II captured Constantinople, which thenceforth came to be known as Istanbul, capital of the Ottoman Empire. Subsequently the Turks conquered most of Greece and its islands, with Rhodes falling in 1522, the Cyclades in 1537, Cyprus in 1573 and Crete in 1669. The fall of Crete ended the fifth of seven wars fought between Venice and the Ottoman Empire between 1463 and 1718. The seventh of these wars reached its climax in 1716, when the Venetians beat back a Turkish attack on Corfu, the last of several unsuccessful attempts by the Ottomans to conquer the Ionian isles.

Corfu, the largest and most populous of the Ionian Islands, was of great importance to the Venetians in establishing their maritime empire in the eastern Mediterranean, so they did everything they could to exploit the resources of the island and to strengthen the defences of its port. Venice offered security against the invaders, who had been ravaging the Greek islands for centuries, but in return the Serenissima demanded absolute obedience to its autocratic rule. Under Venetian rule many of the upper classes spoke Italian and joined the Roman Catholic Church, but the great majority of the islanders retained their Greek language and Orthodox religion.

Early in the sixteenth century a *Provveditore Generale del Levante* was established in Corfu, with absolute authority over the Ionian islanders and command of the Venetian naval forces in the Ionian Sea. The highest body of local government, the Grand Council, was composed entirely of aristocrats, those whose names were inscribed in 1572 in the *Libro d'Oro*, the Book of Gold. A burgher class of merchants also came into being early in the Latin period, and some of them eventually merged with the aristocracy. The Greek peasants were in most cases tied as serfs to the estates of the nobility, with the exception of artisans in the towns and those who made their living from the sea. The Venetians were particularly interested in producing olive oil, and to encourage this they gave the islanders a subsidy for every olive tree they planted. This policy produced the vast olive groves that one sees today on the Ionian isles, more than five million trees in all, so that they are among the greenest of all the Greek islands.

During the early part of the Latin period Kythera, or Cerigo, as it was then called, was administered by the Venetian governor of Crete. But after Crete fell to the Turks in 1669 Cerigo came under the control of the Venetian governor of Corfu, the *Provveditore Generale del Levante*, thus effectively becoming one of the Ionian Islands. This arrangement was continued by all the foreign powers that in turn occupied the archipelago, and even though Kythera today is administered separately from the others, being an eparchy of Piraeus, it is still referred to as one of the Ionian Islands.

The Ionian isles prospered under Venetian rule, and their harbours were always busy with trade passing back and forth between Venice and the Levant. Most of the Ionian islanders were never cut off from the outside world, unlike the Greeks living under the Ottoman Empire, and so throughout the Latin period they were influenced by political and cultural developments in Western Europe. (Lefkas was the only Ionian Island that was occupied by the Turks for any considerable period.) The Ionian isles also became a haven for Greeks fleeing from the advancing Turks, an exodus that began with the fall of Constantinople in 1453 and reached another peak with the final Turkish conquest of Crete in 1669. The latter exodus included among its refugees a number of Cretan painters, who adorned the churches of the Ionian isles with some of the finest paintings in the history of Greek art in the post-Byzantine period. This was part of a cultural renaissance that began on the Ionian isles in the late Venetian period and continued on into the early nineteenth century, while mainland Greece and the Aegean isles were cut off from Western civilisation under the Ottoman Empire.

The Venetians continued to hold the Ionian Islands until 1797, when the Serene Republic of Venice surrendered to Napoleon I, who then sent garrisons to occupy all the isles. After a brief occupation by the French the Ionian Islands were then placed under Russian protection, and became an autonomous state called the Septinsular Republic. Napoleon took control of the Ionian Islands again in 1807, and the French occupied them until their garrisons surrendered one by one to the British navy during the years

1809–1814. Then in 1815 the Ionian Islands became a British protectorate, a well-administered state that was to last for nearly half a century.

The Ionian isles benefitted from both French and British rule, under whose administrations the islands' first roads and schools and other public works were built, early in the nineteenth century. One Corfiot who rose to international prominence in the early nineteenth century was Count John Capodistrias, who began his career in the service of the Septinsular Republic, of which he became Secretary of State in 1807, at the age of 30. He then entered the Russian diplomatic service, serving as Secretary of State for Tsar Alexander I at the Congress of Vienna in 1814. Capodistrias looked after Greek interests while serving the Tsar. This was reflected in one of the articles that Capodistrias was influential in writing into the Treaty of Paris, signed on 5 November 1815, whereby the Ionian Islands became 'a single, free, and independent state under the exclusive protection of His Britannic Majesty'. The treaty also specified that the British would appoint a commissioner, whose first task would be the convocation of an assembly that would draft a constitution for the new state.

The first Lord High Commissioner for the British Protectorate of the Ionian Islands was Sir Thomas Maitland, whose imperious ways gained him the nickname of 'King Tom'. One of his many critics on Corfu described Maitland as 'insufferably rude and abrupt, particularly dirty in his person, and consistently drunk and surrounded by sycophants'. The 'Lord High' had little patience with the idea that the Greeks on the Ionian Islands could be left to govern themselves. As he wrote at the time: 'Any man who has seen much of them would agree with me that colonial assemblies are injurious to the people, and disadvantageous to good government.' Maitland completely controlled the Constituent Assembly that he convened in Corfu town in April 1817. Within a fortnight the Assembly had agreed on the constitution that Maitland had drawn up and submitted to them, one that would leave all power in the hands of the Lord High Commissioner.

Maitland's constitution remained basically unaltered for the next 32 years, giving the Lord High Commissioner exclusive control of the police, postal services and sanitation, with the power to arrest, imprison or exile anyone without benefit of trial. Foreign affairs and military matters were handled directly by the British government, and most of the important posts in the protectorate were held by appointees sent out from England, including the Treasurer General, the Principal Secretaries, the Residents in the seven islands, and the members of the Supreme Judicial Court. The Greeks on the Ionian isles played a part in the government almost solely through the weak and ineffective bicameral legislature, which comprised a Senate with five members and an Assembly with 40 representatives, each body headed by a President. General Sir Charles Napier, who as a young colonel was Resident on Cephalonia from 1822 to 1830, wrote of this first era of the protectorate: 'Elsewhere history is the biography of societies, here it is the biography of the Lord High Commissioner.' Nevertheless, the Ionian isles were well governed throughout the protectorate, with Maitland and his successors administering justice fairly and building roads, bridges, police stations, jails, post offices, hospitals, asylums and schools, including a university founded at Corfu in 1824, the first institution of higher learning in modern Greece.

The Ionian Islands played an important part in the Greek independence movement. When the Greek War of Independence began in 1821, some 3,000 volunteers from the Ionian isles crossed over to the mainland to join in the struggle. But Maitland pursued a policy of strict neutrality, disarming the islanders and reducing the flow of volunteers to a trickle. When Maitland died in 1824 he was succeeded as Lord High Commissioner by Sir Frederick Adam, who continued his predecessor's policy of neutrality, preventing the patriots of the Ionian Islands from joining in the struggle for Greek independence. Three years later Capodistrias was elected President of the Third National Assembly, whereupon he began a tour of the European capitals trying to get support for the Greek cause, but when he tried to stop off at Corfu on his return voyage Adam prevented him from landing. After Capodistrias was assassinated at Nauplia, on 9 October 1831, his body was brought back to Corfu town for burial in the convent of Panagia Platytera, where his tomb is now a national shrine.

The first changes in the constitution of the Ionian Islands were instituted during the first ten days of May 1849 by Lord Seaton, who was then completing his six-year tenure as Lord High Commissioner. As one observer remarked of Lord Seaton: 'In ten days he hurried the wandering Ionians through more political changes than England had undergone in ten generations. On 1 May 1849 the Lord High Commissioner had more power than Queen Elizabeth. On the tenth of the month he was left with less power than Queen Victoria.'

Seaton's constitutional reforms gave the Greeks of the Ionian isles a greater voice in their government, and they immediately used this to call for *enosis*, or union with the rest of Greece. In 1863, after the approval of the other four powers that had signed the Treaty of Paris – Russia, France, Austria and Prussia – the Assembly of the Ionian Islands was convened by Sir Henry Storks, the last 'Lord High', and the members voted unanimously for 'a perfect union with Greece', whereupon they conveyed their message to Queen Victoria along with a note of gratitude. The final documents for the British cession of the Ionian Islands were signed on 21 May 1864, and by noon on 2 June of that year the last of the British troops on Corfu were evacuated. Four days later King George of the Hellenes landed in Corfu town and celebrated a Te Deum in the church of Agios Spyridon, the patron saint of the island.

Thus the Ionian Islands rejoined the Greek world to which they had belonged since the beginning of recorded history, for the men of these isles fought in the siege of Troy, at Salamis and Plataea, and in the Greek War of Independence. They were occupied by the Italians and the Germans during World War II, along with virtually all of the other Greek islands, and Corfu town suffered considerable damage in aerial bombardments. But that damage has now been repaired, as has most of the destruction wrought by the earthquakes in 1948 and 1953.

There are a number of museums of various types on the Ionian Islands that preserve objects from all periods of the archipelago's past. These include museums and galleries devoted to archaeology, Byzantine art, Ionian art, folklore and numismatics, as well as memorials to famous writers, artists and statesmen, of which the Ionian Islands seem to have had more than any other region of Greece in times past.

The most prominent historical monuments in the Ionian Islands are the fortresses that still dominate many of its principal towns, dating in their origins from the Byzantine, Angevin, Venetian and Turkish periods, sometimes with elements of all these eras represented in the same structure. There are also a number of fortified villages dating from these periods, when many of the islanders were forced to flee from coastal towns because of corsair raids, resettling in the mountainous interior. Besides walled villages, there are also medieval *pyrgoi* and fortified monasteries, where the islanders took refuge in times of corsair raids. Some of the monasteries are still inhabited by a few monks, who carry on a way of life that has not changed since the medieval Byzantine era.

There are many churches and monasteries on the islands dating from both the Byzantine and Venetian periods. Some of these have icons by leading artists of the post-Byzantine period from both Crete and the Ionian Islands, when a brilliant school of art flourished under Venetian rule. Besides churches and monasteries, the architecture of the island also includes public and private buildings of both the Venetian period and the era of the British protectorate, the most prominent examples of which are to be seen in Corfu town. More humble examples include the houses and farm buildings in the villages of the Ionian isles, which range from Venetian-style dwellings in the isles of the Ionian Sea to the Cycladic architecture of Kythera.

One of the most characteristic elements of Greek life, particularly on the islands, is the cycle of religious festivals and other celebrations that enliven the year. The two major religious holidays are Christmas and Easter, followed closely by the Feast of the Assumption of the

Virgin, known in Greek as *Koimisis tis Panagia Theotokou*, on 15
August. Then there are the other *paneyeria*, the holy days
dedicated to Christ, the Virgin Mary and the multitudinous
saints of the Greek Orthodox Church. These *paneyeria* are the
survival of the *Dionysia* and other religious festivals of ancient
Greece, which were themselves based on even more ancient
ceremonies connected with important events of the agricultural
year during the Bronze Age. Every town and village on the islands
has several of these *paneyeria* during the year, one for every church
or chapel in the community and its environs dedicated to the
saint who is being venerated on that day. (In Greek, Christ is
Christos, or *Sotir*, the Saviour; the Virgin Mary is the *Panagia*, or
All-Holy, and also *Theotokos*, the Mother of God; saint is *Agios*
(m.), *Agia* (f.) or *Agioi* (pl.).

Usually the observance of a *paneyeri* begins with a service in the
church on the eve of the festival, with music and dancing and a feast
in the church courtyard or village square the following evening.
Sometimes, as on the festival of the Assumption, the celebration
will go on for two or three days, with people coming from all over
the island.

The most exuberant participants at these *paneyeria* are those
named after the saint, for Greeks celebrate their *yiorti*, or name day,
rather than their actual birthday. When a man is celebrating his
yiorti his wife prepares a feast to which his family and friends are
invited, all of them greeting him with '*Chronia Pola!*', or 'Many
Years!'. In the evening they all go to a taverna, where the celebrant
dances in turn with all the women in his family, and then in a
group with all his relatives and friends. Endless glasses of ouzo are
sent out to him, which he pauses momentarily to knock back with
a toast, until he is finally helped back to his table, exhausted and
feeling no pain.

Aside from *paneyeria*, the most joyous occasions in Greek life
are weddings, particularly when they are celebrated in the old-
fashioned way on the islands. Traditional marriages take place on
Sundays at all seasons of the year, except during the month of May.

The favourite times are the last weeks before Lent, in late autumn after the vintage and the olive gathering, and especially the last Sunday after the Advent feast begins. One very important member of the wedding party is the *koumbaros*, or best man, a role taken far more seriously in Greece than in the United Kingdom or United States. The *koumbaros*, who is ideally a well-to-do friend, or at least not a pauper, is the master of ceremonies at the wedding, and beyond that he assumes a lifelong responsibility looking after the couple and their children. Then, when the first child is born, the *koumbaros* is usually asked to be the godfather, who in Greek is also called *koumbaros*.

A great deal of planning and negotiation goes into a Greek marriage, and there are many intricate rules to be observed. For example, it is improper for the son to marry until all of the daughters have been wed; and the girls in a family ideally marry in order of seniority, so that a younger sister should not become engaged while an older sister remains unwed. A primary responsibility for a family with marriageable daughters is to provide all of them with a suitable *proika*, or dowry, which forms one of the most important elements in a marriage settlement. The bride brings her *proika* with her into the marriage, and even if the couple should separate the woman retains her dowry, which among the islanders often involves a house and land, including olive trees. But it is almost unheard of for people on the islands to separate, because Greek marriages are for life – or, at least, they were in the good old days.

The marriage ceremony itself, along with the associated rituals, wedding feast and *glendi*, or party, is one of the most charming of Greek celebrations, particularly in the traditional manner in which it is observed on the islands. There the *koumbaros* usually hires a small band of musicians for the day, and their first task is to go to the home of the bridegroom and serenade him while he dresses for the ceremony. Then they do the same for the bride, after which they serenade her as she walks with her family to the church. The high point of the marriage ceremony itself is when the *koumbaros* holds the crowns of orange blossoms over the heads of the bride and groom, and then changes them when the priest pronounces that they are man and wife.

After the ceremony the marriage party and close relatives return to the bridegroom's house for the wedding feast, following which they and the other guest go to a taverna or the village square for a *megalo glendi*, or big party. The festivities begin when the bride dances alone with the groom, after which her father takes his turn and then the *koumbaros*. On the islands the bride and groom invariably do a *ballo*, a courting dance from Venetian times. The demure bride moves about nimbly with her hands clasped behind her back, playing the part of a coy turtle dove, while the groom soars through the air as he gyrates around his love like an eagle.

The bride and groom, together with her father and the *koumbaros*, are then joined by other guests in a series of group dances, usually a *syrto*, of which there are many regional variations. The *syrto* is one form of the ancient 'circling dance' that Homer describes in the *Iliad*, comparing it to Ariadne leading Theseus and his companions from the Cretan labyrinth.

The Ionian Islands are famous for their folk songs, which combine both Venetian and Greek elements. The most characteristic of the folk songs are the Italianate *cantadas*, which are sung in the island tavernas and at *paneyeria* as well as wedding celebrations. There one will invariably hear the most famous of the old *cantadas*, 'Na Chamilonan ta Vouna,' ('Oh That the Mountains were Lower'), which begins with these verses:

> Oh that the mountains were lower
>
> So that I could see the Levant
> And also Cephalonia
> And little Zante.
>
> Off to sea, off to sea we went,
> And only of you we spoke.
> By sea you go, by sea return –

Remember my words

Corfu and Cephalonia,
Zante and Lefkas –
These four islands
Adorn Greece.

The Ionian Islands have prospered in the past quarter-century, the major source of income being tourism, for the beauty and salubrious climate of Corfu and the other isles have been attracting visitors since the days of the British protectorate. As the painter Edward Lear wrote to a friend in England on 6 December 1857, after complaining about the boredom of life among the British community in Corfu:

> There is one thing here that simply cannot be grumbled at:
> – at present at least. The weather, it has been simply
> cloudless glory, for 7 long days and nights. Anything like the
> splendour of olive-grove & orange-garden, the blue of sky
> & ivory of church and chapel, the violet of mountain rising
> from peacock-wing-hued sea, & tipped with lines of silver
> snow, can hardly be imagined. I wish to goodness grass-
> hoppers you were here.

Mass tourism, particularly the development of beach resorts with their bars and discos, has to some extent spoiled the natural charm of the islands, attracting crowds of sunbathers to stretches of pink-white sand where we could once swim alone in the turquoise sea, and bringing sightseeing buses up to village festivals where tourists sometimes outnumber locals. But the old island life is still there, and one can find it by leaving the tourist centres behind and hiking up to remote mountain hamlets along goat-tracks over thyme-scented hills, passing only the occasional farmer on his mule, who will bid you the time of day and welcome you to his village, just as I remember from our first visits to the Ionian isles half a lifetime ago.

CORFU

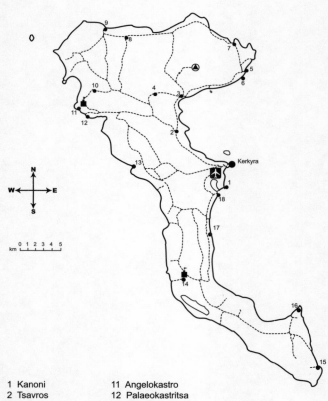

N
W ← → E
S

km 0 1 2 3 4 5

Kerkyra

1 Kanoni	11 Angelokastro
2 Tsavros	12 Palaeokastritsa
3 Pirgi	13 Ermones
4 Korakiana	14 Gardiki Castle
5 Kouloura	15 Kavos
6 Kalamai	16 Alikes
7 Kassiopi	17 Benitses
8 Karousades	18 Perama
9 Sidari	▲ Mt Pantocrator
10 Pagi	✈ Airport

two

Corfu I: The Town

Most travellers who approach Corfu by sea cross on the ferry services that connect the Italian Adriatic ports with Igoumenitsa, the little port town in the north-westernmost corner of mainland Greece. On our first visit to Corfu we boarded a ferry at Ancona, embarking on a 24-hour voyage that began and ended around midnight under successive full moons. During the second evening of our voyage I recalled the memorable lines that Lawrence Durrell wrote of this same sea crossing in *Prospero's Cell*: 'Somewhere between Calabria and Corfu the blue really begins... you are aware of the horizon beginning to strain at the rim of the world; aware of islands coming out of the darkness to meet you.'

As we approached Corfu I saw three clusters of lights off our starboard bow, looking like low-lying constellations between the midnight blues of sea and sky. When I checked my map I learned that they were the Othonian Islands, the northernmost satellites of Corfu. These are a tiny triad of islets, with Othoni to the west, Erithoussa to the east and Mathraki to the south, the three of them forming an equilateral triangle whose centre is six to seven nautical miles north-west of Corfu.

Othoni, the ancient Fano, is the north-westernmost possession of Greece, a maritime outpost on the seaway along which mariners since antiquity have approached Corfu from Italy. On the summit of the island, a 400-metre (m) high crag called Kastri, there are the ruins of a Byzantine castle. Local legend has it that the last royal resident of this castle was a Byzantine princess, who fled there with her gold and jewellery when the Turks invaded Epiros, but the buried treasure has never been found. The French, when they were occupying Corfu, identified Fano with Ogygia, the isle where Odysseus long dallied with the nymph Calypso, the 'shining goddess', before he set out on the last two stages of his homeward voyage, sailing first to Scheria and then to Ithaka. Most modern Homeric scholars reject the identification of Fano with Ogygia, for it took Odysseus 18 days to sail from Calypso's isle to Scheria, the land of the Phaiakians, which almost everyone now identifies with Corfu. Nevertheless, there are romantics who still identify this Othonian isle as Calypso's home, where the castaway Odysseus found the 'queenly nymph' in the great cavern that was her home, 'singing inside the cave with a sweet voice/ as she went up and down the loom and wove with a golden shuttle'.

Once past the Othonian Islands there was a string of lights that I could identify as the northernmost villages on Corfu, and looming above them in the moonlight I could see the massive silhouette of Pantocrator, the highest mountain on the island, its summit 911m above sea level. Here again one thinks of Odysseus, for this mountain would have been his landfall as he approached the land of the Phaiakians after his long voyage from Calypso's isle. 'Seventeen days he sailed, making his way over the water, and on the eighteenth day there showed the shadowy mountains of the Phaiakian land where it stood out nearest to him, and it looked like a shield lying on the misty face of the water.'

Pantocrator and its surrounding slopes form the north-eastern corner of Corfu, where the island is separated from Albania by a channel that at one point is only around one and a half kilometres (km) wide. The Albanian cape opposite Pantocrator is the site of ancient Buthrotum; according to legend, this city was founded by Helenus, a son of King Priam, who settled there after the fall of Troy with Andromache, widow of his brother Hector. Virgil, in the

Aeneid, has Aeneas visit Buthrotum as the guest of Helenus, who prophesises the course of the hero's future wanderings. A legend from Byzantine times has it that Judas Iscariot ended his days in Buthrotum, from where some of his descendants crossed to Corfu.

Corfu is the northernmost of the Ionian Islands, extending southward from Greece's border with Albania along the coast of Epiros. It is the second largest of the Ionian isles, surpassed in area only by Cephalonia, but is by far the most populous, its populace in the most recent census, taken in 2005, numbering 111,041, more than all the other islands in the group combined. The high population of Corfu is due to its high rainfall and fertile soil, with some 60 per cent of its area covered by farms and olive groves.

The island is long and narrow, extending for some 70km north-west to south-east, tapering from a width of 30km in the north to only 4km in the south. It is divided by two mountain ranges into three regions: the northern, central and southern. The northern region is divided into two parts, with Oros to the east and Gyros to the west. Oros is essentially the massif of Mount Pantocrator, which is densely planted with olive trees, its slopes falling precipitately into the sea to form a series of capes separated by coves and sandy beaches. Gyros is a succession of wooded highlands separated by narrow and verdant valleys, fringed by a coastal plain. The central region of the island, Mesi, is made up of a mosaic of high hills and small plains. Lefkimi, the southern region of Corfu, is almost entirely a monotonous plain, whose fertility makes it the principal agricultural region of the island.

Corfu town, the Greek Kerkyra, is the capital and principal port of the island. The town is on the east coast of the Mesi region, directly across the strait from the Greek–Albanian border, built on a promontory that forms the southern horn of a great gulf whose northern side is formed by the massif of Mt Pantocrator. It has a population of some 30,000, making it the largest town in the Ionian Islands, as it has been since antiquity, when it was the city state of Kerkyra.

It is the oldest and most distinguished of all the towns on the Ionian isles, and since it has been spared the earthquakes that have hit the other islands to its south it still has monuments dating from virtually every period of its rich and varied past. The town traces its origin back to the colony founded on Kerkyra by Corinth in 733 BC. Archaeological excavations have shown that the original site of Kerkyra was south of the present town, at the base of the Kanoni peninsula. Kerkyra was centred there up until AD 562, when the city was destroyed by the Ostrogoths under Totila. Some exiguous ruins of the original city of Kerkyra can be seen at Palaeopolis, just south of the suburb of Anemomilos, and objects excavated there are exhibited in the Corfu Archaeological Museum.

During the medieval Byzantine period a new town emerged on what is now Palaion Frourion, the Old Fort, a miniature Gibraltar that forms the promontory between the Gulf of Kerkyra to the north and Garitsa Bay to the south. This is separated from the rest of the town by a channel called the Contrafossa and by the public garden and square known as the Spianada, which in English is called the Esplanade. The promontory's twin peaks (in Greek, *koryphia*, or *korphous* in the accusative) led the Italians to call it Corfu, a name that was applied to the whole island early in the Latin period. During the late Byzantine era Corfu was for the most part contained within the walls of this citadel, but then in the early Latin period it spread out into what is now the Old Town.

The Old Fort endured three sieges by the Turks during the Venetian period, in 1537, 1571 and 1716, the latter occurring in the third year of the seventh and last war between Venice and the Ottoman Empire. During that last conflict the Venetians entrusted the defence of Corfu to Count Matthias von der Schulenburg, a Saxon soldier of fortune, who greatly strengthened the fortifications of the town in preparation for the expected siege, which began with the arrival of a Turkish fleet under Kara Mustafa Pasha on 6 July 1716. The siege lasted for seven weeks, an epic struggle in which Schulenburg distinguished himself by his extraordinary valour, with the Turks finally giving up the attempt and sailing away suddenly on the morning of 19 August. (The Corfiots attributed their deliverance to the intervention of Agios Spyridon, who saved them from many other perils across the centuries.) The war ended officially on 21 July 1718 with the signing of the Treaty of Passarowitz, in which the Serenissima was confirmed in her possession of Cerigo and Santa Maura, as Lefkas was then known, the latter island having been recaptured from the Turks by Schulenburg. News of the treaty had barely reached Corfu when the town was struck by one of the greatest catastrophes in its history. This occurred on 28 October of that same year, when the powder magazine in the Old Fort was struck by lightning and exploded, destroying all the buildings within the fortress and killing some 2,000 people, including the Venetian commander, Captain Andrea Pisani.

Within five years of the war's end Schulenburg had drawn up plans for the reconstruction of the Old Fort, as well as for the building of new fortresses on the two hills to the west of the town, known as San Rocco (in Greek, Sarokka) and Lofos Avrami (the Hill of Abraham), which had been used as artillery positions by the Turks during the siege of 1716. The eastern end of the town, which in earlier times had been a market square known as the Bazaro, was cleared of houses during this period, so as to give an open field of fire across the Contrafossa for the defenders in the Old Fort. This open area, measuring some 600m by 150m, was used by the Venetians as a military drill field. Then at the beginning of the French occupation it was planted with trees and flowers to create the Spianada, whose northern half now serves as the Plateia, the principal public square of Corfu town.

During the second period of French occupation, 1807–1814, the north-western side of the Spianada was closed in with a row of arcaded mansions known as the Liston; these were designed by Baron de Lesseps (father of Ferdinand de Lesseps, builder of the Suez Canal), and were patterned on the rue de Rivoli in Paris. Then in the first decade of the British protectorate a monumental edifice was erected on the northern side of the square to house the Lord High Commissioner and the Ionian Senate. It also served as the headquarters of the Most Distinguished Order of St Michael and St George, which Sir Thomas Maitland founded in 1819 'for natives of the Ionian Isles and of the island of Malta and its dependencies, and for other subjects of His Majesty as may hold high and confidential situations in the Mediterranean'. The architect was Colonel Thomas Whitmore of the British army's Corps of Engineers, who in his memoirs compares his accomplishment to that of constructing the Tower of Babel, writing that 'there were no less than eight or nine languages spoken in it by the workmen, who rarely understood any alphabet but their own'.

The palace on the Esplanade housed the Lord High Commissioners until the end of the British protectorate, where-upon it became one of the imperial residences of the Greek Kingdom. The Royal Palace, as it was thenceforth called, fell into disrepair after 1913, when it was abandoned by the royal family of Greece in favour of Mon Repos, a newer and more secluded palace on the Kanoni peninsula. The old palace suffered additional damage when it was used to house refugees during the Greek Civil War that followed World War II, but then in the early 1950s the building was restored and reopened as a museum, with its upper floor now housing the Museum of Asian Art and the Collection of Christian Art. The former Palace of St Michael and St George, as it was originally called, is the oldest monument of modern Greece, and its handsome Doric portico of 32 columns makes it one of the most outstanding examples of neoclassical architecture in the country. As Nigel Nicholson wrote of it in Sacheverell Sitwell's *Great Palaces*: 'It stands, fairly mottled by time and tribulation … as much loved by Corfiots … as if it had been erected by Greeks for Greeks, instead of a frustrated Colonel of Engineers for the rather surly representatives of a foreign power.'

The Museum of Asian Art is the only institution of its kind in Greece. It was originally founded in 1927 as the Manos Collection of Sino-Japanese Art, after the donation of 1,500 objects by Gregorios Manos. After the donation of collections of objects from various places in Asia by Nikolaos Hadzivassileiou, Harilaos

Chiotakis and others it was renamed in 1974 as the Museum of Asian Art. The most important works in the museum are: statuettes from China, dated to the T'ang dynasty (seventh to eighth centuries AD); bronze ritual vases from China of the Shang dynasty (AD 130–1028); bronze ritual cauldrons from China of the Ming dynasty (1368–1644); statuettes of Chinese deities from the Ming dynasty; statuettes in ivory and semi-precious stones from China of the Ch'ing dynasty (1644–1912); porcelain vases and plates from the Ch'ing dynasty; Samurai armour of the Han dynasty from Japan (206 BC – AD 202); wooden statuette from Japan of the Kamakura period (1192–1338); masques of the No Theatre from Japan, dated to the Edo period (1614–1868); Japanese screens of the Edo period; Hindu woodcarvings of the seventeenth to nineteenth centuries; Hellenistic-Buddhist sculptures in schist from the Indian province of Gandhara (second century AD); woodcuts of Kitagava Utamoro from Japan (1753–1806); Chinese porcelain vases of the green group with *famille verte* decoration, dated to the K'ang-Hsi period (1662–1722); bronze statuettes from Nepal (fourteenth to seventeenth centuries); and *thangkas*, or sacred painted banners of the Himalayas (seventeenth to eighteenth centuries).

The lavishly decorated former throne room of the palace was used by the Lords High Commissioners for official functions. The room contains two huge paintings of St Michael and St Gabriel, along with a portrait of King George I of Greece.

The same wing of the palace contains the Collection of Christian Art. The first room exhibits architectural and fragments of mosaic floors from the church of SS Jason and Sosipater on the Kanoni peninsula, south of Corfu town, dating from the early eleventh century. The second room contains fragments of wall paintings from the ruined Byzantine church of Agios Nikolaos at Korakiana, dating to the eleventh, thirteenth and eighteenth centuries. The third and last room has a collection of icons of the sixteenth to eighteenth centuries, brought here from various churches in Corfu town. The most notable exhibits are: 'SS Sergius and Bacchus', by Michael Damaskinos; 'St John the Baptist', by Emanuel Lombardos;

'St Nicholas', with scenes from his life, by Theodore Poulakis; 'St John of Damascus', by Ioannis Tzenos; 'St Cyril, Patriarch of Alexandria' (from the church of SS Jason and Sosipator), by Emanuel Tzane Bounialis; 'The Archangels Gabriel, Michael and Raphael', by Giorgios Kortezos; and 'St John the Hermit', with scenes from his life, by Ieremias Palladas.

During the early years of the British protectorate the Esplanade was the scene of a day-long festival held annually on St George's Day, which in Greece is usually celebrated on 23 April. The first of these festivals was held to commemorate the official opening of the Palace of St Michael and St George, which was dedicated by Sir Thomas Maitland on 23 April 1823. This festival is described in one of the letters of Private William Wheeler, of the King's Own Yorkshire Light Regiment, who served in the Ionian Islands during the years 1828 to 1838.

> The people assembled presented one of the most curious sights I ever saw, Greeks in the dress of the various islands they belong to, Albanians, soldiers and sailors, etc., all mingled together, each taking part and striving to be conquerors in the different games. Many surprising feats were performed by the Greeks, who are a fine robust race ... The games over, the prizes distributed, the knights then escort the general and his lady home, who are followed by all the Greek nobility and gentry, and officers of the army. All kinds of games continued until dark. Wine and all kinds of refreshment were in abundance. The day passed without a single incident or row.

Private Wheeler also writes of the gala ball that 'King Tom' gave that evening in the palace, where the leading members of the British establishment were joined by the Corfiot aristocracy, headed by Baron Theotoki, President of the Ionian Senate and a Knight of the Order of St Michael and St George.

> An illumination took place at night, the palace was all in a blaze, a grand ball was given at the palace by the Lord High Commissioner protempo. I was in the guard of honour

so that I was in the thick of the fun all evening. Manly of the 32nd was one of the waiters, consequently I came in for some of the good things of the feast. The dancing continued until 5 o'clock, when we escorted Baron Theotoki home, attended by the military bands, and all of the colours of the different regiments in the Garrison, roused all the good people from their morning slumbers, then marched on to our barracks.

The palace was the centre of social life in Corfu throughout the half-century of the protectorate, but the British and the Corfiots had little to do with one another apart from official events held by the Lord High Commissioner. As Viscount Kirkwall wrote in the last year of the protectorate: 'It was a matter of general remark that the English were asked to dinner at the Palace only to meet each other, the Ionians made a similar observation regarding themselves.' Ansted, writing in 1863, makes a similar observation. 'The habits of the English at Corfu are somewhat monotonous; and our countrymen do not mix with the natives... Few of the resident officers take any interest in anything beyond the ordinary occupations of their respective professions.'

The atmosphere of life during the last years of the protectorate is brilliantly evoked in the letters of Edward Lear, who first came to Corfu for a brief visit in 1848 and then returned for a longer stay beginning in 1855, when he began painting his extraordinary landscapes of the Ionian isles. Lear was entranced by the visual beauty of Corfu, as he wrote in a letter to his sister Anne in April 1848:

> I wish I could give you any idea of this island; it is really a Paradise. The extreme gardeny verdure, the fine olives, cypresses, almonds, and oranges make the landscape so rich, and the Albanian mountains are wonderfully fine. All the villages appear clean and white, with here and there a palm-tree overtopping them.

But the letters that he wrote during his later years in Corfu show that he felt stifled by the boredom and monotony of the British social scene in particular and by Corfiot town life in general.

(6 December 1857): Just figure to yourself the conditions of a place where you can never have any extent or breadth of intellectual society, & yet cannot have any peace or quiet: – suppose yourself living in Picadilly, we will say, taking a place with a long surface, from Coventry Street to Knightsbridge say. And suppose that line your constant and only egress and ingress from the country, and that by little and little you come to know all and every one of the persons in all the houses, and meet them always and everywhere, and were thought a brute and a queer if you didn't know everybody more or less! Wouldn't you wish everyone of them, except a few, at the bottom of the sea?

(1 December 1861): Everyone was hospitable, from the Palace downwards: – but as the balls, and small monotonous whist or tea-parties are wholly out of my line in this very very very small tittetattle place, & as moreover night walks from this side of the city to the other don't suit me, not to speak of late hours & a multitude of new and uninteresting acquaintance, I decline all visiting on the plea of health & antiquity or what not... O! if I could but come back to London, bringing with me the gold & blue & lilac & pink of the air, sun, hills & snow.

Directly in front of the palace there is a statue of Sir Frederick Adam, the second Lord High Commissioner, who served from 1824 until 1832. Adam's memorial is surrounded by an ornamental pool, symbolising the modern waterworks that he built on Corfu, including a 13km aqueduct that conducted water from the springs of Benitses to the town. At the southern end of the Esplanade there is a statue of Capodistrias, and some 80m north of this there is an Ionic peristyle honouring Sir Thomas Maitland.

Along the north-eastern side of the Esplanade, just above the north end of the Contrafossa, there is a memorial to the eccentric philhellene Lord Guilford, who in 1824 founded the Ionian Academy, the first university in modern Greece. Guilford's statue shows him dressed in the ancient Greek costume that he wore during the years that he headed the academy, a mode of dress sarcastically described by Napier. 'Lord Guilford is here again, a queer fish but very pleasant. He goes about dressed like Plato with a golden band around his mad pate and flowing drapery with a purple hue. His students' dress is very pretty and is said to be taken from ancient statues.' Napier also mocked the academy, describing Guilford and his faculty as they appeared one evening for supper with the Lord High Commissioner: 'He dined with Sir Thomas, and entered the room at the head of twelve men, professors in black, and with powdered heads, bandy legs, cocked hats under their short arms, and snuff-boxes in hand – brimful of snuff... All the Greeks would speak Greek, the Italians Italian, and the French all the languages together,' while 'Guilford would address every person in a different language, and always that which the person addressed did not understand'.

Nevertheless, Guilford made a genuine contribution to the renaissance of Greek learning, as Papadopoulos Vretos remarked in his biography of the Earl, published in 1846: 'What would have been the condition of learning in Greece when she became a kingdom, I know not, if there had been no Earl of Guilford, and if he had not founded a university in Corfu which gave instruction to nearly all the doctors, lawyers, professors, teachers, and civil functionaries of the present kingdom.'

Midway along the eastern side of the Esplanade, to the left of the bridge that crosses the Contrafossa to the Old Fort, there is a statue of Marshal Schulenburg. This monument was erected by the Venetian Senate in 1716 and originally stood inside the Old Fort, moved to its present location after the British occupied the citadel. On 11 August each year, during one of the four annual feast days of Agios Spyridon, a procession pauses here to pay tribute to Schulenburg, while a 24-gun salute is fired from a battery in the Old Fort. The ironwork bridge across the Contrafossa is flanked by two Venetian cannon dated 1688. This span replaces the original Venetian drawbridge, which was still in place up until the beginning of the last century. On the far side of the bridge a Venetian gateway and a more recent covered passageway lead to the main square of the citadel, and from there a walkway leads out along the southern side of the promontory.

The medieval town of Corfu developed on this promontory after the abandonment of the ancient city of Kerkyra at Palaeopolis. According to tradition, the twin peaks of the promontory were first fortified by the Byzantine Emperor Leo III (reigned 717–741). There were still houses on the promontory as late as the last war between Venice and the Turks, but these were destroyed in the great explosion of 1718 and never rebuilt. Thenceforth the Old Fort was inhabited only by the troops of the garrison and the government officials in the Palazzo of the *Provveditore Generale*, the Venetian governor. Part of the Venetian barracks still survives today, but the governor's palace was blown to bits by a German air raid on the night of 13–14 September 1943, when a third of Corfu town was destroyed.

The surviving parts of the Venetian barracks, dating from 1558, can be seen on the northern side of the promontory. Below them is the marina known as Mandraki, a fortified harbour built by the Venetians in the fifteenth century to moor ten of their galleys. This gave its name to the Panagia Mandrakina, the little seaside chapel on the other side of the Contrafossa facing Mandraki, which dates from 1700. The only other monument on the islet itself is the church of St George, a neoclassical structure built by the British in 1830 on the southern side of the promontory. St George served as the chapel of the garrison in the Old Fort from then until 2 June 1864, when the last British troops were evacuated from Corfu along with the remaining officials of the protectorate, headed by Sir Henry Storks, the last 'Lord High'. The previous day the Municipal Council of Corfu had published a farewell address to the British garrison, which the members had passed with but two abstentions.

> By a generous decision of your August Queen the wishes of this Grecian land have been granted, and you are about to leave this island, on which you have resided for half a century, and nobly have you behaved towards us … Farewell, Brave Sons of England. Forget as we do whatever

may tend to mar our mutual love. Love us as we love you,
and desire that we may imitate your national virtues.

One vestige of the British presence on Corfu that still lingers on
is cricket, which in Greek is known as '*To (the) Game*'. At the time of
our last visit the Corfu Cricket Club was playing a match on the
Esplanade against a team from the Royal Navy. And some of those
who were watching the match, as we did, from one of the cafes
on the Liston, were drinking *tsintsin bira*, or ginger beer, another
heritage of the protectorate, still made according to its original
nineteenth-century recipe.

At the northern end of the Esplanade a portal to the left of the
palace, the Gate of St Michael, leads to Odos Arseniou, the cliff-
hanging street that winds around the north-eastern tip of the Old
Town and down to the port. This street and the old houses along its
landward side are known locally as Mouriya, or the Walls, from the
Venetian fortifications that once extended along this promontory.
At its upper end Arseniou intersects Odos Kapodistriou, the main
street that runs along the west side of the Esplanade, passing behind
the Liston at its upper end.

The house at 1 Odos Arseniou is the Solomos Museum.
Dionysios Solomos (1798–1857) was acclaimed as the national
poet of Greece after the publication in 1822 of his 'Hymn to Liberty',
the first two stanzas of which became the Greek national anthem.
When the hymn was published in French two years later Goethe
called Solomos the 'Byron of the East'. Solomos was born in
Zakynthos, but for the greater part of his life he lived in this house
in Corfu. It was here that he wrote most of his 'Free Besieged', a
major poem about the heroic Greek defence of Mesolongi in 1823.
The museum preserves memorabilia of Solomos, including his
writing desk and many old editions of his 'Hymn to Liberty'.

At the upper end of Kapodistriou a very pretty Venetian mansion
houses the Corfu Reading Society, founded in 1836 by the Corfiot
diplomat and scholar Peter Vrailas-Armenis. The society's library,
the oldest in Greece, has more than 30,000 books, which together
with its collections of manuscripts, icons, prints and photographs

cover all aspects of life on the Ionian isles. One of the most important documents preserved here is the sole surviving copy of the famous *Libro d'Oro*, the 'List' of the 112 noble Latin families of Corfu, the only other copy having been burned by the French when they occupied the island.

Nearby, at the upper end of Kapodistriou, there is another Venetian mansion that once housed the Nomarchion, or Prefecture. This neoclassical edifice was built in 1835 by the Corfiot architect Ioannis Chronis for Count Agostino Capodistrias, brother of John Capodistrias, who was born in 1776 in an earlier family house on this same site.

Continuing along Arseniou, one commands a stunning view of the whole north-western coast of Corfu across the gulf towards Mount Pantocrator. At its upper end Arseniou passes the palace of the Greek Orthodox Bishop of Corfu, which houses an important collection of Byzantine and post-Byzantine icons.

On the seaward side of the street a ramp leads down to a quay at the north-eastern end of the port, where there is a chapel dedicated to Agios Nikolaos, patron saint of Greek mariners. The chapel stands beside the site of the Porta San Nikolo, one of the original gateways in the Venetian sea walls.

Just beyond the ramp there is a splendid line of tall old tenements that stand along the landward side of Arseniou. These buildings follow the line of the defence walls that the Venetians built along the northern shore of the town in 1572, a year after they and their allies had defeated the Turks at the Battle of Lepanto. During the British occupation these houses were known as 'the Lines', or 'Line Walk'. Edward Lear moved into one of them in 1861, when he rented an apartment in an upper floor of the five-storey apartment house that still stands next to the National Bank of Greece. One vignette of Lear's life in Line Walk is described in a letter dated 21 January 1862: 'The woes of painters: just a minute ago I looked out of the window at the time the 2nd were passing by – I having a full palate of brushes in my hand; whereat Colonel Bruce saw me and saluted. Not liking to make a formillier nod in the presence of the hole harmy I put up my hand to salute, and thereby transferred all my colours into my hair and whiskers, which I must wash in turpentine or shave off.' Another appears in a letter dated 2 February 1862: 'There is a man in a boat here under my window – who catches fish all & every day with a long 5 pronged fork: a waistcoat & drawers being his dress. Why should I not do the same?'

Odos Arseniou forms the seaward side of Campiello, the oldest and most picturesque quarter of Corfu town. Campiello dates back to the thirteenth century, when the town first expanded out beyond the bounds of the Old Fort. The quarter is built on a hill (in Greek, *vouno*), and the highest parts of it are reached by stepped streets known as *skalinades*.

At the top of one of these step streets stands the chapel of the Panagia Antivouniotissa, one of the oldest churches in Corfu town, probably dating from the fifteenth century. The chapel now houses a museum of Byzantine and post-Byzantine icons and treasures, including works by such renowned painters as the Cretans Emanuel Tzane Bounialis, Emanuel Lombardos and Father Stephanos Tzangarolos, along with the Corfiots Constantine Contrarinis and Dimitrios Foscalis. The congregation of the Antivouniotissa included a number of noble Venetian families, whose coats of arms can be seen on their tombs in the narthex. The arms of one of these families also appears on an icon by Emanuel Tzane Bounialis, dated 1657, depicting the scene known as '*Noli me tangere*' ('Touch me not'), in which Christ appears to Mary Magdalene. I was particularly interested to see this picture here, because there is a Corfiot tradition that places Mary Magdalene on Kerkyra in her latter days, still dreaming of Christ.

Other notable icons in the museum include: the 'Theotokos Hodegitria', the legendary protectress of Constantinople (end of the fifteenth century); 'St Dimitrios of Thessalonika' (ca 1600); 'St Cyril of Alexandria', by Emanuel Tzane Bounialis, dated 1654; and 'SS Sergius and Bacchus and St Justina', painted by Michael Damaskinos to commemorate the victory of the Christians over the Turks at the Battle of Lepanto in 1571.

Another venerable Campiello chapel is the Panagia Kremasti, which is entered from a picturesque piazza centring on a Venetian well head. Kremasti means 'Hanging', and it is believed that the church takes its name from a sacred icon of the Virgin that in times past was hung on its façade, perhaps as a talisman in times of plague. The church was built in the late seventeenth century and is dedicated to *Isoudia tis Theotokos*, the Presentation of the Virgin. The icon from which the church takes its name now hangs on the right side of the marble *iconostasis*; this is dated 1771 and is signed by the Corfiot painter Spyridon Sperantzas. Set into the pavement in front of the *iconostasis* there are three tombstones bearing the coats of arms of noble Corfiots; one of these marks the tomb of the Theotokis family, the most illustrious in Corfu, tracing its lineage back to Byzantine Constantinople.

The Venetian *pozzo*, or well head, in the centre of the square before the church is known as the Kremasti Fountain. This is a fine work in marble decorated with scrolls and inscribed Byzantine crosses. Dedicatory inscriptions in both Greek and Latin record that the well was built for the common good in 1699 by a Venetian nobleman named Antony Cocchini, whose coat of arms and initials are inscribed in the conches on two sides of the structure.

Two other interesting old chapels in Campiello are dedicated to Christ Pantocrator (the Almighty) and Agios Nikolaos ton Yerondon, St Nicholas of the Old Men, a curious name whose origins are now lost. Both chapels date from the sixteenth century and have icons by Emanuel Tzane Bounialis. The chapel of Agios Nikolaos was originally the cathedral of the Great Protopapas, or High Priest, who headed the Greek Orthodox Church on Corfu before the restoration of the archbishopric in 1841. (The Orthodox archbishopric on Corfu had been suppressed by the Roman Catholic archbishopric under Venetian rule.) The eighteenth-century *iconostasis* in Agios Nikolaos was painted by George Chrysoloras. Three paintings on the doors of the *iconostasis* are by Emmanuel Tzane Bounialis (seventeenth century).

The largest and most important church in Campiello is the Panagia Spiliotissa, Our Lady of the Cave. This three-aisled basilica was erected in 1571, taking its name from an older cave sanctuary of the Virgin on this site, and since 1841 it has served as the Greek Orthodox Cathedral of Corfu. The church has three icons by Emanuel Tzane Bounialis, one by Michael Damaskinos and one in the Western European style by the eighteenth-century painter Panagiotis Paramythiotis.

The cathedral is also dedicated to Agia Theodora, Empress of Byzantium, whose remains are preserved in a silver casket on the right side of the *iconostasis*. Theodora was the wife of the Emperor Theophilus the Unfortunate, who reigned from 829 to 842, and the mother of Michael III, the Sot, who ruled for a quarter of a century after his father's death. When Michael succeeded to his father's throne he was only six years old, and so his mother acted as regent until he came of age. Theodora took this opportunity to restore icons to the churches of the empire, from which they had been banned by the Iconoclasts since the previous century, and for this she is revered as a saint in the Greek Orthodox Church. After the conquest of Constantinople in 1453, her remains and those of Agios Spyridon were brought to Corfu by a priest named Giorgios Kalochairitis. (He transported them in wicker baskets on either side of a mule.) Agios Spyridon's remains were eventually placed in the predecessor of the church that now bears his name in another quarter of Corfu town, while those of Agia Theodora were finally laid to rest here at the Panagia Spiliotissa.

The church of Agios Spyridon stands in the midst of another old quarter south of Campiello. The main entrance is on Odos Spyridon, a street that leads westward from the Esplanade, the guiding landmark being the extremely tall belfry of the church, the highest on the Ionian Islands. The church was built in 1589, replacing an earlier chapel of Agios Spyridon in the Sarokka quarter, destroyed when the Venetians began building their new fortifications after the Battle of Lepanto. The church is a single-nave basilica, its belfry and clock tower surmounted by a red dome, reminiscent of the bell tower of the Greek Orthodox church of San Giorgio dei Greci in Venice, built at about the same time.

The ceiling of the church was originally painted on seventeen cloth panels by Panagiotis Doxaras in 1727, depicting the miracles of St Spyridon. But the paintings rotted away, and all that is left of the original decoration are the gilt-scrolled frames. The present ceiling paintings are inferior copies done in the mid-nineteenth century by N. Aspiotis. St Spyridon's mummified remains are visible in his ornate casket, which is enshrined in the side chapel to the right of the main altar.

Spyridon first came to fame at the Council of Nicaea in 325, where as Bishop of Tremithious on Cyprus he was one of the most forceful of those who supported the doctrine of the Trinity, performing several miracles to make his point. Agios Spyridon became the patron saint of Corfu soon after his remains and those of Agia Theodora were brought to the island in 1456 by Giorgios Kalochairetes. His casket is carried in procession around the town in four annual processions commemorating his miraculous salvations of Corfu, ending a famine in the late fifteenth century, a plague in 1629, another plague in 1673 and the Turkish siege in 1716, the latter miracle being commemorated on 11 August with a three-hour parade involving all the island's civic and religious organisations and its marching bands, along with contingents from the Greek armed forces. (These and other miracles of Agios Spyridon are depicted in several of the icons in the church, which include works by Emanuel Tzane Bounialis, Constantine Contarinis and Spyros Prosalentis.) Agios Spyridon is also honoured on his name's day, 12 December, when all the many men on Corfu and elsewhere in Greece who are named Spyros celebrate their birthday, while the saint's remains are exposed to public veneration beside his church. One hears that his slippers have to be resoled from time to time because of his nocturnal rambles through the town, for he is always vigilant in protecting Corfu. As the Corfiots often say when they part company, 'O Agios Spyridon mazi sou', meaning 'May Saint Spyridon be with you'.

There are several other old Venetian churches in the quarter south of Spyridon's church, including two in the Plateia Ioniki. This square takes its name from the Ionic and Popular Bank, founded during the protectorate with British capital and housed in a neoclassical edifice built in 1840 by Ioannis Chronis.

One of the two churches on the square is the Panagia ton Xenon, Our Lady of the Strangers, founded in 1689. The name comes from the fact that this was the parish church of refugees from Epiros, who in the first two decades of the nineteenth century fled to Corfu to escape from the tyranny of the Albanian warlord Ali Pasha, the Lion of Tebelen. The icons in the church include works by Emanuel Tzane Bounialis and Constantine Contarinis, as well as by Michael Tzenos of Crete and Nicholas Coutouzis of Zante.

The other church in the square is St John of the Cisterns, deriving its name from the Venetian reservoirs beneath it, which Sir Frederick Adam incorporated into the water supply of Corfu in 1831. Among the icons are works by Tzenos and Chrysoloras. A tombstone in the church marks the grave of a Russian captain who was buried here in 1799, one of the casualties in the battle between Admiral Ousakov's Russo-Turkish force and the French garrison on Corfu. Another monument in this quarter is the belfry of the Roman Catholic church of the Annunciation, the rest of which was destroyed by German bombers in World War II. A plaque on the belfry records that the church was the last resting place of Christian sailors who were killed at the Battle of Lepanto.

The town hall of Corfu is some 200m south of Plateia Ioniki. This baroque edifice was built during the years 1663–1690 as the Loggia dei Nobili, an arcade designed as a meeting place for the aristocracy of Corfu. It was rebuilt in 1732 to accommodate performances of plays, concerts and operas, the first institution of its kind in modern Greece. Thereupon it came to be called the Teatro San Giacomo, taking its name from a church across the square now known as Agios Ioakovas, or St James. The building was used as a theatre until 1903, when it became Corfu's town hall, at which time the present top floor was added. Representatives of the Serbs, Croats, Slovenes and Montenegrins met here on 20 July 1918 to sign the Pact of Corfu, creating the modern state of Yugoslavia. (The defeated Serbian army, numbering about 80,000, had encamped on the islet of Vido off Corfu harbour early in 1916, along with the government-in-exile and Prince Alexander, heir to the throne.) The building was badly damaged during World War II, but it has since been splendidly restored. The main façades, to north and south, are decorated with medallion portrait heads and theatrical masques in relief. Between the two windows on the eastern side of the building there is a marble relief honouring Francesco Morosini (1624–1694), who commanded the Venetian forces throughout the sixth war between the Serenissima and the Turks; in that conflict he recaptured the Morea and briefly held Athens, destroying the Parthenon in the process, and then ended his career as Doge of Venice. The monument is dated 1691.

The nearby church of San Giacomo was erected by the Venetians in 1632, and since 1718 it has been the Roman Catholic Cathedral of Corfu. It was for long the parish church of the Maltese community, which originated when stonemasons from Malta were brought here to build the Palace of St Michael and St George. The church was badly damaged during World War II, but it has recently been restored, so that its elegant baroque façade once again adorns the little Venetian *piazetta* on which it stands.

There is another historic public building about 100m to the south of the town hall, standing at the western end of Odos Moustoxidou. This is the former Parliament of the Ionian Islands, built in 1852 by the Corfiot architect Ioannis Chronis to replace an older building that had housed the Ionian Assembly, destroyed by fire in 1852. The main entryway to the building is flanked by a pair of plaques, one in Greek and the other in English; these record the historic vote taken here on 23 September 1863, in which the Ionian Parliament voted unanimously for union with Greece. Six years later the building was given to the British community of Corfu, who converted it into an Anglican church. It was destroyed in World War II and then completely restored in 1962, after which it was converted into an exhibition gallery.

The gallery now houses the Numismatic Museum, a rich collection of banknotes, coins, stamps, documents and other objects once used in the bank, and a reproduction of the modern process for manufacturing banknotes.

Among the other structures destroyed in this neighbourhood during World War II was the Condi Terrace, an apartment building in which Edward Lear had a flat during the years 1856–1858. At that time the Condi Terrace was considered to be one of the most fashionable residences in Corfu town, and in one of his letters Lear writes: 'We are all more or less swells as live in it.' But in a letter dated 6 December 1857, after he had been living at the Condi Terrace for more than a year, Lear reveals that the lack of privacy in the apartment house was beginning to get on his nerves.

> Then you live in a house, one of the best it is true, where you hear everything from top to bottom: a piano on each side, above and below, maddening you: and you can neither study nor think, nor even swear properly by reason of the proximity of the neighbours. I assure you that a more rotten, dead or stupid place than this existeth not… The constant walking and noise overhead prevents my application to any sort of work, and it is only from 6 to 8 in the morning that I can really attend to anything… Just at this moment I think I must have a piano: that may do me good. But then I remember that Miss Hendon over my head has one, and plays jocular jigs continually. Then what the devil can I do? Buy a baboon and parrot and let them rush about the room?

And it was probably in such a frustrated mood that Lear wrote one of his most famous limericks, 'The Old Man of Corfu'.

> There was an Old Man of Corfu
> Who never knew what he should do;
> So he rushed up and down,
> Till the sun made him brown,
> That bewildered Old Man of Corfu.

There are several Venetian mansions still standing in this quarter, most notably those of the Ricci family on Odos Moustoxidou and that of the Giallina on Kapodistriou. Both these mansions have loggias that would have been used by the Venetian aristocracy to observe the festivals and other events taking place on the Spianada. One of these was the May Day festival, in which the Gypsies of Corfu played an important part. During the early Latin period the Corfiot Gypsies belonged by feudal right to a succession of noble Venetian families. The first nobleman known to have held this right was Gianello degle Abitabuli, who in 1464 transferred the possession of his Gypsies to Michele degli Ugoti. Later the lordship of the Gypsies on Corfu passed to the Prosalendis family, who held this feudal right until it lapsed late in the Venetian period. The Gypsies marched as a separate unit in the May Day parade, reviewed by their feudal lord from his loggia on one of the streets leading into the Spianada, a spectacle described by Count Lunzi, writing in 1858:

> On the first day of May the gypsies, led by their captain, their baronial banner carried by their standard-bearer, and with pipes and tambourines, all proceed to the city, carrying the 'May'. This is a branch decorated with flowers, ribbons, gold and baby chicks. This branch is put with great merry-making in the square in front of the baron's house. He prepares a banquet for the people and feasting and revelling to go on for the whole day. The next day the baron holds a muster of his vassals, each of whom presents his tribute. This was 17 aspri (pennies) and a pair of chickens for married couples, and a gold coin from the standard-bearer. In the month of August and on New Year's Day every married couple must pay 15 aspri, and one chicken, and when a gypsy takes a wife he pays two perperi (shillings) and two good chickens.

Another notable Venetian mansion that survives only in ruins stands at the southern end of the Esplanade, at the corner of Kapodistriou and Akadamias. This was built in the mid-Venetian period and was originally known as the Grimani barracks; in 1840 the Ionian Academy was housed here, and later still it served as the

Law Courts, continuing as such until the time of its destruction in a German air raid in 1943.

The Municipal Gallery of Corfu is housed in the old Dalietos mansion on 1 Odos Akadamias. Old maps of Corfu are on display in the entrance hall and some of the corridors. The first room on the right is devoted to portraits of the former Greek royal family. The following room has two outstanding post-Byzantine icons from the funerary chapel of the First Cemetery of Corfu town, along with a painting of the assassination of President John Capodistrias at Nauplion, a scene depicted in other paintings in the collection.

Most of the collection in the gallery is made up of works by nineteenth-century Corfiot painters. The most notable paintings are: 'The Assassination of Capodistria', by Haralambos Pachis; 'Markas' and 'The Herd', by Angelos Giallinas; the 'Fighter of the 1821 War', by Spyros Prossalendis; the 'Arab Musician', by Pavlos Prossalendis the Younger; 'The Giallinas House' and 'The Vianellos Alley', by Nikos Ventouras; the 'Piano Tuner', by Giorgios Samartzis; and the 'Sphinx', by Spyros Skarvelis.

The gallery also houses the Baxter Collection, a beautifully illustrated study of the flora of Corfu by the English artist and botanist Miss Baxter.

Several other monuments can be seen by strolling generally westward along Nikiforou. The first of these is the building that houses the Corfu Choral Society, the oldest musical group in Greece, which stands directly across the street from the church of SS Basil and Michael, built in 1757. Continuing along the arcaded street one then passes the seventeenth-century Venetian church of St Francis, closed because the Roman Catholic population in Corfu is now greatly diminished.

A short distance beyond this is the Greek Orthodox church of SS Anthony and Andrew. The original church on this site, founded in the fourteenth century, was destroyed in the Turkish siege of 1536. The present church dates from 1753 and is renowned for its *iconostasis* of white Carrara marble, the work of Alexander Trivoli-Pierri. The paintings on the *iconostasis* are by Spyridon Sparantzas and Panagiotis Paramythiotis. There are also two other notable paintings by unidentified artists; one of these is a representation of St Anthony, dating from the fifteenth century, and the other, a work of the early seventeenth century, is of the type known as '*Rhodon to Amaranthon*', the 'Undying Rose', in which the Virgin and Christ-child are shown with the four prophets who foretold the birth of Mary and her role as the Mother of God.

The original church on this site had an association with John VIII Palaeologos, the next to last Byzantine emperor, who ruled from 1425 to 1448. The Emperor and the Patriarch of Constantinople, Joseph II, stopped briefly on Corfu in 1439 on their way to the Council of Ferrara-Florence, where they agreed to a union of the Greek Orthodox and Roman Catholic Churches in a vain attempt to obtain aid from the West. Their arrival in Corfu coincided with the feast day of St Anthony, and so the Emperor and the Patriarch attended services here before going on to Italy, the last time a reigning monarch of Byzantium ever set foot on the Ionian Islands.

At its western end Odos Nikiforou Theotoki opens into the *plateia* known in English as Harbour Square, which is dominated on its western side by the New Fort, the fortress built by Marshal Schulenburg after the Turkish siege of 1716.

The New Fort connected the two lines of fortifications that the Venetians began building after the Battle of Lepanto, with one set of walls stretching along the sea and the other extending in a great arc around the landward side of the city. There were four main entryways through these walls, two on the seashore and two inland. The latter two were the Porta Reale, or Royal Gate, which led out through Sarokka to the interior of the island, and the Raimondo Gate, which led to the suburb of Garitsa and Palaeopolis on the Kanoni peninsula. Both of these land gates were demolished during the protectorate, when the British built the first roads on the island. The other two gates were the Porta San Nicolo, the eastern anchor of the sea walls, and the Porta Spilia, the Gate of the Cave, which was built at the western end of the harbour beside the New Fort. Part of the Porta Spilia still survives, built into a hotel where Odos

Nikiforou Theotoki enters Harbour Square. Just to the west of the square there is a Venetian gateway that once led into the New Fort, its lintel carved with a relief of the winged lion of St Mark.

Odos Solomou veers off to the left from the end of Nikiforou and leads into the north-western corner of the town, which is enclosed in an angle of the New Fort. Up under the walls of the New Fort there is an abandoned chapel known locally as the church of Tenedos. The first church on this site was built by refugees from Tenedos, who settled here after their island was captured by the Turks in 1663. This church was destroyed during the siege of 1716. Seven years later the Venetians replaced it with a new chapel dedicated to Our Lady of Carmel, but so strong is local tradition that even now it is still called the church of Tenedos. The church was badly damaged during World War II and has since been abandoned.

Above its entryway one can still see the winged lion of St Mark flanked by a pair of Venetian coats of arms, along with these inscriptions: 'To God alone, praise and glory' and 'Under the shadow of thy wings, do protect us – 1723'.

Odos Velissariou leads south from Solomou into the former Jewish quarter of Corfu, where one finds the only remaining synagogue on the island. The synagogue is still used by the few Jews who remain in Corfu, their community having been nearly wiped out when the Germans shipped them off to concentration camps in 1943–1944.

When Benjamin of Tudela visited Greece, in the years 1160–1173, he found only a single Jew living in Corfu, a man who made his living as a dyer of cloth. The first substantial Jewish community on Corfu developed during the Angevin period, 1267–1368, when they were encouraged to settle in the town to develop its commerce. When the Corfiots petitioned Venice to govern the island in 1386, after the end of the Angevin dynasty, there were two Jews among the six delegates, a measure of the size and influence of their community. The Corfiot Jews continued to flourish under the Venetians, who protected them from the Inquisition. Nevertheless, the Jews in Corfu town were still confined to a ghetto, originally in the Campiello quarter and then later under the New Fort. The population of the ghetto, known as the Hebraica, increased with the arrival of Sephardic Jews from Spain and Portugal beginning in 1492, and more refugees arrived from southern Italy in the following century. By 1665 there were 500 Jewish families on Corfu, and by the end of the nineteenth century they constituted one-ninth of the town's population. The walls of the ghetto were demolished by the French when they first occupied Corfu in 1797, but the Jews continued to live in their quarter under the New Fort. Jervis, writing in 1870, notes that up until the arrival of the French the Jews in the Corfu ghetto had to be protected by the police during Easter week.

> But this protection extended only as far as their lives were concerned, for they were ever the sport and jest of the people; so much so, that, to ensure their personal safety, they were confined every night in the Jews' Quarter. Upon the arrival of the French in 1797, any one of that race who ventured out of the Jews' Quarter during Easter week exposed himself to the danger of being assassinated, and that feeling is by no means diminished, being kept in check by the strict attention of the police on those occasions. (At eleven o'clock on Good Friday, the Corfiots throw all their old pottery into the streets and fire guns and pistols at Judas the rest of the day.) [...] The Jews still live separate in the Jews' Quarter, but it is, happily, no longer closed at sunset with ponderous gates and guarded by detachments.

The custom of throwing crockery into the streets is still observed by Corfiots on Good Friday evening, though they now light fire-crackers rather than firing pistols and exploding dynamite. This custom appears to have developed from the apocryphal legend that has the descendants of Judas settling on Corfu after his death in Buthrotum, across the Corfu Channel in Albania. Lawrence Durrell writes of this strange tradition in *Prospero's Cell*, in which he notes that in his time there was in Corfu town a Jewish shoemaker named Iscariotes. This had been pointed out to Durrell by his friend Dr Theodore Stephanides, who, he says, had made 'the discovery that Judas Iscariot has a direct connection with Corcyra...'.

Walking through the verminous and crooked streets of the Hebraica with Theodore we discuss the problem from all its angles. The cobbled streets are slippery with excrement. The little shops, made for the most part of the flimsiest materials, are worm-eaten and decayed. Yet counters groan with cheap dress materials, mounds of sweets, and every-where the tap of shoemakers' hammers emphasises the gnome-like quality of the place. It is natural, of course, that until today we have never noticed the name of Theodore's shoemaker: ISCARIOTES. It is painted in lopside capitals on a sagging board. The man himself is a deaf mute with some of the lowering gloomy aspect of Dr. Faustus.

Such is the town of Corfu, which still preserves monuments as well as memories of every aspect of its many-layered past, including the now-vanished Jewish ghetto.

three

Corfu II: The Kanoni Peninsula

T he next excursion will take us to the southern suburbs of Corfu town and then around the Kanoni peninsula, the long cape that extends southward to almost enclose the Chalkiopoulous Lagoon, where the airport runway is laid out.

The port quarter in the north-east part of town beyond the New Fort and Lofos Avrami is known as Mandouki. In 1817 the population of this quarter was greatly enlarged by Greeks from Parga in Epiros, who had fled to Corfu when their town was occupied by Ali Pasha of Tebelen.

From Mandouki a road leads around Lofos Avrami to the south on its approach to the Sarokka quarter, and at the first intersection we come to the Platytera monastery. This was founded in 1743 by a monk from Lefkas, who dedicated it to the Panagia Platytera, the Virgin Wider than the Heavens. The monastery was destroyed in 1798 when the French bombarded Mandouki after the people there rose up against them during the Russo-Turkish siege of Corfu. The present building and its *katholikon*, or chapel, were completed in 1801, the belfry in 1864.

The *katholikon* is generally considered to have the finest baroque façade on Corfu, and its intricately carved wooden *iconostasis* is also notable, bearing a series of Italianate icons by N. Koutouzis, a pupil of Nicholas Cantounis. Other notable icons include a 'Madonna and Child', by Emanuel Tzane Bounialis; the 'Apocalypse', by

Theodore Poulakis; the 'Last Judgment', by George Clotzas; and two large paintings by Nicholas Cantounis, the 'Washing of the Feet' and the 'Last Supper', on the north and south walls, respectively. Behind the altar there is a tomb containing the remains of a number of eminent Corfiots. Here lies Count John Capodistrias (1776–1831), who served as President of Greece from 1827 until his assassination in 1831.

The road around Lofos Avrami ends at Sarokka, the Venetian San Rocco, a quarter that centred on an ancient market square described by Ansted, writing in 1863:

> San Rocco is the third principal suburb of Corfu. It contains about 800 inhabitants, and is a very busy place, both by day and night. It is passed through on going southwards or westwards from the town. By day it is a principal horse and cattle fair – horses, mules, donkeys, pigs, goats, and other animals – herding in the road, and pushed about by every comer. Here also are the blacksmiths; and here, at night, every stall is open, and brilliantly illuminated for the sale of meats and drinks, and an infinite variety of sundries.

Odos Marasli follows the course of the old Kanoni road southwards from Sarokka, passing on its right the British Cemetery. This burial ground dates back to the beginning of the British protectorate and continues in use today, including the graves of 44 men of the Royal Navy who died when their ships, HMS *Saumarez* and *Volage*, were sunk by Albanian mines in the Corfu Channel in 1946.

Beyond the cemetery Odos Marasli passes the grounds of a police station and prison, whose entrance is at the south-east end of the enclosure on Odos Menekratous. Just inside the entrance to the grounds there is one of the few monuments of the ancient city of Kerkyra. This is the Tomb of Menekrates, a circular cenotaph of finely worked limestone in six courses, capped with a circular roof. The tomb itself is dated ca 600 BC, and has an archaic inscription reading from right to left around the top of the wall. This states that Menekrates was consul of Kerkyra at his native city of Oianthe, near

Galixide on the north shore of the Gulf of Corinth, and that the Kerkraeans built this memorial to him when he lost his life at sea.

The present roof of the monument is a much later addition, though probably similar to the original. A number of clay and bronze funerary objects of the archaic period (ca 700–480 BC) were discovered when the tomb was excavated in 1843, and some of these are now exhibited in the Corfu Archaeological Museum. These finds indicate that the Tomb of Menekrates stood in the necropolis of ancient Kerkyra. This burial ground was established outside Kerkyra's defence-walls, which extended across the neck of the Palaeopolis peninsula from the Bay of Garitsa to the Chalkiopoulos Lagoon, the ancient Hyllaic Harbour. The latter was one of two ports that served the ancient city; the other, known as the Harbour of Alkinoos, is believed to have been at the southern end of the Bay of Garitsa, probably the silted-up area that is now just westward of the seaside suburb of Anemomilos.

Odos Menekratous leads westward from Marasli to the seaward end of Leoforos Alexandras. Here we see an obelisk commemorating Sir Howard Douglas (died 1841), who served as Lord High Commissioner in the years 1835–1841. During his term of office Douglas wrote to the Colonial Minister concerning the Ionian Islands, remarking that 'the internal state of the country, the moral and physical state of the people have not been benefited by the British connection so far as to protect us hereafter from the reproach of having attended less to their interests than to our own'.

We now head north along the shore on Vassileos Konstantinou to the Corfu Palace Hotel, on whose south side we come to the Corfu Archaeological Museum. The museum has an extensive collection of antiquities from sites all over Corfu, ranging in date from the prehistoric period up through the Graeco-Roman era.

The most important exhibit in the museum is the spectacular Gorgon pediment, the most impressive work of its kind that has survived from the archaic period, some 17m long and 3m high, with its sculptures in relief including several unique and beautiful works. It was discovered in fragments behind the old church of Agioi

Theodoroi, whose ruins are near the north-west corner of the Palaeopolis peninsula a short distance inland from the Chalkiopoulos Lagoon. This surmounted the west front of the archaic Temple of Athena, dated 590–580 BC, the oldest large stone pediment in Greece. At the centre there is a fiendishly grinning Gorgon, her tongue stuck out through her bristling teeth, snakes writhing in her hair and a pair of serpents confronting one another at her waist.

She is flanked by a pair of fabulous beasts known as '*iopanthers*', a combination of lion and leopard, with tiny male figures in the angles of the pediment and a larger one just to the right of the centre.

Another outstanding exhibit in the museum is an archaic lion that served to decorate a funerary monument. This was discovered near the Tomb of Menekrates and was once thought to have surmounted that monument, but it has now been dated to the end of the seventh century BC and attributed to a famous Corinthian sculptor of the archaic period.

Other notable exhibits in the museum are: the left part of an archaic pediment from the area of Figareto, on the road towards Kanoni, dated 500 BC; the base and part of a late archaic *kore*, or young woman, found in an ancient pottery workshop in the Figareto area; a case containing terracotta statuettes found in a small sanctuary of Artemis at Kanoni; the head of a small *kouros*, or young man, found in 1966 during excavations on the estate of Mon Repos, dated 535–530 BC; a bronze statuette of a running young reveller, or *commastes*, probably from a Laconian workshop; a marble torso of Apollo, a copy of the 'Parnopios Apollo' by Pheidias, of the type known as the 'Kassel Apollo', dated to the second century AD; four cases with ancient coins found at various sites on Corfu; and a torso of a late archaic *kouros* found during the excavations at Figareto, dated ca 525 BC. In the courtyard there is a huge capital and the fragment of a column from a temple of Artemis.

The oldest Christian sanctuary on Corfu is reached by continuing along the Kanoni road and then taking the second left into Anemomilos, the suburb that forms the southern horn of Garitsa Bay. This is the church of SS Jason and Sosipator, built early in the eleventh century, one of only two intact structures on Corfu that can be dated definitely to the Byzantine period, the other being the church of Agios Mercurios on the north-east coast of the island. SS Jason and Sosipator were two followers of St Paul, who left their bishoprics in Asia Minor to introduce Christianity to Kerkyra. They were martyred by the Romans here late in the first century along with St Kerkyra, a maiden who had been one of their first converts on the island. The grave of SS Jason and Sosipator was enclosed within a small church early in the Byzantine period, while another chapel nearby was dedicated to St Kerkyra.

The entryway to the church is flanked by two Cufic inscriptions in decorative brickwork; they are both in the style of the early eleventh century, with the one on the right recording that the building was erected by the priest Stephanos on the site of an older and smaller sanctuary originally dedicated to St Andrew. The plan of the building is that of a typical Byzantine church of its period, a Greek cross with a dome set over the intersection of the two arms and carried on a high drum, cylindrical within and octagonal on the exterior, with windows in each of the eight faces. The exterior is decorated with a course of tiles, while inside the church there are two monolithic columns of green stone. The only surviving fresco is in the narthex, an eleventh-century work by an unknown artist depicting St Arsenius, a tenth-century bishop of Kerkyra. A pair of icons in the narthex representing SS Jason and Sosipator are attributed to Michael Damaskinos. There are also icons in the church by Emanuel Tzane Bounialis, including two of the paintings on the elaborately carved eighteenth-century *iconostasis*, one of them representing the Pantocrator and the other the Virgin and Christ Child, as well as two other icons, one representing St John Damascene and the other St Gregory.

Openings in the base of the *iconostasis* allow one to look down into the crypt. A sign identifies this as the tomb of SS Jason and Sosipator, but actually it contains the remains of two historic figures from the last days of Byzantium. One of these is the historian George Sphrantzes, who survived the fall of Constantinople in 1453 and came to Corfu, where he spent the next quarter-century writing a monumental history of the fall of Byzantium. The other is Catherine Palaeologos, wife of Thomas Palaeologos, a younger brother of Constantine XI who ruled as Despot of the Morea. When Constantine was killed in the fall of Constantinople in 1453 Thomas became Pretender to the throne of Byzantium, but three years later the Turks overran the Peloponnesos and he was forced to seek refuge on Corfu with his wife Catherine and their daughter Sophia. Catherine and Sophia remained on Corfu while Thomas crossed to Italy in a vain attempt to obtain help from the West, taking the head of St Andrew from Patras and giving it to the Pope as a present. (The head was finally returned to Patras in the 1960s.) Thomas died in Rome and was interred in St Peter's basilica, where his tomb can still be seen today. His widow, Catherine, became a nun in a convent attached to the church of SS Jason and Sosipator, where she was interred after her death in 1463.

The imperial line of the Palaeologi was perpetuated through Catherine's daughter Sophia, who went on to marry Ivan III, Grand Prince of Moscow. At the time of her marriage the Byzantine princess became the Tsarina Sophia, of whom the Russian historian Kluchevsky wrote: 'As heiress to the declining house of Byzantium, the new Tsarina of Russia had transferred the supreme rights of the Byzantine house to Moscow, as to a new Tsargrad, and there shared them with her husband.' And as the Russian monk Philotheus wrote in the sixteenth century, referring to the fact that Moscow was now called 'the third Rome' and the Russian ruler was the 'Tsar of all Orthodoxy', 'Two Romes have fallen and a third stands, while a fourth is not to be.'

The church was most recently restored in 1978 and still functions today, though it does not belong to a parish. The treasury of the church preserves an embroidered robe that belonged to Catherine Palaeologos.

A short way to the north-west of SS Jason and Sosipator is the ruined church of Agios Athanasios, where a section of the sea wall of the Harbour of Alkinoos was excavated in 1965.

South of Anemomilos the road to Kanoni veers inland to go around the Palace of Mon Repos, whose grounds take up the north-eastern quarter of the Palaeopolis peninsula. This edifice was commissioned by Sir Frederick Adam and designed by Colonel George Whitmore to serve as a summer residence for the Lord High Commissioners of the Ionian Islands. Mon Repos was completed in 1824, just a year after the dedication of the Palace of St Michael and St George, an extravagance that led Charles Napier to comment that it was folly to build two such monumental edifices 'within gunshot of each other'. After the end of the British protectorate Mon Repos served as a summer residence for the Greek kings up until 1967, when the monarchy effectively ended, whereupon it reverted to the Greek government. Prince Philip of Edinburgh was born here in 1921.

The ruins of the church of St Kerkyra can be seen close to the entrance of Mon Repos, to the right of the crossroads south of Anemomilos on the Kanoni road. This is also called the Palaeopolis church, since it stands in what is believed to be the centre of the ancient city of Kerkyra. The church was destroyed during an air raid in World War II, and all that remain are its roofless nave and the splendid arcade of its narthex. The triple entryway there has two Corinthian columns obviously inherited from an ancient sanctuary, along with pillars, capitals, lintels and other architectural members. The inscription on the lintel over this portal records that the church was built in the fifth century by Jovian, Bishop of Kerkyra, who used in its construction materials from pagan altars that he himself had destroyed.

Archaeolgical study has revealed that Jovian's church was a five-aisled basilica, which he built on and from the ruins of a Doric temple of the fifth century BC and a Roman odium, along with other ancient structures. The basilica was destroyed several times, by the Vandals and the Goths in the sixth century, by the Saracens and Normans in the eleventh century, by the Turks in 1537, and finally in World War II. It was rebuilt twice: first after its destruction in the eleventh century, and again in 1680, by the Cretan monk Arsenios Caloudis. The mosaic floor of the church was restored in 1960, and then in 1968 the mosaics and all the early Christian architectural parts were removed to the Old Palace Museum, where they now form part of the Collection of Christian Art. Architectural members in and around the church have been identified as fragments from two ancient temples of Palaeopolis, one dedicated to Artemis and the other to Hera.

The remains of the temple of Artemis are approached by a footpath that leads out to the north-western corner of the Palaeopolis peninsula, the landmark near the site being the old convent church of Agioi Theodoroi. Archaeological investigations have revealed that the temple was of the Doric order and was probably erected in the second decade of the sixth century BC. Virtually all that remains of the temple, aside from the Gorgon pediment and other fragments in the museum, is its great altar, 25m long and carved with triglyphs and plain metopes.

The footpath leads on to a fragmentary tower of the ancient city wall, behind the Proto Nekrotaphio, or First Cemetery. The tower, which dates from the fourth century BC, is roughly rectangular in form and nearly 6m high, and it is believed to have guarded one of the city gates. Known as the Tower of Nerandzicha, it survived because it was used as a church dedicated to the Blessed Virgin.

The funerary chapel of the First Cemetery was built in 1840 and is still functioning. It formerly contained a large number of important icons of the sixteenth and seventeenth centuries, including five signed works by Michael Damaskinos, but most of these are now in the Collection of Christian Art in the Old Palace.

The road divides into two one-way branches beyond the grounds of Mon Repos, with the right fork for traffic south to the Kanoni peninsula and the other for the return journey. But one should really walk this loop, which is about one and a half kilometres each way, for, as Edward Lear wrote after a stroll out to Kanoni, 'The colour and scenery were enough to delight a dead man,' with cypresses, orchards and vineyards still flourishing amidst the remnants of the vast olive grove that once completely covered this luxuriant peninsula.

This is the landscape that led early European travellers to believe that they had found here the celebrated Gardens of Alkinoos, which Homer describes in Book VII of the *Odyssey*. William Cowper's translation perhaps best evokes the Homeric landscape of these romantics:

> There grew luxuriant many a lofty tree,
> Pomegranate, pear, the apple blushing bright,
> The honied fig, and unctuous olive smooth...
> Pears after pears to full dimensions swell,
> Figs follow figs, grapes clust'ring grow again
> Where clusters grew, and (ev'ry apple stript)
> the bows soon tempt the gath'rer as before.

The view from the cliff-top cafe at Kanoni is one of the most celebrated in Greece, with the two islet chapels of Vlachernae and Pondikonisi floating in the still waters just outside the mouth of the Chalkiopoulos Lagoon, the verdant mountains of southern Corfu rising above Perama on the opposite shore.

Vlachernae, the nearer of the two, is connected to the tip of the Kanoni peninsula by a causeway. The chapel and convent there are dedicated to Our Lady of Vlachernae, named for a famous shrine of the Virgin founded at Constantinople in the seventh century. Pondikonissi, or Mouse Island, has a chapel dedicated to the Pantocrator. Travellers in times past identified Pondikonissi with the petrified ship of the Phaiakians, turned to stone along with its crew by Poseidon, who was enraged that King Alkinoos had helped Odysseus return to Ithaka.

At the end of the return leg of the Kanoni loop there is a road to the right that leads off to Analypsis, or Ascension. This pretty village is perched on the heights about halfway down the west coast of the Palaeopolis peninsula, with a superb view to the north of Corfu town and its citadel against the background of Mount Pantocrator, the mountains of Albania and Greek Epiros looming to the east across the Corfu Channel. Edward Lear came here frequently during the autumn and winter of 1856–1857 to paint this scene, producing the first of his immense and magnificent Corfu landscapes, entitled 'View from above the Village of

Ascension'. Lear first mentions this project in a letter dated 19 February 1856, soon after he arrived on Corfu for his first long-term stay: 'I still think of making Corfu my headquarters, & of painting a large picture of the Ascension festa in June, for 1857 exhibition... When I get a house, you must come out and have a run, & I'll put you up: I'll feed you with Olives & wild pig, and we'll start off to Mount Athos.' In a letter dated 9 October of that same year he mentions the project again: 'I trust to paint a magnificent large view of Corfu, straits and Albanian hills. This I trust to sell for 500 pounds as it will be my best, and is 9 feet long. If I can't sell it I shall instantly begin a picture 10 feet long. Nothing like persisting in virtue. O dear! I wish I was up there, in the village I mean, now on this beautiful bright day!' Then in a letter dated 11 January 1857 he indicates that he is well along on his landscape. 'It is Mr. Kakali's opinion & compliment that the painting I am now doing of Corfu will prevent all other Englishmen coming here, for... where's the good of people coming so far if they can see the very same at home.'

Analypsis takes its name from a hilltop chapel dedicated to the Ascension, where the festival mentioned by Lear still takes place every year 40 days after the Greek Easter. This is one of the oldest *panereyia* in Greece, the survival of an ancient festival celebrating the return of life to the world after the annual desolation of winter. On the morning of this day the women of Analypsis in times past, and perhaps still today, went down to the shore and each filled an amphora with water, which they sprinkled throughout their home while reciting an incantation: 'As Christ rose to heaven, so may calumny, sickness, the evil eye and all other evils arise from our house and disappear.' And then the entire family would walk up to the chapel of the Analypsis to celebrate Christ's Ascension, as Jervis describes them doing in the last year of the British protectorate.

> The show festa of the island is that which takes place... on Ascension Day. Numerous booths are erected in the olive groves, where jars of wine are in constant circulation, where lambs roasted whole are soon divided amongst the hungry crowd. Cheered with wine, the countrymen form

into sets, and dance the Romaica in rings, averaging from twenty to thirty in number, each man holding his neighbour's handkerchief, and, beginning with a gradual cadence, they finally whirl around at a rapid pace, which presently evinces a necessity for fresh libations. It is on such occasions that the women display their beautiful native costumes; and, every village having adopted one of its own, the variety gives a most pleasing effect... To these festas the peasantry come from great distances, bringing their offerings of candles; and, on such occasions, the wife, being adorned with holiday attire, is allowed to ride pillion.

Near road's end in Analypsis a footpath leads off to the left, heading down to the seashore below the village. This brings one to the Fountain of Kardaki, a spring issuing from an ancient well head with an eroded relief of the lion of St Mark. The fountain was originally designed to supply water for a cave sanctuary of Apollo on the hillside just above; this is within the bounds of Mon Repos, and thus closed to the public, but its scattered columns and other architectural members can be seen through the fence that surrounds the palace grounds. The sanctuary was discovered by Colonel Whitmore in 1822, when he was building Mon Repos, and subsequent excavations have revealed that it was a Doric temple with 11 columns along each side and six at the ends, dedicated to Apollo towards the end of the sixth century BC. This monumental temple would have replaced an earlier and much smaller shrine of Apollo in a hillside cave at Kardaki.

The shrine of Apollo at Kardaki has an almost forgotten association with the legend of Jason and the Argonauts. According to one version of this saga, perpetuated in the *Argonautica* of Apollonius Rhodius, Jason and Medea were married in the cave sanctuary of Apollo on Kerkyra, which thereafter was called Medea's Cavern. 'The sacred grot, recorded still by fame, bears to this day Medea's name.'

After seeing the Fountain of Kardaki we make our way back to Corfu town, having completed our tour of the Kanoni peninsula.

four

Corfu III: Around the Island

O ur next tour will take us entirely around the island, starting north along the shore from Corfu town. The road north from the town goes through Mandouki and then around the New Harbour, with Vido islet dominating the seaward view from its strategic position about 1,000m northward in the Gulf of Corfu.

Vido played an important part in several sieges of Corfu, most recently in 1798–1799, when the Russo-Turkish forces captured the islet and set up artillery there to bombard the Old Fort, thus forcing the French to surrender. During the last two years of World War I some 80,000 Serbian refugees were encamped on Vido under primitive conditions, and about a third of them died and were buried there in a large cemetery. Other unfortunates of earlier times lie buried in unmarked graves on the smaller islet to the west of Vido, the Lazaretto, just off the promontory at Kontokali. This was the station where all those intending to land on Corfu were confined in Venetian times, allowed ashore only after they survived an extended quarantine period. This and other such quarantine stations took their name from the monastery of San Lazaro off the Lido in Venice.

Further along the view north across the gulf is dominated by the great conical mass of Mount Pantocrator, its bare rocky peak contrasting with the lush greenery of the olive groves and colonnades of columnar cypresses through which the coastal road passes. The coast south of Pantocrator has now been completely taken over by tourism, with hotels, holiday villas, restaurants and shops lining every swimmable stretch of the shore. This has somewhat diminished the once paradisical beauty of this coast, which Lawrence Durrell put on the map in his *Prospero's Cell*, beginning with an entry dated 10 April 1937.

> We have chosen Corcyra because it is an anteroom to Aegean Greece, with its smoke grey turtle backs lying low against the ceiling of heaven. Corcyra is all Venetian blue and gold – and utterly unspoiled by the sun. Its richness cloys and enervates. The southern villages are painted out boldly in rich brush strokes of yellow and red while the Judas trees punctuate the roads with their dusty purple explosions. Everywhere you go you can lie on the grass; and even the bare northern reaches of the island are rich in olives and mineral springs.

Beyond Kontokali the road curves around the deeply indented Bay of Gouvia. Off to the left of the road at Kontakali there are the remains of a Venetian arsenal, principally the beautifully boned arches of the boathouses in which the galleys of the fleet were laid up and repaired during the winter. An inscription on the gateway to the arsenal bears the date 1770, just 27 years before the downfall of the Serenissima.

Beyond the village of Gouvia a road on the left leads to the Castello Hotel, built by the Italian Mimbelli. The hotel is a replica of a fourteenth-century Venetian *palazzo*, with period furniture and decor, evoking the atmosphere of late medieval Venice. The turning to the right at the same crossroads leads to Dassia beach, one of the most popular resorts on the island.

At the northern end of the bay the road passes through the village of Tsavros, where on a tiny islet just a few metres offshore there is a church dedicated to the Panagia Ipapandi. On the left there is a turn-off for the main east–west road across the island to Palaeokastritsa, its distances marked by old-fashioned English milestones. This road was built by British soldiers for Sir Frederick Adam so that he could travel more expeditiously to Palaeokastritsa, where he spent all his holidays during his tenure as Lord High Commissioner.

At the north-western corner of the gulf there is a crossroads at Pirgi, where there are two interesting diversionary routes to choose from before continuing around the coast. One of these leads eastward across the waist of the island via Korakiani, while the other goes northward around the west flank of Pantocrator via Spartillas and Episkepsis, with a side road winding up to the summit of the mountain.

There are two interesting churches at Agios Markos, which is a little over a kilometre along the Korakiani road. One of these is Agios Mercurios, the only other intact Byzantine church on Corfu besides SS Jason and Sosipator, with rather fragmentary frescoes dated to 1075. The other is the post-Byzantine church of the Pantocrator, which has exceptionally well-preserved wall paintings dated by an inscription to 1576.

The second diversionary route from Pirgi takes one to Spartillas, beyond which a turn-off on the right leads to the mountain village of Strinilas, where a road to the right leads up to the summit of Pantocrator. The road to the peak passes the old Venetian chapel of the Taxiarchis, or Archangels, which retains part of its original fresco decoration. The summit is surmounted by the Monastery of the Pantocrator, which commands a panoramic view of the whole island and its surroundings, with Paxos and Antipaxos strung off to the south of Corfu and the skyline to the east dominated by the beetling mountains of Albania and Greek Epiros.

The Monastery of the Pantocrator was founded in 1347 by the Angevins, but the only part of the original structure that survives is the barrel vault of the *katholikon* with its palimpsest of faded frescoes. The monastery was destroyed during the Turkish siege of 1537 and then completely rebuilt in 1689, with the present façade dating from a nineteenth-century reconstruction. The monastic church celebrates the feast of the Transfiguration on 6 August, with pilgrims keeping a week-long vigil in the cells of the monastery before the *paneyeri* begins. This important feast, which undoubtedly goes back to pagan rituals associated with midsummer, is described by George A. Megas in his *Greek Calendar Customs*.

> On this day it is the custom to bring the first baskets of grapes to church to be blessed. The grapes are then distributed among the congregation. The fast is broken, as on Annunciation Day and Palm-Sunday, and a special dish is prepared, usually cod or some other fish, cooked in various ways.

> No one is supposed to work on this day except fishermen, who are allowed to go out fishing in order to draw omens concerning the success of their calling during the rest of the Year. Many Greeks believe that the heavens burst open during the night from 5 August to 6 August and that any wish uttered at this moment will come true. For this reason many people sit up all night to see the divine light.

The coastal highway veers eastward at Pirgi to go round the seaward flanks of Pantocrator, where Corfu bulges out towards the Albanian coast. Side roads on the right lead down to a series of beach resorts, the most popular of which are Barbati and Nissaki, to which there is a regular boat service from Corfu town.

After winding for a short way up into the eastern foothills of Pantocrator, the road comes down to the sea again at Kouloura, a pretty village on the Corfu Channel, with the Albanian coast only about one and a half kilometres distant across the narrowest part of the strait. The village is set in a crescent cove embowered in cypresses and olive trees, its most prominent structure being a Venetian *pyrgos*, in this case a fortified manor house, with iron cannon balls surmounting its gateposts.

The Turks sacked Kouloura during their siege of Corfu in 1537, carrying off the surviving women and children and selling them in the Istanbul slave market. One of these captives was a young Graeco-Venetian girl known in Turkish as Nur Banu, who became the wife of Sultan Selim II and the mother of Murat III. During the reign of her son, 1574–1595, Nur Banu was the power behind the throne, influencing the power of the Ottoman Empire in favour of Venice. But despite her power Nur Banu remained a virtual prisoner in Topkapi Sarayi, the great palace of the Ottoman sultans, never returning to Corfu and her native village of Kouloura.

From Kouloura a secondary road leads south around a headland to the seaside hamlet of Kalamai. Lawrence Durrell and his wife Nancy lived here from April 1937 until September 1939, in an idyllic setting that he describes at the beginning of *Prospero's Cell*.

> It is April and we have taken an old fisherman's house in the extreme north of the island – Kalamai. Ten miles from the town, and some thirty kilometres by road, it offers all the charms of seclusion. A white house set like a dice on a rock already venerable with the scars of wind and water. The hill runs clear up into the sky behind it, so that cypresses and olives overhang this room in which I sit and write. We sit upon a bare promontory with its beautiful clean surface of metamorphic stone covered in olive and ilex: in the shape of a *mons pubis*. This is become our unregretted home. A world. Corcyra.

On the following page Durrell describes the magnificent view from Vigla, a mountain village directly above Kalamai.

> Climb to Vigla in the time of cherries and look down. You will see that the island lies against the mainland roughly in the form of a sickle. On the landward side you have a great bay, noble and serene, and almost completely landlocked. Northward the tip of the sickle almost touches Albania and here the troubled blue of the Ionian is sucked harshly between ribs of limestone and spits of sand. Kalamai fronts the Albanian foothills, and into it the water races as into a swimming-pool: a milky ferocious green when the north wind curdles it.

From Kouloura the highway cuts northward across the base of Corfu's north-easternmost cape to come out to the sea again at Kassiopi, an ancient port that has in recent years become a popular holiday resort. Kassiopi was founded during the reign of King Pyrrhus of Epiros, who ruled Kerkyra and Lefkas during the first quarter of the third century BC. The Romans built a temple here dedicated to Jupiter Cassius, to whom mariners dedicated offerings if they survived the dangerous voyage around the promontories at the north-eastern corner of the island, Capes Kassiopi and Varvara. Cicero stopped here in 48 BC, when he had the captain of his ship put in at Kassiopi because of a storm that was raging in the Corfu Channel. His fellow passengers were impatient and persuaded the captain to sail on, but Cicero had the satisfaction of seeing them again the following day when their ship was wrecked off Cape Kassiopi. Cicero remained in Kassiopi for a week and then sailed off to Italy in fine weather, presumably after having offered up his thanksgiving at the temple of Jupiter Cassius.

Two Roman emperors are known to have visited Kassiopi. Tiberius, who succeeded Augustus in AD 14, is believed to have had a villa here, which he would have used when crossing between Italy and Greece in the course of his eastern campaigns. Nero landed in Kassiopi in AD 67, the last year of his reign, while on his way to participate in the Isthmian Games at Corinth as a singer and lutist. During his brief stay he took the opportunity to give a performance of his songs at the temple of Jupiter Cassius, accompanying himself on the lyre.

The strategic importance of Kassiopi led the Byzantines to construct a fortress on the heights above the port, where its ruins can still be seen today. The fortress was captured in 1081 by Count Bohemund of Taranto, son of Robert Guiscard, at the outset of the first Norman invasion of Greece. Three years later it was recaptured by a Byzantine force led by the Emperor Alexius I Comnenus, who defeated the Normans in a series of three naval battles in the Corfu Channel off Kassiopi. The fortress passed to the Angevins in 1267, and then in 1368 it was taken by the Venetians, who dismantled it so that it could not be used as a base by invaders or rebellious islanders. Thus during the Turkish sieges of 1537 and 1716 Kassiopi had no defences and was pillaged by the invaders, who on both occasions enslaved all the townspeople who had not fled into the interior. The Venetians eventually rebuilt the fortress after the siege of 1716, but by then the town had been virtually abandoned, the survivors having moved to more secure villages high up on Pantocrator.

Aside from the fortress, the only remnant of old Kassiopi is the little chapel of the Panagia Kassiopitissa. The original church of the Virgin on this site was a three-aisled basilica, which in the early Byzantine period was erected upon the ruins of the temple of Jupiter Cassius. The basilica was destroyed by the Turks in 1537, and the present church dates from after the siege of 1716. During the Venetian period the Panagia Kassiopitissa was the most venerated church on Corfu after that of Agios Spyridon, and the ships of Christian nations sailing through the Corfu Channel always fired a salute in honour of the Virgin. Those who survived the sinking of their vessels off Capes Kassiopi and Varvara offered up their thanksgiving at the shrine of the Panagia Kassiopitissa, just as survivors in earlier times had expressed their gratitude at the sanctuary of Jupiter Cassius. One can still see their ex-votos today on the walls and *iconostasis* of the church, mostly tin images of ships ranging in type from Venetian galleons and Greek caiques to modern steamships.

The most beautiful icon in the church is itself a thanksgiving offering by the artist who painted it. This is a representation of the Virgin and Christ-child by Theodore Poulakis, who presented the icon to the church in 1670 after he survived a sinking in the Corfu Channel. The icon soon became renowned for its miracle-working powers, as George Wheler noted after he and Jacob Spon visited the Panayia Kassiopitissa in 1675:

> This little church is famous for a picture of Our Lady to which they attribute Miracles, and whereof I had a mind to try the skill. The way is thus: Strangers, that have a mind to know whether their Friends are alive or dead, go to the Picture, and clap a piece of money upon it, thinking of some friend. If the person they think of be alive, the piece

> will stick fast, but if dead it will drop down into a Sack
> placed underneath; so that, dead or alive, the Priest is sure
> of the money.

Beyond Kassiopi the road continues around the northern coast of Corfu, with turn-offs to the left leading up to the villages on Pantocrator. Halfway around the northern coast the road passes the seaside hamlet of Roda, near which there are the fragmentary ruins of a temple of the fifth century BC. Some architectural fragments of the temple are on exhibit in the Corfu Archaeological Museum.

The road comes next to Karousades, a picturesque village on the slope of a hill above the north-west coast. The most notable building is the fortified Venetian manor house of the Theotokis, the most distinguished family on the island, who came to Corfu from Constantinople after the fall of the Byzantine capital to the Turks in 1453. The oldest parts of the manor house probably date from the latter half of the fifteenth century.

The last village along the north coast as one drives west is Sidari, which is renowned for the extraordinary rock formations and eroded promontories that flank its little port and long sandy beach. One sea-carved channel at Sidari is known as the Canal d'Amour, and a local tradition has it that any girl who is able to swim its length can have the man her heart desires.

From Sidari the main road leads southward and eventually brings one to Palaeokastritsa, while a turn-off to the right just outside the town leads to the villages in the north-western corner of the island. It has been said that the north-western coast of Corfu fits the description of the inhospitable shore off which Odysseus was almost drowned when he approached Scheria, with its succession of precipitously cliffed and wave-lashed promontories, beginning with Cape Drastis and continuing all the way down to Palaeokastritsa. Homer describes the scene in Book V of the *Odyssey*:

> But when he was as far away as a voice can carry he heard
> the thumping of the sea on the jagged rock-teeth, for a big
> surf, terribly sucked in from the main, was crashing on the
> dry land, all was mantled in salt spray, and there were no

harbours to hold ships, no roadsteads for them to ride
in, but promontories out-thrust and ragged rock-teeth
and boulders.

The place where Odysseus swam ashore has been identified
with a number of sites on the western coast of Corfu, the leading
candidates, from north to south, being Afionas, Palaeokastritsa
and Ermones, all of which have a sandy cove with a river of
sorts running into the sea, fitting the description in Book V of
the *Odyssey*.

> He got clear of the surf, where it sucks against the land, and
> swam on along, looking always toward the shore in the
> hope of finding beaches that slanted against the waves or
> harbours for shelter from the sea, but when he came,
> swimming along, to the mouth of a sweet-running river,
> this at last seemed to him the best place, being bare of rocks,
> and there was even shelter from the wind there.

The village of Afionas perches on the neck of Akri Arilas, the
second promontory south of Cape Drastis, where archaeological
excavations have unearthed evidence of a settlement dating back to
the Neolithic era. The ruins of this ancient town are undoubtedly
the source of a local legend that stems from the Homeric sagas. As
this story goes, Afionas was once the capital of a kingdom ruled by
a queen named Pamphlyagona, whose younger sister was Kerkyra,
the nymph for whom the island was named. Pamphylagona's
husband had gone off to fight in a foreign war, and on his way home
he had been beguiled by a witch whom he had brought back to
the island and tried to install as his queen. But when their ship
approached Cape Arilas Pamphylagona called upon St Nicholas, the
Christian reincarnation of Poseidon, who turned the vessel and
its passengers and crew into stone. The petrified ship is identified
in local tradition with the offshore islet known as Gravia, which
is midway between Akri Arilas and Akri Agios Stefanos, the next
promontory to the north.

The main road south from Sidari takes one through a classical
landscape that would have pleased Odysseus after his long voyages

over the 'barren sea', winding along among hills and valleys covered with vast groves of olive trees and occasional stands of spectral cypresses, with wide-ranging views occasionally opening all the way across the island from the Corfu Channel to the west coast, a scene totally unspoiled by modern tourism.

At Arkadades there is a turn-off to the right for Pagi, a drive of 6km. At Pagi a secondary road leads down for another 4km, passing through the most beautiful olive groves on the island to Agios Giorgios, where there is a superb sand beach some 5km long, fringed by olive groves and stands of cypress trees.

Beyond the village of Kastellani Gyrou the main road comes to a fork, with the road to the turns heading through the Troumpeta Pass (its name means 'the Trumpet') and thence back to Corfu town, while the road on the right winds down to the coast at Palaeokastritsa.

Lawrence Durrell and his party passed this way on 7 April 1938, as he notes in *Prospero's Cell*, describing a *paneyeri* they could see being celebrated below in Kastellani Gyrou.

> Coming over the crest of the hill behind Kastellani we see that a dance is in progress. From the grassy glades below, the shadow of the olive trees is broken by clouds of dust, and the afternoon silence by the terrific giggling of donkeys – like pantomime comedians. Smoke from the fires, upon which whole kids were turning upon spits, rises lazily. Through the hum of human voices one can hear the scratch and squeak of the violin and guitars, and the hollow beat of the drum, resonant and vulgar as a full stomach struck with the palm of the hand. 'Ah look,' says N. 'Just look at the dancers.'

Durrell then goes to describe the dancing, in which the women were wearing the beautiful old costumes that have now virtually disappeared from the Ionian Islands except for special occasions.

> A multicoloured circle of flowing head-dresses moves slowly about the axis of the musicians, reversing and advancing with slow rhythmic measures. In the centre of

the circle, moved by the current, but free, the young men dance, each improvising his improvisations upon the theme, hand on hip, head thrown back, face devout and abstract. In the luminous shadows among the trees the crowds are laughing and chattering, the pedlars of ikons, talismans, or bread or sweets, resting for a while upon the boles of olive trees in expressive poses. Whiffs of roasting lamb and wine come across the clearing where the old men and women are sitting in groups upon the grass like birds, eating and drinking... Several of the girls from our northern villages are in the outer circle; one recognises them by the sobriety of their costume – black clothes with white head-dress; and in Corfu the women of Gastouri are justly renowned as the most beautiful and most colourful. Here in the line of dancers you can see the famous full pleated skirt of shot silk and the old-fashioned bodice, under a bolero heavy with gold stitching – the crust of embroidery. Gold drops dangle at the ear, while the coiffure is a marvellous erection – built up towards the back of the head in tiers, worked over little pads, and tied with red ribbon. A lace-edged handkerchief turned back from the crown, frames the handsome olive face.

The road to Palaeokastritsa passes through Krini, a hamlet in the hills above Akri Falakron, the third cape south from Akri Drastis. At Krini a track leads seaward towards the cliff-top site of Angelokastro, the principal medieval site on the western coast of Corfu.

The site takes its name from the Castle San Angelo, whose ruins are perched on a sheer-sided crag 330m above the sea near Cape Falakron, where the shoreline bends sharply eastward towards Palaeokastritsa and the Bay of Lipiades. The fortress was erected in the mid-twelfth century by one of the Despots of Epirus, either Michael I Angelos or his son and successor Michael II. In 1272 the fortress was taken by the Angevins, who had gained control of the rest of Corfu five years earlier. It was then that the fortress was first called Castrum Sancti Angeli, the Castle of the Holy Angels, known to the Venetians as Castello San Angelo and the Greeks as Angelokastro. The Venetians took the fortress from the Angevins in 1387, and from then until the end of the sixteenth century Angelokastro was the official capital of Corfu, for the *Provveditore Generale del Levante* resided there.

During the Latin period the fortress served as a refuge for the people of the surrounding villages when the island was attacked, and these invaders in turn included the Catalans, Navarese, Sicilians, Genoese and Turks. In 1403 an army of 10,000 Genoese mercenaries under the French Marshal Boucicault stopped off in Corfu while on their way to join the crusade in the Holy Land; they landed at Palaeokastritsa and besieged Castel San Angelo for a year without success, until they were finally driven away by a force of armed peasants from the surrounding villages. During the Turkish siege in 1537 some 3,000 people from these villages took shelter in the fortress, while 20,000 others who had not been able to take refuge there or in the citadel of Corfu town were either slaughtered or enslaved. When the Turkish Admiral Kilich Ali Pasha invaded the island in 1571 he sent two-thirds of his troops to attack Angelokastro, while the remainder of his force besieged Corfu town. The garrison at Angelokastro, mostly peasants from the surrounding villages, held out against the Turks and forced them to lift their siege. Then, when the Turks withdrew, the peasants sallied forth from Angelokastro and harried their retreating enemies, rolling boulders down upon them as they made their way through the mountains back to Corfu town, forcing Kilich Ali Pasha to end his siege and sail away. Angelokastro once again served as a refuge for the islanders during the Turkish siege of 1716, but this was its last defence and thereafter it was allowed to fall into disrepair, degenerating into the romantic ruin that one sees today.

After the detour to Angelokastro, we continue from Krini along the hilltop road towards the village of Lakones. About a kilometre before Lakones there is an old roadside cafe known as Bella Vista, whose sign records the names of the kings and other heads of state who have paused there to enjoy the magnificent seascape, with the surpassingly beautiful promontories and coves of Palaeokastritsa spread out below, the greenery of the olive groves and cypresses contrasting vividly with the turquoise of the shallower water close inshore and the deeper blue further asea. Edward Lear depicted this scene in two of his Views of the Ionian Isles, one of them entitled 'Palaiokastritza' and the other 'Castle Sant' Angelo'. Lear usually had the view to himself, but in a letter dated 'Easter Sunday, April 20, 1862' he complains about the day trippers who would inevitably be disturbing the serenity of the scene on the following day:

> At this beautiful place there is just now perfect quiet, except only a dim hum of myriad ripples 500 feet below me, all round the great rocks which rise perpendicularly from the sea: – which sea, perfectly calm and blue stretches right out westward unbrokenly to the sky, cloudless that, save a streak of lilac cloud on the horizon. On my left is the convent of Palaiokastritza, and happily, as the monkery had functions at 2 a.m., they are all fast asleep now and to my left is one of the many peacock-tailed bays here, reflecting the vast red cliffs and their crowning roofs of Lentish Prinari, myrtle and sage – far above them – higher and higher, the immense rock of St. Angelo rising into the air, on whose summit the old castle still is seen a ruin, just 1,400 feet above the water. It seems to me that such a life as this must be wholly another from the drumbeating bothery frivolity of the town of Corfu, and I seem to grow a year younger every hour. Not that it will last. Accursed picnic parties with miserable scores of asses male and female are coming tomorrow, and peace flies – as I shall too.

The road then passes though the picturesque village of Lakones before finally winding down to the sea at Palaeokastritsa. Palaeokastritsa forms the northern side of the Bay of Lipiades, where the island begins to narrow southward after bending in sharply at Cape Falakron. The village of Palaeokastritsa itself, now wholly given over to tourism, stretches along the shores of two bays and the necks of the two peninsular rocks that bound them to the west. The westernmost of the two peninsulas is Palaeokastritsa proper, while the eastern one is called Agios Nikolaos, between which there are a total of six coves, three of them forming a cloverleaf.

Palaeokastritsa means Our Lady of the Ancient Castle, named for an old monastery on the summit of the tree-clad promontory. The monastery, which is dedicated to the Dormition of the Virgin, was founded in 1228, though its *katholikon* dates only to 1722. Among the icons in the church are works by Theodore Poulakis, Emanuel Lombardos and George Chrysoloras.

Palaeokastritsa has sometimes been identified as the place where Odysseus swam ashore when he reached Scheria, and some writers have placed the Palace of Alkinoos here. The offshore rock of Kolovri is said by legend to be the petrified boat of Odysseus, while another story says that it is the ship of an Algerian pirate, turned to stone when he tried to sack the monastery.

Another site that has been identified as the landing place of Odysseus is Ermones, the next beach-fringed bay to the south. The route from Palaeokastritsa to Ermones goes south through the plain known to the Venetians as the Val di Ropa. This was once a miasmal swamp known as 'the Enemy of Youth', because of the many people whose lives were cut short there by malaria, but within the past century it has been drained and it is now the island's largest level area for farming and grazing.

A huge hotel complex now surrounds the cove at Ermones, which is dominated on its southern side by Mount Agios Giorgios. And the stream that flows into the cove is dried up in summer, making it even more difficult to evoke the scene described in Book VI of the *Odyssey*, in which Nausikaa and her maids play ball on the beach as they wait for their laundry to dry, awakening Odysseus in the thicket where he had fallen asleep after he swam ashore. Odysseus emerged and confronted the girls, whereupon they all ran away except Nausikaa, who spoke to him and heard his story, after which she invited him to her father's palace. 'Rise up now, stranger,' she said, 'to go to the city, so I can see you to the house of my prudent father, where I am confident you will be made known to the highest Phaiakians.'

A road goes south from Ermones around the eastern flank of Mount Agios Giorgios, passing a turn-off to Glifada beach. At the north end of the beach there is an old monastery called Myrtidiotissa, Our Lady of the Myrtles, a title of the Virgin often associated with seaside chapels on the Greek islands. According to tradition, the Myrtidiotissa was founded in the fourteenth century by the son of a Turkish pasha who converted to Christianity after he was captured by the Venetians. The monastery stands in an olive grove on the south slope of Mount Agios Giorgios, surrounded by a stand of cypresses and the only banana trees on Corfu.

Just beyond the turn-off to Glifada the road passes through Pelekas, a village noted for its superb setting high in the hills above the west coast of Corfu. One famous spot near Pelekas is the Kaiser's Throne, so called because Wilhelm II loved to sit there and enjoy the view during his vacations on Corfu in the years 1908–1914.

Beyond Pelekas the road joins the main highway leading back to Corfu town, but one can turn right at the crossroads and continue driving south via Sinarades, beyond which there is a turn-off for the beach at Agios Gordis. Beyond the Agios Gordis exit the road passes through Kato Garouna, a village high in the beautiful pass west of Mount Agioi Deka, the second highest peak on the island. The mountain and the village on its north-eastern slope are named for the Holy Ten, Cretan martyrs who were executed by the Romans during the reign of Decius, 249–251.

Beyond the pass the road continues south through Agios Mattheos, a charming village of old stone houses on the western slope of a mountain of the same name, the third highest on Corfu, covered with olive groves and oak trees. A secondary road leads down to Paramona beach on Makroula Bay.

A pathway leads up from the village to the summit of the mountain, where there is a monastery dedicated to Christ Pantocrator. Near the monastery there is a cavern in which archaeologists have discovered Neolithic remains, the oldest evidence of human existence on Corfu, dated ca 6000 BC. This cave supposedly connects with the sea below, and locals who have explored it report that they can hear the surf pounding ever louder as they make their way down into the bowels of the cavern.

South of Agios Mattheos there is a turn-off to the right that, after a short distance, leads to the ruins of a medieval fortress known as Gardiki Castle. This was built in the fourteenth century by one of the Despots of Epiros, either Michael I or Michael II. The fortress consists of eight towers connected by curtain walls to form an octagonal enclosure, with decorative courses of ceramic tiles set into its structure, along with fragments of ancient buildings that once stood in the vicinity.

Beyond the turn-off to Gardiki Castle one comes to a crossroads, where the main north–south road down the spine of the island crosses the road that leads from Agios Mattheos to Messongi and Moraitika on the east coast. Turning right at the crossroads, one can then begin the long drive down to the south-eastern end of the island, a route that must be retraced on the way back to Corfu town.

South of the crossroads the road veers to the south-east as it passes between Mount Kavalovouno and the enormous lagoon known as Lake Korission, which is bounded on its seaward side by a sandbar some 6km in length. Beyond the lagoon there is a turn-off to the right for Agios Giorgios beach, a 7km stretch of sand that extends all the way from Lake Korission to Cape Mega Choro.

Just beyond the turn-off to Agios Giorgios the road passes through Argyrades, where there is a turn-off to the left to the group of villages that cluster around the great promontory known as Boucari Point. This cape forms the western horn of the Bay of Lefkimmi, whose more elongated eastern horn is formed by Cape Lefkimmi. The main road goes to the village of Lefkimmi, where roads branch off in three directions along the south-easternmost peninsula of Corfu. One road leads north to Alikes, which is at the near end of the salt flats extending out to Cape Lefkimmi; a second road leads south along the spine of the outermost peninsula to the hill villages on the eminence known as Vouris; while the third road leads out along the north-eastern shore of the peninsula to the little port of Kavos, where some boats stop on their way to Paxos.

The road continues beyond Kavos and becomes a dirt track as it goes out to Cape Asprokavos, the south-easternmost tip of Corfu.

Out near the cape there is a ruined monastery dedicated to the Panagia Arkoudilas. A partially effaced date over the gateway records that it was built in the first decade of the eighteenth century, but little else is known of the history of this romantic ruin, perched on the most remote promontory of southern Corfu.

Driving back from Cape Asprokavos one can turn right at Lefkimmi village to make a brief detour to Alikes, a hamlet near the shining salt flats that extend out to Akri Lefkimmi, the cape known in antiquity as Leukimme. During the years 435–433 BC the navies of Kerkyra and Corinth fought two great battles in the strait between this cape and the Syvvota Isles, a tiny archipelago just off the mainland of Epirus. The Kerkyraeans won the first battle and erected a trophy on Cape Lefkimmi to commemorate their triumph. The second battle was inconclusive, though the Corinthians claimed victory and erected a trophy on one of the Syvvota Isles. Thucydides writes of this second battle in his account of the prelude to the Peloponnesian War.

> Many ships had been engaged on both sides, and the action had been an extensive one, so that, once battle was joined, it was not easy to make out who was winning and who was being defeated. Indeed, so far as numbers of ships were concerned, this was the biggest battle that had ever taken place between two Hellenic states.

The return route takes one up the east coast of the island from Moraitika, just beyond the turn-off to Messongi, where the density of hotels and other touristic establishments is even greater than on the coast north of Corfu town. This coast was apparently a resort era even in ancient times, for remains of villas of the Roman imperial era have been found in both Messongi and Moraitika as well as in Benitses, a pretty little fishing port on the shore east of Mount Agioi Deka. The villa at Benitses dates from the third century AD, as do the Roman baths that have also been excavated there. These baths relied on the springs above Benitses, which were the source of the water supply system that Sir Frederick Adam built during his tenure as Lord High Commissioner, one that still functions today.

North of Benitses there is a turn-off for Gastouri, a place that Margaret Hopkins, in her excellent book on the island, describes as having 'long had the reputation of having the prettiest women, the most beautiful costumes and the best dancers of any village on Corfu'. As the road enters the village it brings one to the Achilleion, a grandiose palace standing on a hilltop above Benitses.

The Achilleion, which is supposed to be a recreation of an ancient Phaiakian palace, was built during the years 1888–1892 for the Empress Elizabeth of Austria, the beautiful but ill-fated wife of the Austro-Hungarian Emperor Franz Joseph. Elizabeth wanted the Achilleion to be a summer hideaway where she could enjoy the beauties of Corfu undisturbed by the outside world, naming it in honour of her hero Achilles, who is represented in his dying moment by a statue in the palace gardens. 'I want a palace with pillared colonnades and hanging gardens,' she wrote, 'protected from prying glances – a palace worthy of Achilles, who despised all mortals and did not fear even the gods.' But Elizabeth had only a short while to enjoy the Achilleion, which she last used in 1896, two years before she was assassinated by an anarchist in Geneva. After Elizabeth's death the palace passed to her daughter, but it was little used during the following decade. Then in 1908 the Achilleion was bought by Kaiser Wilhelm II, who thereupon had the following dedication inscribed on the base of Achilles' statue: 'To the greatest of the Greeks from the greatest of the Germans.' (The inscription has since been removed.) The Kaiser used the Achilleion until the outbreak of World War I in 1914, and after the German defeat four years later the palace was acquired by the Greek government. The palace is now a museum by day and a casino by night, an anachronistic monument to colossal bad taste that nevertheless has a touch of the romantic because of its association with Elizabeth of Austria, whose statue stands in a niche overlooking the palace gardens.

The last stretch of the route back to Corfu town goes up the coast as far as Perama, where the road turns abruptly inland to go around the Chalkiopoulos Lagoon and the airport, joining the main inland road from the south. Perama was where the Durrells settled when they first came to Corfu, living in a house that they called the Strawberry Pink Villa. The villa has long since disappeared, demolished to make way for the airport, but the vanished scene is evoked in Gerald Durrell's *My Family and Other Animals*.

> The villa was small and square, standing in a tiny garden with an air of pink-faced determination… Its shutters had been faded by the sun to delicate creamy-green, cracked and bubbled in places… The warm air was thick with the scent of a hundred dying flowers, and full of the gently soothing whisper and murmur of insects.

Halfway between Perama and the main inland road one passes the rivulet known as the Cressida Stream, which here flows into the lagoon, the ancient Hyllaic Harbour. Cressida, in Greek mythology, was the daughter of the seer Kalchas, who in Book I of the *Iliad* is described as a man 'who knew all things that were, the things to come and the things past,/ who guided into the land of Ilion the ships of the Achaians…'. But Cressida herself is not mentioned in the *Iliad*, and the story of her tragic love affair with Troilus, son of King Priam of Troy, is a medieval invention. Waller Rodwell Wright, who was Consul General of the Septinsular Republic from 1800–1804, believed that this was where Nausikaa and her maids discovered Odysseus, and he gives a lyrical description of the scene in his *Horae Ionicae*:

> Such is the spot where flows Cressida's stream;
> The peasant's solace, and the poet's theme;
> From the cold rock her limpid fount distils;
> A rocky bed receives the falling rills.
> Twas here, sequester'd midst the embow'ring shades,
> The bright Nausicaa sported with her maids,
> What time Laertes' god-like son address'd
> His tale of sorrow to her pitying breast…

These romantic verses carried us around the Chalkiopoulos Lagoon and past the airport into Corfu town, ending our tour of the island. The following morning we were scheduled to leave Corfu, and so that evening we had a last dinner at our favourite restaurant on the Liston, where we were serenaded by an old fiddler named Spyros. When I told him that we would be leaving the following morning he sang for us as a parting song the favourite of all Corfiots, a *cantada* called 'Perdika', or the 'Partridge'.

> In this neighbourhood, in a small lane,
> The little partridge built her nest.
> She is praised, she is well-known
> Wherever she goes or wanders or stays.
> Little partridge: who is so well-known,
> And in the village is the envy of all.
> Corfu, my Corfu, my golden one,
> You are the most beautiful of islands.

I was still humming the words of Spyros' song when our ferry left Corfu the following morning, as we stood on the fantail for a long last look at the old Venetian town, wondering when we would return. As the town faded from view in the Ionian Sea I was reminded of the lines that Edward Lear wrote just after he departed from Corfu, in a letter dated 18 April 1864. 'I hope you got a letter from me just before I left Corfu – of which place I am now cut adrift, though I cannot write the name without a pang.'

Corfu (Kerkyra): population 111,041; area 588 sq. km; highest peak: Mt Pantocrator (911m); airport: international charters and flights from Athens and Thessalonika; ferries: boats to Corfu town from Igoumenitsa, Sagiada and Patras, as well as from the Italian ports of Ancona, Bari, Brindisi and Venice; also a weekly boat to Lefkimmi from Igoumenita.

PAXOS AND ANTIPAXOS

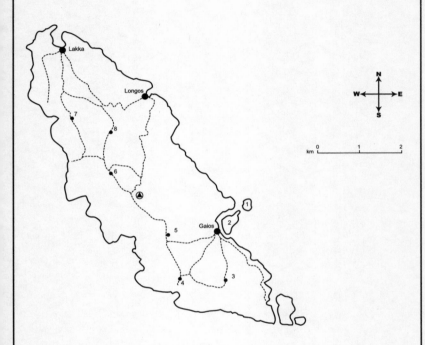

Paxos and Antipaxos

1 Panagia Island
2 Agios Nikolaos Island
3 Ozias
4 Veliantatika
5 Bogdanatika
6 Magazia
7 Ipapanti
8 Mastoratika
9 Agrapidia
10 Vigla
⊕ Mt Agios Ysavros

five
Paxos

P axos is the smallest and least populous of the seven main isles that together form the Eptanisa. Its area is only 19 sq. km, while its population in the 2005 census was just 2,448. The island is 11km long, extending from Cape Lakka on the north-west to the Mogonisi and Kalkionisi islets off its south-east coast, with its greatest width about 4km. Cape Lakka is only about eight nautical miles (15km) from Cape Asprokavos, and so Kavos on Corfu is a convenient port for ships sailing down to Paxos, but in summer there are also frequent boats from Corfu town.

Paxos has three ports: Lakka, on the northern tip of the island; Longos, some 3km down the eastern coast from Cape Lakka; and Gaios, the principal harbour and largest town of the island, which is 4km beyond Longos on the east coast. Boats also cross between Gaios and Parga, the nearest port on the mainland, a route that has been used since antiquity by Epirots moving across to Paxos to escape from wars or tyrannies on the mainland. Many of the present Paxiots are descendants of those who fled from the Turkish warlord Ali Pasha of Tebelen when he took control of Epiros during the first two decades of the nineteenth century.

Paxos is the greenest of all the Ionian Islands, with virtually its entire landscape covered with olive groves, stands of cypresses, and other trees and plants, of which over 250 species have been identified, including 15 different kinds of orchid. But it is the olive tree that dominates the landscape of Paxos, a heritage of Venetian days. It is estimated that there are more than 300,000 olive trees on Paxos, making it the most densely planted of the Ionian isles in that quintessentially Greek tree. And the olive oil that they yield is reputed to be the best on the Ionian isles, as Ansted reports in his description of Paxos and the Paxiots, whose good looks and longevity he attributes to the healthy climate of the island.

> Its inhabitants are among the best looking and most comfortable of the whole group, and are different, in this respect from most of the small islands. Its olive trees are celebrated as among the finest trees and as yielding the largest crops and the best oil of any of the islands ... The air of this little island is regarded as very healthy and the people attain a great age. The women are remarkable for their good looks when young; but, as elsewhere in this part of the world, the beauty of the lower classes is worn off before the girls are out of their teens.

Gaios, the capital of Paxos, is probably where Antony and Cleopatra had their headquarters before the Battle of Actium, which took place some 48km to the south-west on 2 September 31 BC, at the entrance to the Ambracian Gulf. Tradition has it that the town is named for the early Christian disciple Gaius, mentioned in *Acts of the Apostles*.

The harbour of Gaios is protected from the sea by two islets, Panagia and Agios Nikolaos, both named after seaside chapels. Larger ships use the northern channel between the islets and the town, first passing Panagia and then Agios Nikolaos, a strait so narrow that Gaios appears to be a river port rather than a harbour on the open sea.

The most distinguished building along the quay is the former mansion of the British Resident, built soon after the beginning of the British occupation of Paxos in 1815. William Gladstone stayed here in December 1858 during his fact-finding tour of the Ionian Islands. During his short stay Gladstone called upon the Bishop of Paxos, a meeting marked by an embarrassing incident described by Viscount Kirkwall:

At Paxos, as everywhere else, he [Gladstone] showed the
most unbounded admiration for the dignitaries of the
Greek Church. In Corfu, he had excited the perhaps illiberal
disgust of the English by publicly kissing the hand of the
Archbishop and dutifully receiving his blessing… The
simple bishop of Paxo appears to have been ignorant of the
etiquette which the High Commissioner Extraordinary
practised with ecclesiastical dignitaries. Mr. Gladstone,
having taking and respectfully kissed the Bishop's hand,
leaned forward to receive the orthodox blessing. The
Bishop hesitated, not knowing what was expected of him
and not imagining perhaps, that a member of the Anglican
church would require his benediction. At last, he perceived
the truth, and, bending forward, he hastened to comply
with the flattering desire of the representative of the British
Crown. But at this moment, unfortunately, Mr. Gladstone,
imagining that the deferred blessing was not forthcoming,
suddenly raised his head and struck the episcopal chin. The
Resident and other spectators of the scene had considerable
difficulty in maintaining the gravity befitting so solemn
an occasion.

The only other building of note in Gaios is the pretty little chapel
in the centre of the town's attractive seaside *plateia*. The church of
Agios Nikolaos, behind the bus stop, has many fine icons. There is
an ancient cistern to the right of the church.

The Junior School, an early twentieth-century building on the
south side of the harbour, houses the Paxos Museum. Outside the
museum there are old olive presses and containers for measuring
oil, as well as millstones, a limestone sink and other stone artefacts.
The exhibits in the first room of the museum include fossils, Stone
Age flint tools and classical pottery, as well as guns and tools from
the Venetian and later periods. The kitchen contains pots, pans,
dishes and other utensils of times past, as well as scales and weights
from the Ottoman and British periods. The main room contains a
seventeenth-century bed with *anapapsolia*, hanging wooden rings
for the lady of the house to rest her feet on. Next to the bed is the
baby's cot and the dressing table of the lady of the house, whose

collection of clothing and undergarments is also on display. In the hall there are a number of other exhibits, most notably a book on Paxos written in 1887 by Ludwig Salvator, Archduke of Austria.

One can hire a boat on the quay to go out to the two islets in the harbour. On the isle of Agios Nikolaos there are two chapels, one dedicated to Agios Nikolaos and the other to Agios Ioannis, as well as the ruins of a fortress almost completely overgrown with trees and shrubbery. This was built in 1423 by the Sant' Ippolito, a noble Neopolitan clan who obtained Paxos as a baronial fiefdom during the Angevin period and continued to rule the island for a time under the Venetians. The fortress was captured by the Turks in the invasions of 1537 and 1716, when most of the people on the island were either killed or enslaved. Those who subsequently repopulated the island were principally refugees from Epiros.

The isle of the Panagia is named for a chapel of the Virgin. The *paneyeri* of the Dormition of the Virgin is celebrated there on 15 August, when everyone goes out to the island in boats to a morning liturgy in the church, followed that evening with music and dancing in the *plateia* of Gaios.

Paxos is so small that in a single day one can walk the length of the island. The island's main road, originally built by the British and asphalted through the generosity of Aristotle Onassis, connects Gaios and Lakka along the spine of the island, with a loop to the villages south of the capital and two turn-offs to Longos. These roads take one through the heart of Paxos to the villages in the interior of the island, where there are a number of old churches of some interest embowered in the dappled shade of the vast olive groves.

A shore road leads south along the coast from Gaios, passing pebble beaches at Plakes and Defteri. It then goes around the headland at Ballos, where there are the remains of a Byzantine church at the end of the beach. The road continues to the southern tip of Paxos, where a causeway crosses the narrow strait to Mogonisi islet.

Another shore road leads north from Gaios to the new ferry port at Gerominachus, where there are the remains of an abandoned village. The road continues north to pebble beaches at Kioni and Kamini, before turning inland. At this point there is a track down to the beautiful secluded beach at Kaki Langada.

The southern loop of the main road inland passes Ozias, where there are the ruins of the oldest church on Paxos, a seventh-century basilica dedicated to Agia Marina. This was destroyed a century or so after it was founded, probably by Saracen raiders, and it was never rebuilt; nevertheless, the presence of recently used devotional objects such as oil lamps and votive candles indicate that local people still worship there.

At the crossroads south-west of Gaios there is a turn-off to Veliantatika, one of several villages that at one time or another in the Latin period supplanted Gaios as the island's capital. Veliantatika's last Venetian mayor, Il Condo, built the village church in the last quarter of the eighteenth century, making the main portal high enough so that he could enter on horseback without dismounting, or so it is said.

At the crossroads west of Gaios the main road north goes through Bogdanatika, and then about half a kilometre further along it passes on its right the church of Agios Haralambos, built in 1727. Haralambos is the patron saint of Paxos, revered for having stopped a plague in 1815; he performed similar miracles in many other places in Greece, and his feast day on 12 February is widely celebrated for that reason. George Megas describes an interesting custom associated with this *paneyeri*.

> The offerings made to this saint differ from the usual gifts: as a rule, the villagers offer St. Haralambos an apron, or a little shirt made of 'one-day cloth', i.e., cloth woven in one night by a group of women and young girls gathered together in one house. The weaving is done according to a number of magical formulae to the sound of incantations, thus endowing the shirt with magical powers.

The road then runs along the western slope of the island's highest hill, Mount Agios Ysavros (248m), near whose summit there is an old Venetian church dedicated to the Holy Cross. After passing a turn-off to Longos on the right, the main road heads towards Magazia, the largest village in the interior of the island, passing en route the hamlet of Arvanatatika, whose name suggests that it was founded by Albanian refugees. Here a turn-off to the left leads to the hamlet of Eleousa, which takes its name from an old Venetian church dedicated to the Panagia Eleousa.

At Magazia there are three churches dating from the Venetian period, none of them of exceptional interest. A turn-off to the left leads out to the village of Boikatika on the west coast, where there are two more Venetian churches; the more interesting of these is Agioi Apostoloi, noted for its beautifully decorated *iconostasis*. This church celebrates a two-day *paneyeri* on 29–30 June, the feast days of SS Peter and Paul. According to Megas, during these two days 'young girls of marriageable age perform various divinatory practices regarding their future marriage, using molten lead, water, mirrors or eggs'.

Beyond Magazia the road splits into two branches, which come together again a kilometre or so south of Lakka, with the right fork joining up with a road that leads to Loggos. The left fork is the more interesting of the two, because it is the old route through the northern villages of Paxos, the most notable of which is Ipapanti. This village is named of the Panagia Ipapanti, the oldest extant church on the island; founded in Byzantine times and completely rebuilt in 1602, it served as the Greek Orthodox cathedral for Paxos throughout the Latin period. The original deed of foundation endowed the church with 800 olive trees, all of which appear to be flourishing still. The Ipapanti has a famous icon of the Virgin, which is carried in procession through the surrounding villages on the feast of the Assumption.

One of the places through which this procession passes is Vasilatika, a virtually deserted village on the north-western coast of the island. Vasilatika is empty throughout most of the year, but some of the villagers return to their ancestral homes in mid-August to celebrate the festival of the Panagia Ipapanti, when their hamlet comes to life once again as the sacred icon of the Virgin is carried by with chanting and song.

Lakka is a pretty village at the end of a deeply indented bay, its buildings clustering around several charming little *plateias*. There are a number of pebble beaches around the bay, with Harami and Kanoni to the west, and to the east Arkoudaki, Orkos, Lakos and Monodendri.

From Lakka one can return to Gaios by boat, stopping en route at the picturesque port of Longos. Just south of Longos there is a good shingle beach at Levericho, where there is a taverna. One can also make the return journey from Lakka on foot, choosing a route that takes one to some of the villages and old churches that were not seen on the outward journey.

At Mastoratika, a village on the road between Magazia and Loggos, there is a church of SS Constantine and Helena dated 1720. The feast day of SS Constantine and Helena is celebrated on 21 May, the principal *paneyeri* of that month throughout Greece. In times past this festival was marked by the sacrifice of bulls or rams, indicating that it is the survival of an ancient fertility rite. In some places the high point of the festival was an extraordinary rite called *Anastenaria*, in which the devotees of the cult of St Constantine, the Anastenarides, danced on live coals, a custom that is still observed in the village of Agia Eleni in Thrace.

A travel company at Gaios offers daily voyages that circumnavigate both Paxos and Antipaxos. This gives one an opportunity to see the extraordinary western coasts of the islands, with their succession of dramatic cliffs, rocks and 'graves', or sea caves. The best description of this coast is by John Davy in his *Notes and Observations on the Ionian Islands and Malta*, published in 1842, in which he writes: 'To the traveller interested in bold and picturesque scenery an excursion to the caverns of Paxo may be safely recommended. No cliff scenery in the Ionian Isles is more deserving of being seen, – none will probably afford greater gratification.' The caves that Davy describes are known locally as Ipapanti, Landros, Achantakas, Achaios, Stachai, Petritis, Sterna and Agrilas, or the great cave. The largest of these is the Ipapanti cave, which in Davy's time was known as Grammatico, 'so called', as he writes, 'from the nearest village being of that name'.

> It is considered one of the largest of the caverns of Paxo;
> I would say it is the largest, and in all circumstances, the
> cliff being about triple that height [i.e., some 600 feet high];
> it is nearly as wide as it is high at its entrance, which
> capacious dimensions it retains some distance inward, and
> it may be some 300 to 400 feet deep. When we were about
> half way within, the view outward was very peculiar, and
> not without grandeur and a certain beauty, produced by
> a combination of circumstances, such as the great arched
> lofty roof, the vast perpendicular walls, the deep and
> transparent blue water beneath heaving up and down, the
> gigantic cliff skirting it on the outside, almost shutting out
> the sea and sky, the beautiful and vivid tint of the rock: the
> extraordinary play of light on the roof, and the clear-
> obscure which belongs to deep shade in a clear atmosphere
> under a bright sun.

The Ipapanti cave is just north of the famous Ermitis cliffs, which take their name from the hermits (in Greek, *ermetis*), who in earlier times lived in eyries high in the rock face of the precipice, lowering a basket with a pulley and line to receive supplies from passing mariners. While Davy was circumnavigating the island he was told of how the Paxiots caught swallows from the top of Ermitis and the other cliffs on the west coast of the island.

> Should the season be spring, the traveller may have an
> opportunity of witnessing a singular species of angling, in
> which, I was informed, the natives indulge from the lofty
> cliffs, not in the sea beneath for fish, but in the air for birds
> – swallows – which then crowd about the cliffs, and which
> they catch with a fly, attached to a fine hook and line,
> thrown and managed in much the same way as in common
> fly-fishing.

Two other notable features of the west coast of Paxos are the natural stone arch at Tripotos and the obelisk-like rock known as Ortholithos. Davy seems to have missed the arch at Tripotos, but he describes the Ortholithos in the account of his visit to the Petritis cave, whose name eluded him.

> Of the many other caverns on this shore I shall mention only one more, the name of which, if it has one, I could not learn. Its relative situation is well marked by a very fine pyramidal rock, insulated in the sea, just opposite to it, nearly two hundred feet [60m] high, and which is so near the cave that its shadow at noon almost reached it. In dimensions this cavern, too, was little inferior to that of Grammatico; and the view from the interior of it, which we entered, was very striking; indeed it was extraordinary, owing to the pyramidal rock standing before it, hiding almost entirely the sea and sky, though not intercepting the light, and producing, by its break-water effect, a mirror-like smoothness of the water.

There are also remarkable cliffs and a sea cave on the islet of Mogonisi, which one passes en route to Antipaxos. On the even tinier islet of Kalkionisi, which is separated from Mogonisi by a very narrow channel, there is a chapel of Agios Spyridon, which is the object of pilgrimages on the saint's four annual feast days.

The north-easternmost promontory of Antipaxos, Cape Katovrika, is about one and a half kilometres south of Kalkionisi. Approaching Antipaxos, one can see the dramatic cliffs that form the north-western ramparts of the island, which is just over 4km long and less than 2km in width at its broadest. Halfway along the east coast of Antipaxos caiques stop at Agrapidia, from where a road leads up to Vigla, the largest village, passing en route a chapel dedicated to Agios Emilianos. The next cove north of Agrapidia is Voutomi, whose superb sand beach is rimmed with spectacular chalk-white cliffs, a perfect place for a swim before heading back to Gaios.

The strait between these northern Ionian isles and Epirus is the setting for a strange tale that was first recorded in Plutarch's *Moralia*, part of an essay entitled 'Why the Oracles Cease to give Answers'. The story, which was told to Plutarch by his friend Epitherses, is set in the reign of Tiberius (AD 14–37).

Epitherses told me that, designing a voyage to Italy, he embarked himself on a vessel well laden with goods and passengers. Towards evening, the vessel was becalmed around the Echinades Isles, whereupon their ship drove on with the tide till it was carried near the Isles of Paxi; when immediately a voice was heard by most of the passengers (who were then awake, and taking a cup after supper) calling unto one Thamus, and with so loud a voice as made all the company amazed; which Thamus was a mariner of Egypt, whose name was scarcely known in the ship. He returned no answer to the first calls, but at the third he replied, 'Here! here! I am the man.' Then the voice said aloud to him, 'When you are arrived at Palodes (Buthrotum), take care to make it known that the great God Pan is dead'. Epitherses told us, this voice did much astonish all who heard it, and caused much arguing whether this voice should be obeyed or slighted. Thamus, for his part, was resolved, if the wind permitted, to sail by the place without saying a word; but if the wind ceased and there ensued a calm, to speak and cry out as loud as he was able. Being come to Palodes, there was no wind stirring, and the sea was as smooth as glass. Whereupon Thamus standing on the deck, with his face towards the land, uttered with a loud voice his message, saying, 'The great Pan is dead!' He had no sooner said this, but they heard a dreadful noise, not only of one, but of several, who, to their thinking, groaned and lamented with a kind of astonishment. And there being many persons in the ship, an account of this was soon spread over Rome, which made Tiberius the Emperor send for Thamus, and he seemed to give such heed to what he told him, and he earnestly enquired who this Pan was; and the learned men about him gave in their judgments that it was the son of Mercury by Penelope.

This curious legend is mentioned by Milton in his 'Ode on the Nativity', lines that came to mind as our caique crossed the strait between Paxos and Parga, evoked by the elegiac Ionian light of an August afternoon. 'The lonely mountains o'er,/and the resounding shore,/A voice of weeping heard and loud lament.'

I also recalled a couplet from Waller Rodwell Wright's encomium to Paxos, which is no longer so far off the beaten track as it was when he was there: 'Blest with whatever a genial clime supplies/Remote from human intercourse it lies.'

Paxos (Paxoi): population 2,448; area 19 sq. km; highest peak: Mt Ysavros (248 m); no airport; ferries: connections with Corfu town and Parga.

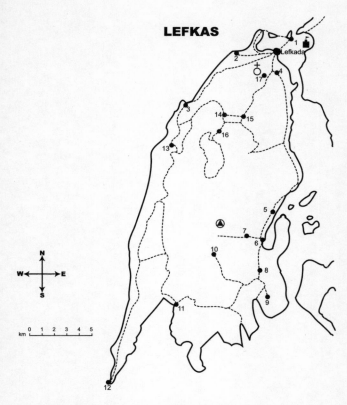

LEFKAS

1 Santa Maura
2 Agios Ioannis
3 Agios Nikitas
4 Kalligoni
5 Nydri
6 Vlycho
7 Charadiatika
8 Katochori
9 Poros
10 Syvros
11 Vassiliki
12 Cape Leucatas
13 Kalamitsi
14 Asprogerakata
15 Lazarata
16 Pygadissanoi

17 Hodegitria Monastery
⊕ Mt Elati

six
Lefkas

Lefkas, the ancient Leucadia, more commonly known to the Greeks today as Lefkada, is a geographical ambiguity among the Ionian isles. It has not always been an island, nor is it quite technically one now, since it is joined to the mainland by two causeways and their connecting bridge. But when the bridge opens so that ships can pass through the coastal waterway, then Lefkas is indeed an island in every sense of the word, one that is perhaps more beautiful than Corfu and certainly far less spoiled by tourism and the modern world.

Lefkas was known to the Latins as Santa Maura. This name came from the famous Castello Santa Maura, which stands halfway across the lagoon between the island and the mainland, just before the bridge that crosses to the second of the two causeways. Stanley Lane-Poole, writing in 1888, describes it as 'that diabolical castle seated like a magician's fortress in the middle of the sea'.

Construction of the castle began on 10 July 1300, when Charles II of Naples permitted John I Orsini to fortify the approach to Leucadia, which he had acquired some five years earlier as a dowry on his marriage to Maria Comnena, a daughter of Nichephorus I Comnenus, Despot of Epiros. The fortress was held by the Angevins from 1324 until 1362, when they were ousted by Leonardo I Tocco, who added Leucadia to his Palatine County of Cephalonia, which also included Ithaka and Zante. In 1388 his son, Carlo I, married

Francesca Acciajuoli, daughter of Nerio I, who earlier that year had taken Athens from the Catalans. William Miller describes the Countess Francesca as 'the ablest and most masterful woman of the Latin Orient, who used to sign her letters in cinnabar ink "Empress of the Romans"'. The countess held court both in Cephalonia and in Castello San Maura, where in 1396 she entertained some of the French knights who had been defeated by the Turks earlier that year at the Battle of Nicopolis on the Danube. Miller writes: 'The ladies were exceedingly glad to have such noble society, for Venetian and Genoese merchants were, as a rule, the only strangers who came to their delightful island.'

Half a century later another remarkable woman held court in the castle of Leucadia. This was the Empress Helena, wife of Manuel II Palaeologos (reigned 1391–1425) and mother of John VIII (reigned 1425–1448) and Constantine XI (reigned 1448–1453). After the fall of Constantinople to the Turks in 1453, Helena fled to the castle on Leucadia, which was then ruled by Leonardo III Tocco. Grateful for her deliverance from the Turks, she endowed a convent within the castle walls and lived out her last days there as a nun, taking the name of Epimoni, or Patience. Living with her in the convent was a daughter of Thomas Palaeologos, the last Despot of the Morea, who spent the rest of her life here, while her more fortunate sister Zoë was reigning as the Tsarina Sophia, wife of the Grand Duke of Moscow, Ivan III. The convent founded by Helena was dedicated to Santa Maura, who was depicted in a sacred icon that the Empress had brought with her from Constantinople, and this in time became the name of the castle and the island, with the present name coming into use only in recent times.

Lefkas first fell to the Turks in 1479, when it was captured by Gedik Ahmet Pasha, Grand Vezir of Sultan Mehmet II. During the conflicts between Venice and the Ottoman Empire Santa Maura changed hands six times, the last exchanges taking place in the sixth and seventh Veneto-Turkish wars. At the beginning of the sixth war the Venetians under Francesco Morosini captured Lefkas on 6 August 1684. During the seventh and last war the Venetians abandoned

Lefkas to the Turks without a struggle in 1714, but two years later Marshal Schulenburg recaptured the island after his successful defence of Corfu. After the end of the Venetian period the island was held in turn by the French (1797–1798), the Russians (1798–1807), the French again (1807–1810) and the British (1810–1864), before finally achieving *enosis* along with the other Ionian isles.

Writers in antiquity all agree that Leucadia was connected to the mainland by an isthmus, which survives in the two causeways leading out to the island. The first canal through this isthmus seems to have been dug by the Corinthians when they established a colony here in the seventh century BC, at about the same time that they founded the city of Kerkyra. This canal, known in antiquity as the Dioryctus, silted up continually, and had to be cleared by all the powers who held the island. During the British protectorate harbour facilities were built for ships passing through the canal, which has been reconstructed on a number of occasions in the past century, the most recent addition being the present bridge linking the two causeways.

Lefkada, the capital and principal town of Lefkas, is linked to the fortress of Santa Maura by the outermost of the two causeways. The town was known in times past as Amaxiki, a name that continued in use up until fairly recent times. The town of Amaxiki dates from the late fifteenth century, though in antiquity this was probably the port of Leucada, the principal city of the island, whose ruins have been identified on the spur of the mountain just to the south of the isthmus. Amaxiki really began its development in the first period of Turkish occupation during the reign of Beyazit II (reigned 1481–1512), son and successor of Mehmet II, who constructed the first causeways along the isthmus, along with an aqueduct, thus linking the town directly to the Ottoman possessions in north-western Greece.

Beyazit also encouraged Sephardic Jewish refugees from Spain to settle in the Ottoman Empire after their expulsion from Spain in 1492, and a large number of them moved into Amaxiki, where they soon dominated the town's commercial life. One of the first travellers to mention the numerous Sephardic community on Santa Maura was William Lithgow, who passed this way in 1610 on his way to Crete; as he writes in his *Rare Adventures and Painefull Peregrinations*: 'On our left toward the main, we saw an island called St Maure, formerly Leucas or Leucada, which is only inhabited by Jews, to whom Bajazet II gave it in possession, after their expulsion from Spain.'

William Martin Leake, in his *Travels in Northern Greece*, published in 1835, describes Amaxiki as it was early in the nineteenth century:

> The modern capital of Leucas, named Amaxikhi, resembles Mesolongi, as well as by its situation on the lagoon as in the form of houses, which are very unlike those of Corfu, being chiefly of wood in a substructure of stone or brick, with galleries supported by wooden pillars. The greater part of them are of one story only, which, as well as the wooden construction, is said to have been adopted in consequence of the frequency of earthquakes... The women are generally handsome, as at Mesongi, and in other situations in Greece which have every appearance of being unhealthy; but many of the men have a sickly complexion.

Travellers in times past invariably complained about the lack of amenities in Amaxiki, the earliest of its detractors being George Wheler, who after his visit in 1675 wrote that 'we had very hard cheere there, but bad Wine, bad Bread, and worse Cheese'. Ansted, writing in 1863, reports:

> The town was described to me by one who knew it well, and had travelled much, as the third worse real town to be found in civilised countries. He knew of two only that were more wretched. I think that my own experience could add but one or two more to the melancholy list. There is no house of public entertainment in which a stranger can take up his temporary abode. Such a thing as an hostel would be simply ridiculous.

But the situation is very different today, for the town was totally – and well – rebuilt after the 1948 earthquake, and Lefkada now has several hotels and restaurants, a measure of the increasing popularity of the island as a summer resort. The height of the season is August, when Lefkada has two cultural festivals, one devoted to folk dancing and the other to literature. The latter festival is a recognition of the role that Lefkas has played in modern Greek literature, for two of the country's most renowned poets were born there: Aristotelis Valaoritis (1824–1879) and Angelos Sikelianos (1884–1951). Another well-known writer who originated in Lefkas is Lefcadio Hearn (1850–1904), famous for his travel books and his stories about Japan, where he ended his days as a Japanese citizen under the name of Yakumo Koizumi. Hearn's father was an Irish surgeon in the British army and his mother a Greek from Kythera; after his birth in Amaxiki he was christened Patrick Lefcadio, his middle name commemorating his native island.

The town's role as a cultural centre is also evidenced by the fact that it has four museums and three musical societies, the oldest of which is the Lefkas Philharmonia, founded in 1850. The Folklore Museum, which is near the church of Agios Spyridon, was founded by the Lefkada musical association known as *Orpheus*. The museum has an interesting collection of memorabilia and objects made and used by the people of Lefkas in times past, including old photographs, maps, dolls, traditional costumes, handwoven items, house utensils, models of a windmill and an olive press. A room of the museum had been converted into a representation of a traditional Lefkadian room.

The Archaeological Museum, on Odos Faneromeni, has exhibits dating back as far as the early Bronze Age, including objects found on Lefkas by the German archaeologist Wilhelm Dörpfeld. The collection includes finds from the cemeteries of the ancient city of Leucadia, from the burial mounds at Steni and Skaros in the area of Nydri, the Chrysospelia cave at Eugeros, the Asvotrypa cave at Fryni, the cave of the nymphs near Agia Kyriaki, and on the isle of Meganissi. The most important exhibits are: a clay sauce boat found in the mound at Steno, dated to the early Bronze Age (3000–1900 BC), a black glazed funerary vase decorated in the 'West Slope' style, and a clay statuette of a standing female figure, both from the north cemetery of ancient Leucadia and dated to the first half of the third century BC.

The Museum of Art, which is housed in the Public Library, has some rare icons of the Byzantine period, as well as works by Lefkadian painters from the eighteenth century onwards. The two most important paintings are an anonymous fourteenth-century 'Entry into Jerusalem', and a 'St Dimitrios' by Panigiotis Doxaras. There are also some Russian icons from the Pontus, as well as a gold-embroidered stole presented to the Archbishop of Lefkas by Catherine the Great.

The Gramophone Museum has a rich collection of gramophones as well as other objects related to the everyday life of Lefkadians, including jewellery, coins, embroideries, old photographs and traditional musical instruments, in addition to many records and tapes of island folk music. One haunting old song is a Lefkadian *miroloyia* or funeral dirge, entitled '*Se Stratokopo*', or 'Lament for a Soldier'.

> On Friday I invited you,
> On Saturday I waited
> On Sunday I came out of church
> to eat and drink with you.
> and on Monday very early
> I came to meet you,
> to put in your bag the world's three good things;
> the sun and the wind and the bright moon.
> The sun for the hard worker,
> the wind for the sailor,
> and the bright moon for you, the soldier.

There are several old churches in the town, some of them dating from the Venetian period. The oldest of these is the church of Christou Pantocrator, which was built by Francesco Morosini to celebrate his liberation of Lefkas from the Turks in 1684. The church has a superb episcopal throne and is splendidly decorated with icons in carved wooden frames. The poet Aristotelis Valaoritis is buried in the garden of the church, which used to belong to his family.

The church of Agios Spyridon was founded in 1685 by a local magnate who had been ennobled by the Venetians after they reoccupied the island. Other churches are Agios Dimitrios, Agios Nikolaos, Agios Minas, Isodia tis Theotokou and Panagia ton Xenon (Our Lady of the Strangers). The latter church, like the one of the same name in Corfu, was founded by refugees from Epiros, the origin of many Lefkadians.

There are only two structures remaining from the period of the British protectorate. These are the twin buildings that served as the courthouse and the headquarters of the British Resident. Ansted writes an account of the memorable party that was given in the Residence early in March 1862, to celebrate the wedding of the Prince of Wales and Princess Alexandra of Denmark. After describing the preparations for the grand ball and supper, to which 200 of the principal Lefkadians were invited, he writes of the other entertainments that took place during the day, including music by the British band and by local musical societies, one of which sounded to him like a group of Highlanders.

> After our return to the Residence, a sound of distant music was heard. I was at the time talking to one of the officers of the garrison, and I stopped to ask if they had any Highlanders, as I thought I recognised bagpipes. The error was soon explained, for the sound proceeded from a drum and fifes played on by villagers from the mountains, whose national music and some of their other pecularities have a similar resemblance to those of the Scotch.

He also describes the dance that the Lefkadian guests performed towards the end of the ball:

> The primates, who were present, were not accompanied by wives or daughters... They did not join in the regular dances, and sat all together in one room, scarcely moving the whole evening; but just before the ball broke up, a request was made that they should take their share, and,

a proper instrument being obtained, they favoured the company with a specimen of the remarkable and most ancient Romaika, a curious measured movement, probably identical with the Pyrrhic dance, and certainly handed down from very remote antiquity... They retained throughout a wavy serpentine line, changing every instant, and from time to time the dancer at the end would detach himself and perform gesticulations much more violent. They afterwards danced again, each holding the hand of his neighbour, but the effect seemed to depend on the wavy line in which they moved.

Our first tour will take us out to the castle of Santa Maura. As we drive out along the causeway we see on our left the submerged piers of the Turkish aqueduct that conducted water to Amaxiki, also serving as a causeway until 1825. According to Leake, who first visited Lefkas in 1806, when the Russians were still occupying the fortress of Santa Maura, the Turkish structure

is supported by about 260 arches, and is 3600 yards [3,300m] in length... The aqueduct is so narrow, that when the wind is very strong it sometimes happens that careless or drunken men fall, or are blown over into the water and smothered in the mud. The Russians in garrison, who have just received a year's arrears of pay and are commanded by a rough Russian colonel, who has learned a few words of Italian at Naples and in these islands, and says that he would prefer the most miserable village in Russia to his present solitary and disagreeable station.

The castle of Santa Maura forms a hexagon of unequal sides, with five massive towers at the corners and bastions guarding the gateways leading to the causeways, where there used to be drawbridges. The present structure is a composite of work done by those who held the castle, beginning with John I Orsini, who in 1300 built the original fortress here. The tower beside the modern lighthouse, which has a vaulted substructure, is surmounted by the tomb of Major-General Davis, Adjutant General of the British forces in Sicily, who died in Lefkas on his way home in 1813. The eighteenth-century chapel in the south-eastern bastion stands on the site of the original church of Santa Maura, built by the Princess Maria Comnena when she married John I Orsini in 1325.

After seeing the castle, we return to town by a circuitous route, driving out along the Yiro, the long sandbank that surrounds the western lagoon. The road passes Yiropetra, the northernmost cape on Lefkada, after which it continues around the southern side of the lagoon on its way back to town.

Our next tour will take us out along the north-west coast of the island to the fishing village of Agios Nikitas, leaving the town centre along Odos Faneromenis. About one and a half kilometres out of town, just before reaching Frini, a turn-off to the right leads to the coastal village of Agios Ioannis. The village is named for an ancient church of Agios Ioannis Andzouzes, built in the last quarter of the thirteenth century by the Angevins, whose name it perpetuates in corrupted form. The nave is built in under a declivity in the rock face behind the church, where local tradition places the first Christian sanctuary on Lefkas.

Beyond Frini the road passes Moni Panagia Faneromeni, the most renowned monastery on the island, standing on a hilltop in a grove of pines. The monastery was founded in 1634, supposedly on the site of an ancient sanctuary. The beautiful *iconostasis* was created by Estathios Prosalendis, whose icon of the Panagia Faneromeni is covered with ex-votos. The monastery was ruined in the 1948 earthquake, and the subsequent reconstruction left little of architectural interest.

After passing through the pleasant village of Tsoukalades, the road finally comes to an end at Agios Nikitas, a pretty little seaside hamlet surrounded by pines, cypresses and olive trees, with the long and beautiful beach of Pefkoulia just to its north.

The main road south from Lefkada leaves town along Leoforos Lefkadas. Some 3km south of the town the road comes to a fork, with the right branch leading southward through the mountains and the one on the left going out to the east coast of the island.

About a kilometre along the left fork the road passes on its right Megale Vrisi, the Great Spring, which since antiquity has been the source of water for the island's capital. Megale Vrisi is enshrined within the church of Panagia Zoodochos Pigi, Our Lady of the Life-giving Well, an old shrine of the Virgin that probably replaces an ancient sanctuary of Artemis, as evidenced by the dedicatory niches cut into the rock face around it.

A few hundred metres beyond Megale Vrisi the road turns sharply right at the village of Kalligoni, 'the Good Corner', after which it heads down the eastern coast of the island. The rocky spur above Kalligoni has been identified as the site of the ancient city of Leucadia. During the Persian Wars contingents from Leucadia fought at the Battles of Salamis and Platea, and during the Peloponnesian War the city was an ally of Corinth. All that remains of the ancient city are a tower and a stretch of its defence walls. According to Leake, the city was originally called Nerikos, a name it retained until after the Peloponnesian War, when it came to be known as Leucas. The city is referred to in Book XXIV of the *Odyssey*, in which Laertes tells his son Odysseus that as 'Lord of the Kephallenians, I took Nerikos, the strong-founded city on the mainland cape'.

The road south from Kalligoni passes on its left a side road that leads out to the salt flats at Alikes. Here the channel between Lefkas and the mainland narrows to less than 400m, its passage further constricted by a tiny islet halfway across. On the islet are the ruins of Fort Alexandros, named for Tsar Alexander I. This is one of two fortresses that the Russians constructed along the channel during their occupation of Lefkas; the other, a few hundred metres to the north, is known as Fort Constantine.

On the mainland just to the south of the channel there are the ruins of a Venetian fortress known as Castro San Georgio, which guarded the southern approach to Amaxiki from the Bay of Drepano. The last time this and the other fortresses across the channel saw action was in 1807, when Ali Pasha made a move to take Lefkas. The defence of Lefkas was commanded by John

Capodistrias, who conscripted all the men on the island between 16 and 60 and directed them in digging trenches on the sandbar of the lagoon and in strengthening Santa Maura and the other fortresses along the channel. Despite a sporadic bombardment from Ali Pasha's artillery, the defences were completed and deterred the invasion, so that by mid-July Capodistrias could report to the government of the Septinsular Republic that Lefkas was secure. Thereupon a great banquet was held in a field beside the channel, where, as one chronicler described it, 'they had toasted the liberation of Greece, and had embraced each other with tears in their eyes'.

Beyond the turn-off to Alikes the main road reaches the sea at Lygia, where one has the first clear prospect of the seascape between Lefkas and the mainland. At Nikiana a turn-off on the right leads inland to Alexandros and other mountain villages in the heart of Lefkas, a number of them clinging to the slopes of the four highest peaks on the island: Efkatos (730m), Agios Profitis Ilias (1,012m), Elati (1,158m) and Pyrgos (925m). En route from Nikiana to Alexandros the road passes through Kollyvata, where a path leads up to the seventeenth-century monastery of Agios Giorgios on the heights of Mount Skaros (663m). Off to the south-west is the fifteenth-century chapel known as Kokkini Eklisia, the 'Red Church'. The village of Alexandros has an interesting church dedicated to the Dormition of the Virgin, with a carved wooden *iconostasis* and fine icons.

The next large village on the coast is Nydri. This is one of the most popular summer resorts on Lefkas, standing as it does on the very beautiful fiord-like Bay of Vlycho, with a view of the Agia Kyriaki peninsula and the archipelago to its south and south-east. The peninsula is named for the tiny chapel of Agia Kyriaki on its northern promontory, just south of Nydri at the narrow mouth of the Bay of Vlycho. Some 200m from the chapel there is a villa that for many years was the home of the archaeologist Wilhelm Dörpfeld (1853–1940), who lies buried there in the garden. Dörpfeld, who had been Schliemann's assistant at Troy, spent his last years excavating two ancient burial sites near Nydri. His findings convinced him that the home island of Odysseus was not Ithaka but Lefkas, but modern archaeologists are not in agreement with his theory. Nevertheless, a number of scholars currently identify Lefkas with Homeric Doulichion. This island is mentioned in Book I of the *Odyssey*, where Telemachus tells Athena of the suitors who have been paying court to his mother Penelope.

> For all the greatest men who have power in the islands. In Doulichion and in Same and in wooded Zakynthos, and all who in rocky Ithaka are holders of lordships, all these are after my mother for marriage, and wear my house out.

A small museum in the village has some of the antiquities that Dörpfeld and others found at archaeological sites in the vicinity. There are a number of ancient sites and monuments to be seen in the countryside around the village, including the remains of a prehistoric settlement, an aqueduct and several circular tombs.

East of Nydri are the small islets of Khelmi, Madouri, Sparti, Skorpido and Skorpios. Madouri was the home of the poet Aristotelis Valaorites, whose Palladian mansion can still be seen there on the shore opposite the Agia Kyriaki chapel. Skorpios was acquired in 1962 by Aristotle Onassis, who six years later was married there to Jacqueline Kennedy, widow of the late President John F. Kennedy. Onassis is now buried on the island, which has passed on to his heirs.

There is a daily caique from Nydri to Meganissi, which is by far the largest of the satellite isles off the south-east coast of Lefkas. The island has two ports, Spartachori and Vathe, which are connected by road with the only inland village, Katomeri. Near Spartachori there is a cave called Spilaio tou Daimoni, the Cavern of the Demons. This was excavated in 1925 by Sylvia Benton, who found early Bronze Age sherds, as well as objects from the Hellenistic and Roman periods. At the north-western tip of Meganissi there is an enormous sea cavern known as Spilaio Papanikolos, named for the Greek submarine that used it as a secret base during World War II. This is the second largest marine cave in Greece, 120m in length, its width tapering from 60m at the entrance to 30m at the inner end.

There are half a dozen other islands scattered in the sea south-east of Lefkas, the largest of which are Kalamos and Kastos, which are well under a kilometre from the Akarnanian coast. These islands, together with Meganissi and the tiny islets to its north, were known in antiquity as the Taphii, or sometimes as the Teleboa. The people of these isles, the Taphians, were renowned seamen and traders who often resorted to piracy. In Book I of the *Odyssey* Athena disguises herself as a Taphian warlord named Mentes, telling Telemachus that she is an old friend of his father's.

> I announce myself as Mentes, son of Anchialos the wise,
> and my worship is over the oar-loving Taphians. Now I
> have come in as you see, with my ship and companions
> sailing over the wine-blue water to men of alien language,
> to Temese, after bronze, and my cargo is gleaming iron...
> Your father and I claim to be guest-friends by heredity...

The drive from Nydri south to Vlycho, the village at the southern end of the bay, is one of the most scenic on the Ionian Islands, with the blue serpentine fiord almost completely enclosed by white sand beaches and vividly green tree-clad hills. Vlycho, a village of boatbuilders, has now become a yachting centre, with a large marina, a perfect base for exploring the fiord and the isles that are scattered around it.

North of Vlycho there is a side road that leads inland to the village of Charadiatika, from where a secondary road leads up to Alatron, a hamlet high on the southern slopes of Mount Elati, the highest peak on the island. Nearby there are two old monasteries, one dedicated to St John and the other to St Dimitrios.

South of Vlycho the main road passes through the village of Katochori, where there are two churches dating from the Venetian period. The thirteenth-century church of Agios Dimitrios has a carved wooden *iconostasis* and an episcopal throne dating from the eighteenth century. The church of Agios Haralambos has wall-paintings dating from the fifteenth century. Some 2km outside the village there is an old church dedicated to Agios Nikolaos.

South of Katochori the road comes to a fork, where we take the road on the left and head out along the south-easternmost peninsula of Lefkas to Poros, a pretty village set in a natural amphitheatre on the verdant slop of a hill overlooking the sea. The oldest church in the village, dedicated to the Analypsis, has some fine icons dating from the seventeenth century.

On the peninsula south of Poros there are the remains of a Hellenistic settlement around the ruins of a *pyrgos* dating from the third century BC. These watchtowers are to be seen on many of the isles around the Ionian and Aegean Seas, almost all of them dating from the early Hellenistic period, when the successors of Alexander the Great were fighting one another for control of the eastern Mediterranean world.

On the road out to Poros there is a turn-off to the right for Poros Beach, a seaside hamlet on Ormos Rouda, the bay enclosed between the south-easternmost peninsula of Lefkas and the next promontory to its west. Down by the bay there is a nineteenth- century church of Agia Marina, one of numerous chapels in Greece dedicated to this saint, who died a martyr in Antioch in 262. Agia Marina is probably a Christian reincarnation of Artemis, as is the Blessed Virgin, as evidenced by fragments of ancient temples of the virgin huntress that have been found at these shrines. And thus the *paneyeri* of Agia Marina, celebrated on 17 July involves rituals that would appear to date back to the beginnings of Greek civilisation. As George Megas writes of this festival:

> Her feast-day coincides with the season when the grapes ripen, and it is celebrated with a general exodus to the vineyards and orchards, and by fruit-offerings in church. In some parts of Greece, as at Damati in Epirus, an ox is sacrificed at the expense of the whole community, so as to ensure health and happiness for all. The ox is cut into thirty or thirty-two pieces, which are distributed among the descendants of an equal number of families – this

probably being the number of the first families to settle in
the village. St. Marina also protects the faithful against
noxious insects. On her feast-day the priest is asked to bless
the house and fields with holy water to keep insects away.

Returning to the crossroads south of Katochori, we now take the
road that heads westward across the southern end of the island. At
the next intersection, a secondary road on the right leads to the
villages of Syvros and Agios Ilias. Some four or five kilometres
along this road, keeping to the left at the first fork, we come on the
left to a path that leads to the ruined monastery of Agios Ioannis sto
Rodaki, St John of the Pomegranate Tree. Most of the monastery
seems to date from the eighteenth century, with some of its frescoes
still visible on the fragmentary walls of its apse. The chapel is built
on the site of and using the architectural members of an ancient
temple that was excavated by Dörpfeld, who believed that this
sanctuary was bigger than those of Hephaestus at Athens or
Poseidon at Cape Sounion. The temple is believed to have been
dedicated to Demeter, the Greek goddess of agriculture, because in
times past the local farmers brought their ploughshares here to be
blessed at the church.

Back on the main road once again, we next pass a side road on
the left leading to Syvota, a pretty seaside hamlet at the inner end of
another fiord-like bay. A short way beyond the Syvota road there
is a turn-off on the left that leads to Evgiros; from there a path leads
south to Khirospilia, the Hog's Cave, where Dörpfeld found pottery
and tools dating back to the early Bronze Age.

The main road across the south side of the island has its terminus
at Vassiliki, a picturesque village at the inner end of an enormous
bay that terminates to the south-west at Akri Lefkatas, the ancient
Cape Leucatas. There is no direct route to the cape from Vassiliki
other than by boat, and so motorists must take the main road north
across the mountains as far as Agios Petros, where a turn-off to the
left leads to Athanion and the road that leads down along the entire
length of the Lefkatas peninsula. A turn-off to the left leads to the
seventeenth-century monastery of Agios Nikolaos, whose *katholikon*

has a carved wooden *iconostasis* and interesting old icons. The road finally brings one to the famous white cliffs of Cape Leucatas, from which the island takes its name.

Cape Leucatas is renowned as 'Sappho's Leap', from the legend that the Lesbian poetess leaped from its white cliffs into the sea. Strabo and other ancient sources refer to a temple of Apollo Leucatas that stood on the heights above the cliff. Nothing now remains of the temple, but Dörpfeld was able to identify its site as the place where the present lighthouse stands. Local tradition has it that this was where Sappho and others suffering the pangs of unrequited love hurled themselves into the sea, and also that it was the launching pad for the extraordinary ritual called *katapontismos*, in which convicted criminals were thrown off the cliff as scapegoats, though every effort was made to save their lives. Strabo gives a vivid account of this ritual in Book X of his *Geography*, along with a description of Cape Leucatas and 'Sappho's Leap'.

> Leucas... was named, as I think, after Leucatas... a rock of white colour jutting out from Leucas into the sea and towards Cephallenia... It contains the temple of Apollo Leucatas, and also the 'Leap', which was believed to put an end to the longings of love. 'Where Sappho is said to have been the first,' as Menander says, 'when through frantic longing she was chasing the haughty Phaon, to fling herself with a leap from the far-seen rock, calling upon thee [Apollo] in prayer, O lord and master.' Now although Menander says that Sappho was the first to take the leap, yet those who are better versed than he in antiquities say that it was Cephalus, who was in love with Pterelas the son of Deineus. It was an ancestral custom among the Leucadians, every year at the sacrifice in honour of Apollo, for some criminal to be flung from this rocky lookout for the sake of averting evil, wings and birds of all kinds being attached to him, since by their fluttering they would lighten the leap, and also for a number of men, stationed all round below the rock in small fishing-boats, to take the victim in, and, when he had been taken on board, to do all in their powers to get him safely outside of their borders.

The story of Sappho's suicide at Cape Leucatas is probably an invention of Menander, but the legend has such romantic appeal that from the Hellenistic period onwards it has been part of the accepted tradition of her life. Nor is there any reference to Leucada in her surviving poetry, though it is possible that she may have passed or stopped at Cape Leucatas on her way to or from Sicily, where she lived for a time in her childhood before returning to Lesbos. Nevertheless, Strabo's description of the *katapontismos* evokes these lines from Sappho's 'Invocation to Aphrodite', in which she describes an epiphany of the goddess.

> Throned in splendor, deathless, O Aphrodite,
> child of Zeus, charm-fashioner, I entreat you
> not with griefs and bitterness to break my spirit, O goddess;
> standing by me rather, if once before now
> far away you heard, when I called upon you,
> left your father's dwelling-place and descended, yoking
> the golden
> chariot to sparrows, who fairly drew you
> down in speed aslant the black world, the bright air
> trembling at the heart to the pulse of countless fluttering
> wingbeats.
> Swiftly then they came, and you, blessed lady,
> smiling on me out of immortal beauty…

This is one of the most romantic spots on the Greek isles, the 'ancient mount' in whose shadow Byron's Childe Harold 'saw the evening star above Leucadia's far projecting rock of woe'. The white cliffs of Cape Leucatas also inspired Thomas Moore, who writes of the fateful plunge in his *Evenings in Greece*.

> The very spot where Sappho sung
> Her swan-like music, ere she sprung
> (Still holding in that fearful leap,
> By her lov'd Lyre) into the deep.

Waller Rodwell Wright also writes of 'Sappho's Leap' in his *Horae Ionicae*.

Lo! next, where Acarnania's shores extend,
Leucate's pale and broken rocks ascend.
Ah, fatal scene! by Venus doom'd to prove
The last sad refuge of despairing love,
For ever sacred be the foaming tide
That breaks against thy hoarse resounding side.
What though thy long forsaken steep retain
No mould'ring vestige of its marble fane,
Yet shall thy cliffs derive eternal fame
From Sappho's plaintive verse, and hapless flame.

Driving back from Cape Leucatas, one can continue north at Athanion on the road to Komili, turning left at the crossroads beyond the village and rejoining the main road north from Vassiliki and Agios Petros. The main road continues north through the villages of Chortata, Exanthia and Drymon, where there is a turn-off to the left for Kalamitsi, and from there a side road goes on to the coast at Agios Nikitas.

Kalamitsi is one of the oldest and most picturesque villages on the island, with 13 windmills still standing. There are four old churches in the countryside around the village, of which the most famous is Panagia stous Kipos, Our Lady in the Garden; the others are Taxiarchoi, Agia Paraskevi and Panagia Theotokos.

The main road then comes to the crossroads village of Asprogerakata. This is the hub of a network of roads that inter-connect the mountain villages in the interior of the island, the largest of them being Karya, whose picturesque *plateia* is shaded by a venerable *platanos*, or plane tree. Some 5km from Karya there is an old monastery dedicated to St John.

The road eastward from Asprogerakata leads to Lazarata, where there are two old churches, one of them dedicated to Agios Spyridon and the other to Agios Dionysios, both of which have a finely carved wooden *iconostasis*. Some 2km from the village there is a cave chapel dedicated to Agios Profitis Ilias, the Prophet Elijah.

South-west of Lazarata are the villages of Pinakochori and Pygadissanoi, and to its north-east is Spanochori. These and several other villages in the vicinity are known as the Sfakhiotes, after the mountainous region in Crete known as Sfakia. Local tradition has it that these villages were founded by refugees from Sfakia after Morosini's recapture of Lefkas from the Turks in 1684.

Pygadissanoi is on the rim of the enormous sunken valley of Livadi. This is the most spectacular of the so-called 'sumps' of the Ionian isles, which Ansted describes in the account of his journey south from Amaxiki to Sappho's Leap.

> On reaching the top of the ridge we look towards the country beyond, and, at first sight, the antiquary might fancy himself in some vast amphitheatre of giants, so perfectly circular is the sweep, and so regular the apparent seats in two or three valleys at his feet. Two such valleys are seen nearly adjacent, one a little behind the other. The nearest is the most perfect, and might well deceive any whose faith in the magnitude of human works was sufficiently great. A much larger one is closer at hand. The bottom is perfectly circular and is absolutely flat. It is, indeed, the bed of a lake; and at the time of my visit the water had only just left the bottom. I had no means of measuring the dimensions, but I think the diameter could not be less than half a mile [about 800m] at the bottom, and the depth to the bottom I estimated at a hundred and fifty feet [just under 50m]. The apparent seats were natural terraces, carried round at intervals of various heights, produced by the action of water that had rested at those levels. The resemblance to an artificial construction is admirable... They are, in fact, portions of the limestone of which so much is to be seen in this part of the world, and they indicate places where hollow cavities have been produced in the interior by the infiltration and passage of water, and where probably the roof of some cavern has fallen in.

The road from Lazarata to Spanochori leads directly back to Lefkada town, passing to the west of Mount Agios Ilias (550m). One site of interest on the last stretch of the way back to town is the ruined Monastery of the Hodegitria, which is to the left of the road some 3km outside Lefkada. This monastery was founded in 1450 by the Empress Helena, wife of Manuel II Palaeologos, at the time that she founded the convent at Santa Maura. The Hodegitria is named for a renowned icon of the Virgin, the talisman that protected Byzantium from its foes until the fall of Constantinople to the Turks in 1453, three years after the founding of this monastery in Lefkas.

We spent one last night in Lefkada before leaving the island, checking in at the Hotel Byzantium because of its romantic name. After dinner that evening we took a stroll along the *paralia*, or waterfront promenade, to catch the *melteme*, the prevailing northerly wind that seldom fails to relieve the heat on summer evenings in the Greek isles. I was reminded of this when I read the last pages of Ansted's description of Santa Maura, which he ends with some remarks on the customs, superstitions and appearance of the Lefkadians.

> In Santa Maura it is the custom for people to walk out after dusk with their wives to enjoy the evening breeze. In such cases the lady walks before her husband, and they do not address each other. Should a gentleman meet his friend thus accompanied, he would not think of addressing the lady, or alluding to her existence; he would not even take off his hat, though acquainted with and visiting the family. The lady is entirely incognito, and must remain so. This is a curious specimen of orientalism preserved intact to the present day, common enough in Greece a few years ago, but now confined to the less visited isles ... Superstition is rife in Santa Maura, especially among the country people. Not long ago a most respectable and wealthy proprietor, the chief of his village and district, allowed it to be known that he had been induced to give upwards of two hundred dollars to a woman who had a reputation as a witch, and who was known to have visited churchyards in the costume of Eve without her innocence. The poor man, being himself in authority, was forced by the authorities to give evidence on the subject, which he would willingly have avoided, and the woman was punished with imprisonment ... for there

was reason to suppose that she was a mischievous and dangerous character... As in Corfu, the women, except when young, are extremely ugly; but the men are handsome, and often seem to improve and gain an appearance of dignity and intelligence when they grow old, which is not observable at an earlier period of life.

Lefkas (Lefkada): population 22,536; area 293 sq. km; highest peak: Mt Elati (1,158m); no airport (the nearest airport is at Parga); ferries: in summer connections between Vassiliki and Frikes in Ithaka.

ITHAKA

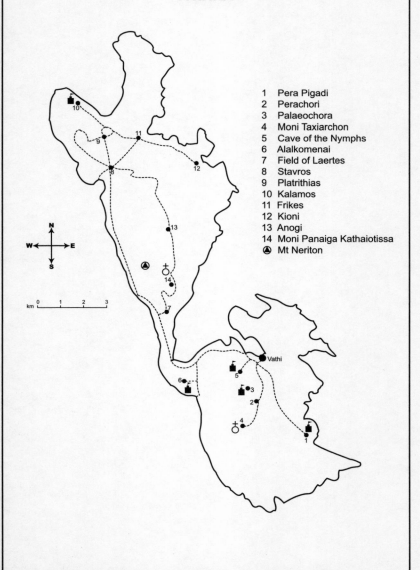

1   Pera Pigadi
2   Perachori
3   Palaeochora
4   Moni Taxiarchon
5   Cave of the Nymphs
6   Alalkomenai
7   Field of Laertes
8   Stavros
9   Platrithias
10 Kalamos
11 Frikes
12 Kioni
13 Anogi
14 Moni Panaiga Kathaiotissa
⬤ Mt Neriton

seven
Ithaka

I thaka is the second smallest of the principal Ionian Islands, after Paxos, with an area of only 90 sq. km. It lies off the Akarnanian coast of Greece south of Lefkas, separated from the much larger (by a factor of seven) island of Cephalonia by a narrow strait. Ithaka and Cephalonia, together with Zakynthos to their south, form the southern group of the six Greek islands in the Ionian Sea, lying off the western end of the Gulf of Patras.

We began our tour of the southern Ionian Islands at Astakos, a little port on the western coast of Akarnania, from which there is a daily boat that stops first at Ithaka and then at Cephalonia. This was our first visit to these islands, after 30 years of travelling around Greece, and as the ferry set out from Astakos I recalled some prophetic lines from Cavafy's 'Ithaka', as translated by John Mavrogordato:

> Setting out on the voyage to Ithaka
> You must pray that the way be long,
> Full of adventures and experiences...
> Many be the summer mornings
> When with what pleasure, with what delight
> You enter harbours never seen before...

En route to Ithaka the ferry passes through a little archipelago known as the Echinades. This group takes its name from the Greek *echinus,* meaning hedgehog or sea urchin, for 'they are indeed like the spines of a sea-urchin, bristling through the clear blue sea-wave'. The Echinades lie off the alluvial delta of the river Acheloos, which there forms the constantly shifting boundary between Akarnania and Aitolia. The lighthouse on Oxeia, the southernmost of the Echinades, has since antiquity marked for mariners the transition point between the Ionian Sea and the Gulf of Patras, known in former times as the Gulf of Lepanto.

Oxeia anchored one end of the two opposing lines of warships in the Battle of Lepanto, which was fought at the entrance to the Gulf on 7 October 1571, with the struggle extending from there 7,000 yards (6,400m) across to the Peloponnesian shore. The fleet of the Christian allies, the Holy League, was commanded by Don John of Austria, the 25-year-old bastard son of Charles V, while the Ottoman forces were led by Ali Pasha, whose second in command was Ochiali, later to be famous as Kilich Ali Pasha. There were 235 warships in the Christian fleet, of which 63 were Venetian and 64 Genoese, the latter contingent led by Gian Andrea Doria, while the Turks had 271 vessels, with Ochiali commanding 93 of them. The battle ended in a decisive victory for the Holy League, with virtually all the ships of the Ottoman fleet sunk or captured except for the contingent commanded by Ochiali, who outmanoeuvred Doria and escaped to fight another day. The Turks had some 30,000 men killed or drowned, with another 8,000 taken prisoner, while the Christian dead numbered about 9,000, a loss compensated for by the liberation of 15,000 Christians who had been serving as galley slaves in Ali Pasha's fleet. The allied victory at Lepanto is still celebrated in the churches of Venice and other former members of the Holy League, while in the English-speaking world it is evoked in the resonances of Chesterton's memorable poem.

> Don John pounding from the slaughter-painted poop
> Purpling all the ocean like a bloody pirate's sloop,
> Scarlet running over on the silvers and the golds,
> Breaking of the hatches up and bursting of the holds...
> Viva Hispania! Domina Gloria!
> Don John of Austria has set his people free!

These remote and seldom visited islands are rarely noted by modern writers, though they have been mentioned by Homer, Herodotus, Thucydides, Strabo and Pausanias. Petala, the largest of the group, was identified by Leake as Homeric Doulichion, though most other authorities tend to disagree with him, preferring the ancient Cephalonian city of Pale. Leake's identification is based on the Catalogue of Ships in Book II of the *Iliad*, in which Homer mentions the contingent from these islands before that of Odysseus, who commanded 12 ships from Zakynthos, Cephalonia and Ithaka.

> They who came from Doulichium and the sacred Echinai
> islands, where men live across the water from Elis,
> Meges was the leader of these, a man like Ares…
> Following along with him were forty black ships.

The ferry from Astakos weaves around the northernmost isles of the Echinades on its way to Vathi, the capital and port of Ithaka. The town is at the inner end of a deeply indented bay at the south-eastern corner of the Moulo Gulf, a huge bight that almost cuts Ithaka into two parts, with the northern and southern peninsulas of the island connected by a rugged isthmus that narrows to a width of only 620m. The peak of the southern peninsula is Mount Petalatiko (671m), also known as Merovigli, and the summit of the northern one is Mount Neriton (806m), the 'leaf-trembling Neritos' of the *Odyssey*. The isthmus between them is dominated to its south by Aetos, the Eagles' Cliff, which some believe to be the site of the palace of Odysseus. Aetos looks out across the Ithaki Strait towards Cephalonia, whose serrated north-western shore is less than 4km from the isthmus of Ithaka as the eagle flies, with Lefkas visible to the north and Zakynthos to the south. This is the scene that Odysseus describes when he identifies himself to King Alkinoos, in Book IX of the *Odyssey*.

> I am Odysseus son of Laertes, known before all men for
> the study of crafty designs, and my fame goes up to the
> heavens. I am at home in sunny Ithaka. There is a mountain
> there that stands tall, leaf-trembling Neritos, and there are

islands settled around it, lying one very close to another ... a
rugged place, but a good nurse of men; for my part I cannot
think of any place sweeter on earth to look at.

Ithaka was famous even in antiquity as the home of Odysseus,
though Strabo (64 BC – after AD 21) comments on some of the
geographical inconsistencies in Homer's description of the island
and its surroundings. Nevertheless, the very existence of Ithaka was
almost forgotten in Europe during the medieval Byzantine era,
when the ravages of barbarians and corsairs forced the few surviving
islanders to flee or to take refuge in the mountains, where they have
left virtually no trace. Ithaka was permanently severed from the
Byzantine Empire in 1185, when the island was taken by the Sicilian
Admiral Margaritone.

During the Latin period the island was held in turn by the
Normans (1185–1209), the Venetians (1209–1218), the Latin
Emperors of Constantinople (1204–1261), the Angevins (1267–
1404), the Tocco dynasty (1404–1479), the Turks (1479–1503) and
the Venetians (1503–1797). When the Venetians regained control of
Ithaka, then (as now) known in the local Greek dialect as Thiaki,
they found it uninhabited, whereupon they invited colonists to
settle there with a five-year exemption from taxes. Thus began the
resettlement of the island, as noted in two documents dating from
the mid-sixteenth century. The first, dated 1545, refers to Vathi as
Val di Compare, the name by which the island was known to the
Latins. 'Under the jurisdiction of Cephalonia there is another
island named Thiaci, very mountainous and barren, in which there
are different harbours and especially a harbour called Vathi or Val
de Compare; in the which island are hamlets in three places,
inhabited by about sixty families, who are in great fear of corsairs
because they have no fortress in which to take refuge.' The second,
dated 1563, describes Ithaka, as 'very well populated, for many
Cephalonians go to live there'.

Leake writes that in his time the population of the island had
risen to 8,000, although he notes that 'about 1200 are absentees,
employed chiefly at Constantinople in importing grain and iron

into that city from the Black Sea, or as sailors working the ships of the island, possessed by these merchants'. By the end of the British occupation the resident population had risen to nearly 15,000, and by the start of the twentieth century some 200 Ithakian ships with native crews were engaged in commerce with ports on the Black Sea and up the Danube. By then the modern Greek diaspora had begun, the greatest exodus being from the rural areas of the country and barren isles such as Ithaka, whose enterprising mariners had first emigrated to Russia and Romania after *enosis* with Greece, with the second wave taking them to America and Australia. The population of Ithaka continued to decline until 1980, when it stabilised at about 3,000, the tide of emigration stemmed by the rise of tourism on the island, which since Leake's time has regained fame as the home of Odysseus.

The first thorough attempt to identify the Homeric sites on the island was by Sir William Gell, whose work on The *Geography and Antiquities of Ithaca* was published in 1807. Byron, who first visited Ithaka three years later, was at first sarcastic about the work of such antiquarians, writing: 'Of Dardan Tours let Dilettanti tell, I leave topography to coxcomb Gell.' But after meeting the author he changed his opinion; as he wrote in the *Monthly Review*, 'That laudable curiosity concerning the remains of classical antiquity, which has of late years increased among our countrymen, is in no traveller or author more conspicuous than in Mr Gell.'

Byron first visited Ithaka in August 1810, crossing over from Cephalonia and staying for eight days as guest of the British Resident, Captain Wright Knox. After being shown the Homeric sites identified by Gell, Byron wrote:

> The hospitality of Captain Knox and his lady was in no respect inferior to that of our military friends of Cephalonia. That Gentleman with Mrs K. and some of their friends conducted us to the fountain of Arethusa – which alone would be worth the voyage – but the rest of the island is not inferior in attraction to the admirers of Nature; – the arts and tradition I leave to Antiquaries, and so well

have those Gentlemen contrived to settle such questions
– that as the existence of Troy is disputed – so that of Ithaca
(as Homer's Ithaka, i.e.) is not yet admitted.

Byron returned to Ithaka in 1823, shortly before his death at
Mesolongi, a visit described by Trelawny in his *Records of Shelley,
Byron and the Author*, published in 1878.

Our party made an excursion to the neighbouring island
of Ithaca; contrasted with the arid wastes and barren red
hills of Cephalonia, the verdant valleys, sparkling streams,
and high land, clothed in evergreen shrubs, were strikingly
beautiful. After landing it was proposed to visit some of
the localities that antiquarians have dubbed with the title
of Homer's school, Ulysses' stronghold, etc.: he [Byron]
turned peevishly away, saying to me, 'Do I look like one
of those emasculated fogies? Let's have a swim. I detest
antiquarian twaddle. Do people think I have no lucid
intervals, that I have come to Greece to scribble more
nonsense? I will show them I can do something better.'

Although Leake, Gell and other scholars had explored the
antiquities of Ithaka, the first systematic archaeological excavations
were made by Heinrich Schliemann, who visited the island in 1868
and 1878. Wilhelm Dörpfeld also explored the island, beginning in
1900, and his findings convinced him that Lefkas was the original
Ithaka of the *Iliad*, a theory that he expounded in his *Alt-Ithaka*,
published in 1927. That same year the opposing view was presented
in two influential books, Victor Berard's *Ithaca et la Grèce des
Achéens*, and *Homer's Ithaca* by Rennell Rodd. Rodd subsequently
sponsored a research programme by the British School of
Archaeology in Athens, which began excavating sites in Ithaka in the
early 1930s under the direction of W. A. Heurtley. These excavations,
which continue to the present day, show that the island was
inhabited continuously from the early Bronze Age down to Roman
times; in addition a number of findings have led most authorities to
conclude that this is in fact Homeric Ithaka. As a result, since 1981
an international congress called the Odessa is held every October

in Vathi, with presentations by Homeric scholars from all over the world. A cultural festival is also held there every summer, with Homer the central theme.

The town of Vathi stretches around the inner end of its harbour, the most spectacular in Greece, measuring 926m from its narrow mouth to the inner end of the port, from where the town looks across the gulf to Mount Neriton. The tiny offshore islet in the port is the former Lazaretto, with a little chapel dedicated to Agios Sotiros, or the Saviour, built by the Venetians in 1668. Everyone goes out in boats to the chapel to celebrate the *paneyeri* of the Saviour on 5–6 August, returning for music and dancing in the tavernas of Vathi.

The town itself was founded at about the same time as the chapel of Agios Sotiros, when the Ithakians first felt secure enough to move down from their mountain villages to the port, which began to thrive as one of the way stations of the Venetian maritime empire. Virtually nothing now remains of old Vathi, for the earthquake of 1953 destroyed 80 per cent of the town's buildings, some of their ruins still haunting the streets above the port. The finest houses in town are those of G. Karavias and G. Drakoulis, neoclassical mansions at the centre of the quay. Another interesting house is the birthplace of Odysseus Adroutsos, the hero of the Greek War of Independence.

Three old churches survive, though all were rebuilt after the earthquake; these are the cathedral, dedicated to the Presentation of the Virgin, with a fine carved wooden *iconostasis*; the church of Agios Giorgios; and the church of the Taxiarchoi, which has an icon of Christ attributed locally to El Greco.

The Folklore and Cultural Museum is located behind the Agricultural Bank. The museum is designed to show the life of Ithaka during the period when it was occupied by the Venetians, British and other foreign powers, with bedrooms, a sitting room and a kitchen fully furnished and decorated as they would have been in those times. There are also photographs showing the devastation of the 1953 earthquake.

The Cultural Centre has a rich library with some rare and unusual books, including the complete works of St Athanasios, dating from 1686, and an edition of the *Odyssey* and *Iliad* in Japanese.

The Archaeological Museum is on Odos Kallinikou, one block back from the quay. The exhibits date from the Geometric period (ninth–eighth centuries BC) to the Roman era, principally from Piso Aetos and the Louizou Cave in Polis. The most important objects in the museum are: a ring-shaped vase, dated to the end of the late Geometric period; and a votive inscription mentioning the goddesses Athena and Hera, found in the Louizou Cave and dated to the late Archaic period.

Near the museum there is a courtyard with a memorial to the Ithakians who have died in the wars of modern Greece, three millennia after Odysseus led his contingent from the Ionian isles in the siege of Troy. This unit is listed in the Catalogue of Ships in the *Iliad* directly after the flotilla from 'Doulichion and the sacred Echinai'.

> But Odysseus led the high-hearted men of Kephallenia,
> those who held Ithaka and leaf-trembling Neriton, those
> who dwelt about Krokyleia and rugged Aigilips, those
> who held Zakynthos and those who dwelt about Samos,
> those who held the mainland and the places next to the
> crossing. Following with him were twelve ships with bows
> red-painted.

A stele in this memorial courtyard commemorates Byron's two visits to Ithaka, with an inscription recording his first impression of the isle of Odysseus: 'If this island belonged to me, I would bury all my books here and never go away.' After his first visit Byron wrote to his friend John Cam Hobhouse, in a letter dated 4 October 1810, telling him that 'I have some idea of purchasing the Island of Ithaka. I suppose you will add me to the Levant lunatics.'

The hydra-headed peninsula that encloses the north side of Vathi harbour has a number of tree-fringed coves with excellent sandy beaches. The most popular of these, all of which can be reached by road, are Skinos, on the north-west side of the peninsula, and

Filiatro and Sarakiniko on the south-east side. The name of the latter cove, frequently found on the Greek isles, derives from the Saracen corsairs who raided the isles in times past. There is also a beautiful beach at Gidaki on the north shore of the peninsula, serviced by several boats a day from Vathi.

One of the secondary roads going out from Vathi leads to Pera Pigadi, a spring at the head of a bay that indents the south-eastern corner of the island. Above the bay there are three Homeric sites, identified by both Leake and Gell: Arethousa's Fountain, the Rock of Korax (the Raven) and the Cave of Eumaios, the faithful swineherd of Odysseus. These are mentioned in Book XIII of the *Odyssey*, in which Athena instructs Odysseus to seek out Eumaios before proceeding to his palace.

> First of all, you are to make your way to the swineherd who
> is in charge of your pigs, but his thoughts are kindly, and he
> is a friend to your son and to circumspect Penelope. You
> will find him posted beside his pigs, and these are herded
> near the Rock of the Raven and beside the spring Arethousa.

The site is described by Leake, who came here by caique in his search for 'the fountain, which by the learned of Vathy is supposed to be the Arethusa of the poet'.

> The spring is in a ravine midway between the shore and
> a long perpendicular cliff which closes the ravine, at a
> distance of a mile [about one and a half kilometres] from
> the sea... The fountain is a natural and never-failing
> reservoir in a cavern, before which a wall has been built for
> the convenience of watering cattle. There is every reason to
> believe that this is really the fountain Arethusa intended by
> Homer, and that the precipice above it is the rock Corax,
> which the poet had in view in describing the station of the
> swineherd Eumaeus... Near the pigadi is another smaller
> cavern, which also contains water. Below them the torrent
> continues its rapid course to the sea along a narrow glen,
> where a deep channel in the lime-stone rock is overhung
> with the trees which cover all the heights around, and
> which consist chiefly of lentisk, agnus-castus, myrtle, and

holly-oak. The scenery of the Arethusa and Corax is
very beautiful, not only in its nearer features, but as
commanding a noble prospect of the sea, seen through
the openings of the woody precipices...

A track leads on to the plateau of Marathia, where at a site called
Hellinico a Mycenaean settlement was excavated. The path goes on
to the promontory that forms the south-eastern tip of Ithaka, where
there is a chapel dedicated to Agios Ioannis stin Pounta, St John
of the Point.

Another road leads from Vathi to Perachori, the only village in
the interior of Ithaka's southern peninsula, perched at an altitude
of 300m on the eastern slope of Mount Petaliatiko. A path on the
outskirts of the village leads north to the ghost town of Palaeochora,
whose most notable remains are the shells of several frescoed
churches. This was the principal community on Ithaka during the
Byzantine and early Latin eras, but it was abandoned after the
island was taken by the Turks in 1479. When the island was resettled
by the Venetians early in the sixteenth century the new village of
Perachori developed south of the medieval town.

Perachori is the largest village in the interior of Ithaka, renowned
for its olive oil, cheese and wine. The principal church in the village
is dedicated to the Dormition of the Virgin. The church is renowned
for its beautiful Byzantine wall paintings, which represent the
Dormition of the Virgin, brought here from one of the ruined
churches in Palaeochora. The church also preserves the carved
wooden *iconostasis* of Moni Taxiarchon, an abandoned monastery
perched at an altitude of 510m some 3km to the south of
Perachori. The monastery was founded in 1645 and remained in use
up until the early years of the twentieth century. It was ruined in the
earthquake of 1953 but has since been rebuilt, though it is normally
open only on the first day of May, when the *paneyeri* of the
Taxiarchoi begins there with a liturgy in the *katholikon* of the
monastery, followed that evening by music and dancing in
Perachori. Perachori also has a wine festival in August, when people
from all over the island, along with Ithakians from abroad and

tourists, gather there to celebrate and drink up the last of the year's vintage and empty the barrels for the next pressing of the grapes in autumn. But one is advised to arrive at the festival early, for an old Ithakian proverb says that 'good wine in the tavern has a short life'.

The main road to the northern peninsula of the island begins at the western end of Vathi's quay. About a kilometre out of town a turn-off on the left is signposted for Spilaio Nymphi, the Cave of the Nymphs, which is some 3km inland. But it is unlikely that this is the cavern that Athena describes to Odysseus in Book XIII of the *Odyssey*, for that would have been on or near the shore by the Harbour of Phorkys, the Old Man of the Sea, which Gell and other authorities have identified with Dexia Bay, a cove just to the west of the entrance to Vathi's harbour. Unfortunately, the grotto on Dexia Bay that Gell identified as the Cave of the Nymphs was destroyed during the British occupation, demolished to make way for the high-way along the shore. According to Gell, this is where the Phaiakians put the sleeping Odysseus ashore, and where upon awakening he saw Athena, disguised as a young herdsman. Athena speaks, describing the landscape that Odysseus has forgotten in his long wanderings:

> Come, I will show you settled Ithaka, so you will believe me.
> This is the harbour of the Old Man of the Sea, Phorkys,
> and here at the head of the harbour is the olive tree with
> spreading leaves, and nearby is the cave that is shaded, and
> pleasant and sacred to the nymphs...and there is the
> mountain Neritos, all covered with forest.

Some 3km out of Vathi there is a turn-off on the left that leads to Piso Aetos, a cove that in times past was used as a landing place for travellers crossing from Cephalonia to Ithaka. As it crosses the saddle the road passes a site known locally as the Kastro tou Odysseus, which Schliemann identified as Alalkomenai, the capital of ancient Ithaka. Since 1930 the site has been under excavation by archaeologists from the British School, who have unearthed there the remains of an Archaic period temple and both structures and pottery ranging in date from the late Mycenaean period to the imperial Roman era. The earliest structure discovered in these excavations is a sanctuary dated ca. 1200 BC, around the time that Odysseus would have returned to Ithaka after his long wanderings.

The main highway continues around Aetos Bay and winds up to the spine of the precipitous isthmus that links the southern and northern peninsulas of Ithaka, with a breathtaking view back across the gulf towards the harbour of Vathi. At the northern end of the isthmus the highway passes two turn-offs; the first, on the left, leads down to the coastal hamlet of Agios Ioannis; the second, on the right, winds up around the slopes of Mount Neriton to the mountain village of Anogi and then down to Stavros, the hub of all the roads in north Ithaka.

The countryside at the northern end of the isthmus is known locally as Agros Laertou, the Field of Laertes. This was so identified by Gell, who believed that he had discovered here 'the site of the gardens of Laertes, to which the father of Ulysses retired during the absence of of his son'. This is the setting for a very moving episode in Book XXIV of the *Odyssey*, in which Odysseus reveals himself to Laertes after an absence of 20 years.

> He spoke, and Laertes' knees and the heart within him went slack, as he recognised the clear proofs that Odysseus had given. He threw his arms around his dear son, and much-enduring great Odysseus held him close, for his spirit was fainting.

Gell's imaginative identification led Schliemann here on the day after he first landed on Ithaka, 11 July 1868, as he writes.

> I soon came to the field of Laertes, where I sat down to rest, and to read the 24th book of the *Odyssey*. The arrival of a stranger is an event even in the main town of Ithaka: how much more so in the countryside! I had scarcely sat down, when the villagers crowded round me and bombarded me with questions. I thought that the best plan would be, to read aloud lines 205 to 412 of the twenty-fourth book of the Odyssey, and to translate it word for word into their dialect. Their excitement was boundless as they listened to the account, in the musical language of Homer, in the

language of their glorious forebears of three thousand years ago, of the terrible sufferings which King Laertes had suffered on that very spot where we were gathered, and to the description of the great joy when he found again, after twenty years' separation, his beloved son Odysseus whom he had held for dead. The eyes of all were swimming with tears, and when I had concluded my reading, men, women and children all came up to me and embraced me with the words: 'You have given us great joy, we thank you a thousand times.' I was carried in triumph to the city, where all competed to give of their hospitality in abundance, without the least sense of being incommoded. I was not allowed to leave until I had promised to visit them a second time in the village.

Driving north on the main road, we soon see down below the seaside hamlet of Agios Ioannis and its white sand beach, which up until recent times was a landing place for boats crossing from Cephalonia.

The coastal road through Agios Ioannis rejoins the main road at Lefki, a pretty village perched 160m above the sea, with an extensive view of the east coast of Cephalonia across the strait. Lefki was founded in the sixteenth century by people from the mountain village of Anogi, who wanted to be closer to the strait between Ithaka and Cephalonia for fishing and maritime trade. Paths lead down from the village to several excellent beaches on the strait.

The road then comes to Stavros, the main market town of north Ithaka, set 110m above the horseshoe-shaped Bay of Polis. Stavros and the village of Platrithias to its north were founded in the sixteenth century by people from the mountain villages of Exogi and Anogi, because the decreasing threat of corsair raids encouraged them to move down closer to the sea.

There are four interesting churches in Stavros, those of Agios Sotiris, Agia Varvara, Zoodochos Pigi and Agios Nikolaos. Agios Nikolaos was originally the *katholikon* of a monastery founded during the Venetian period, but the rest of the institution was destroyed in the earthquake of 1953. The church of Agios Sotiris celebrates its *paneyeri* on 5–6 August, when people come from all over the island to take part in the festivities.

All the old houses in Stavros were destroyed in the 1953 earthquake except for the Tzovanatos mansion, another survivor of the Venetian era. In the centre of the village there is a small park with a monument surmounted by a bronze bust of Odysseus, for local tradition holds that his capital was just north of Stavros on the Hill of Pelikata.

Just outside the village, on the road that leads to Exogi, there is a small but interesting archaeological museum with exhibits from sites in the area around Stavros. The most important of these is part of a female face mask with an inscription recording that it was 'Dedicated to Odysseus'. This ex-voto, which dates from the Roman era, was found in a cave sanctuary on the Bay of Polis known as Spiliou Louizou. The cave was first excavated in 1930 by archaeologists of the British School, who discovered there sherds ranging in date from the Mycenaean age down to the Roman period. This led them to conclude that Spilia Louizou was a *heroon*, or shrine of a deified hero, dedicated to Odysseus, whose memory was celebrated on Ithaka as late as the third century BC in games known as the Odysseia. Other interesting objects in the museum from the Spiliou Louizou are: fragments of large bronze tripods, dated ninth to eighth centuries BC; a clay plate with the representation of a cock, seventh century BC; fragments of a clay masque with an incised inscription, first or second century AD; and a stone relief with the figures of dancing nymphs, dating from the Hellenistic period.

The name 'Polis', which means 'City', has led some authorities to suggest that the ancient capital of Ithaka was located on this bay. No ancient settlement has been discovered here, but locals say that in the bay there are the submerged ruins of a Byzantine city known as Ierousalem, which was destroyed and inundated by an earthquake in AD 967.

Other objects in the Stavros museum are from a site just to the north of the village on the Hill of Pelikata known as Kastro, where excavations by the British School in 1930 uncovered remains dating from the early Bronze Age down to the Mycenaean era. These finds and the geographical position of the site have led a number of authorities to identify this as the ancient capital of Ithaka, rather than Aetos. Those who favour it as the Homeric capital point to the position of the Hill of Pelikata, which has Mount Neriton to its south, Mount Marmarakas to its north-east and Mount Exogis to its north-west, with the latter two mountains rising from peninsulas that define Frikes Bay to the east and Afales Bay to the north. This agrees with the description in the *Odyssey*, where the capital of Ithaka is situated between 'three mountains' and looks out upon 'three seas', the three bodies of water being the two large bays and the Ithaki Strait. Such is the speculative science of Homeric geography.

The road divides north of Stavros, with the left fork leading to Exogi and the right going through Platrithias and then on to the north-eastern corner of the island, passing through the pretty seaside villages of Frikes and Kioni.

Exogi is one of the oldest villages in Ithaka, and excavations on its eastern side have unearthed both ancient and Byzantine ruins. The principal church in the village is dedicated to Agia Marina, whose *paneyeri* on 17 July attracts celebrants from all over the island.

At the top of the village a track leads up to the mountain top at a site known as Pernarakia, ending at an abandoned monastery dedicated to the Panagia, which was inhabited up until 1945. The view from the monastery is superb, looking out across the strait towards the northern end of Cephalonia.

Platithrias had been inhabited since antiquity, since it is in the centre of a fertile and well-watered area, with easy access to the sea at the Bays of Afales and Frikes. Nearby on a hilltop is the abandoned monastery of the Taxiarchoi, which was inhabited up until the end of the nineteenth century. The monastery was destroyed in the 1953 earthquake, and today only the *katholikon* remains.

A dirt road leads north from Platithrias to Kolieri, a pretty hamlet on the west coast of Afales Bay. A local scholar, Dr S. Vrettos, has converted his house into a small but interesting folklore museum, with household utensils, tools, furniture and other objects from all over the island.

Ancient remains have been found in the vicinity of Platithrias, where excavations have unearthed structures and graves from the Mycenaean period. The only ancient structure that is visible above ground can be seen at Agios Athanasios, a ruined chapel between Platithrias and Exogi. All that remains of the structure are some courses of its polygonal wall, which form the foundations of the chapel. The ruins, which local tradition have identified as 'the School of Homer', are thought to be Mycenaean, as evidenced by a few sherds of that period found on the site. Gell agreed with this identification after he visited the site in 1806, and thereafter it became one of the regular stops on the tour of Homeric Ithaka. The philhellenic poet Donald MacPherson writes of the School of Homer in the second verse of 'A View from Mount Neritos, in the Island of Ithaka', one of the poems in his *Melodies from the Gaelic*, published in 1824.

> See yonder pile, torn by the teeth of Time,
> In moss-grown fragments scattered all around!
> Oft did these walls to many a theme sublime,
> In matchless eloquence of verse resound.

Two more supposed Homeric sites can be seen along the road that leads north-west from Platithrias. The first of these, halfway along the road, is Pige Melanidros, or Blackwater Spring. Local tradition attributes therapeutical properties to this spring, where Homer is supposed to have regained his sight by bathing in its healing waters. The spring is enclosed within a chapel dedicated to the Panagia Melanidros, whose feast day is celebrated in a *paneyeri* held on 15 August in the village square of Platithrias.

The second of the two sites, at road's end, is the Fountain of Kalamos, the principal water source for what seems to be the most fertile valley on Ithaka. Local tradition identifies this as the Fountain of Arethusa, and when Leake explored Ithaka in 1806 he was shown a nearby precipice called Koraka, the Rock of the Raven. His guides also pointed out a sea cavern that they believed to be the Homeric Cave of the Nymphs. This led Leake to ponder the possibility that Frikes was a corruption of Phorkys, the Old Man of the Sea. He also speculated that Frikes Bay was the Harbour of Phorkys, and that the Melanidros Spring was where 'the noble swineherd Eumaios' brought his pigs 'to eat the acorns that stay their strength, and drink of the darkling/water, for these are nourishing for pigs, and fatten them'. But after considering the evidence he rejected these identifications in favour of the competing places in south Ithaka, though locals in the north continue to point out their Homeric sites to travellers.

Two roads lead from Platithrias to Frikes, the more northerly route passing through the pretty villages of Agia Saranda, Mesovouno and Lachos, surrounded by trees and beautiful gardens.

The beautiful seaside hamlet of Frikes is set at the inner end of the enormous bay of the same name, which deeply indents the north-east corner of the island. The village was founded at the end of the sixteenth century, first by a few people from Exogi and then from Stavros, after the threat of piracy had diminished. The villagers made their living then from fishing and marine commerce, and now from tourism. During the summer ferries leave Frikes daily for Fiskardo in Cephalonia and Vassiliki in Lefkas.

The picturesque village of Kioni is set in a natural amphitheatre around an almost enclosed bay on the north-western coast. The village was founded at the end of the sixteenth century by people from the mountain village of Anogi, who ventured down to the sea with the decline of piracy under Venetian rule. The monastery of Agios Nikolaos was founded at that time by the villagers of Kioni, who credited St Nicholas with protecting them from corsairs. The monastery was destroyed in the 1953 earthquake, and now all that remains is its *katholikon*, where a column in the altar was probably taken from the ruins of an ancient temple on the site.

Another road heads eastward from Stavros and then turns south to climb up along the slopes of Mount Neritos to Anogi, a mountain village perched at an altitude of 500m. Anogi ranks with Exogi as one of the oldest villages on the island, its remoteness and elevation making it a safe haven from the pirates who ravaged Ithaka during the medieval Byzantine era. The villagers have a distinct accent that dates back to Venetian times, as do many of their customs The village church of the Panagia was founded in the Byzantine era, with local tradition holding that it was constructed on the ruins of a temple of Hera. The church has been rebuilt a number of times, its frescoes a faded palimpsest of post-Byzantine art dating from several dates in the Latin era. Like the other mountain villages of Ithaka, the population of Anogi is only a small fraction of what it was in times past, for the villagers began to move back down to the coast when the threat of piracy diminished. Gell noted at the time of his visit that more and more families were moving down from Anogi to Kioni in particular, 'tempted by the convenience of the port to forsake the security which the mountain offered'.

The countryside round Anogi is strewn with large rocks, the most enormous of which, standing some 8m high, is known as Arakles, from the tradition that it was a statue of the god Herakles, the Roman Hercules.

The road continues south from Anogi to the crossroads at Argos Laertou, with a turn-off to the right leading to Moni Panagia Kathariotissa, a monastery perched 550m above sea level on the southern slope of Mount Neriton. The monastic church was founded in 1696 to house a miraculous icon of the Panagia, which pious local tradition attributes to St Luke. Tradition also holds that the church was built on the ruins of an ancient temple, dedicated to either Artemis or Athena. The church is noted for its remarkable wall paintings and reredos, an ornamental screen behind the altar. The church has its feast day on 8 September, when the people of Anogi and its dispersed villagers on the coast gather together in the monastery courtyard to celebrate what is probably the oldest *paneyeri* on Ithaka.

The drive back down from Kathara to Vathi is spectacular, with continually changing views of hydra-headed Ithaka and its surrounding seas and islands. This is the panorama that inspired MacPherson to write his poem 'A View from Mount Neritos, in the Island of Ithaka', the first verse of which comes to mind as one begins the long descent from 'leaf-quivering Neritos'.

> Hail, rugged Isle! whose mountains wild are seen
> Heaving abrupt their heads of hoary gray,
> With here and there a lively spot of green,
> Like Winter mingling with the bloom of May;
> Yet, to fair plains, to courts luxurious, gay,
> Did thy sage chief prefer these barren hills –
> Full twenty years a wanderer did he stray,
> Of life, for thee, despising all the ills –
> Much can the man endure whose breast the patriot fills.

But in the end it is Homer who once again comes to mind, perhaps the lines in Book XIII of the *Odyssey*, where the disguised Athena speaks to Odysseus after he has landed on the Harbour of Phorkys, now visible below as one drives back across the isthmus to south Ithaka.

> This is a rugged country and not for the driving of horses...there is abundant grain for bread grown here, it produces wine, and there is always rain and the dew to make it fertile; it is good to feed goats and cattle; and timber is there of all sorts, and watering places good through the seasons; so that, stranger, the name of Ithaka has gone even to Troy, though they say that it is very far from Achaian country.

We spent another night in Vathi before catching the ferry to Cephalonia. The boat took us round the southern peninsula of Ithaka before heading across the strait towards Sami, with Mounts Nerovoulo and Neritos remaining in sight until we rounded Cape Dichalia and approached the port. As the Ithakian mountains finally faded in the distance I stood out on the fantail and recalled the last stanzas of Cavafy's poem, remembering the years when I had dreamed of finally arriving on Ithaka, when now I was leaving it behind.

You must always have Ithaka in your mind. Arrival there is your predestination. But do not hurry the journey at all. Better that it should last many years; Be quite old when you anchor at the island, Rich with all you have gained on the way. Not expecting Ithaka to give you riches. Ithaka has given you your lovely journey. Without Ithaka you would not have set out. Ithaka has no more to give you now. Poor though you find it, Ithaka has not cheated you. Wise as you have become, with all your experience, You have understood the meaning of an Ithaka.

Then I remembered lines from an Ithakan song I had heard at a *paneyeri* on the island, a favourite of Ithakians in exile.

I'm leaving with a fond farewell
My poor Ithaka,
Taking only my body
Since my mind is left behind.

Ithaka (Ithaki): population 3,052; area 90 sq. km; highest peak: Mt Neriton (806m); no airport; ferries: connections with Astakos on the mainland and Sami on Cephalonia; in summer connections between Vassiliki on Lefkas and Frikes on Ithaka.

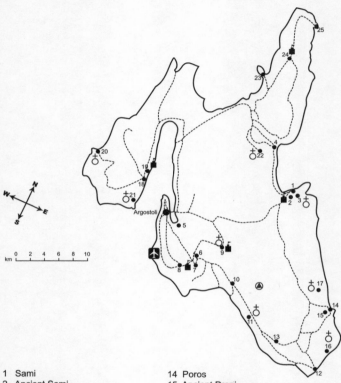

CEPHALONIA

1 Sami
2 Ancient Sami
3 Agrilion monastery
4 Agia Evfimia
5 Ancient Krani
6 Castle of St George
7 Peratata
8 Metaxata
9 Monastery of Agios Gerasimos
10 Vlachata
11 Sision monastery
12 Nea Skala
13 Markopoulo

14 Poros
15 Ancient Proni
16 Agios Giorgios chapel
17 Moni Panagia Atrou
18 Lixouri
19 Palaeocastro
20 Panagia Kipourion monastery
21 Agia Paraskevi monastery
22 Moni Theotokou Themata
23 Assos
24 Enosis
25 Fiskardo
⊕ Mt Aenos
✈ Airfield

eight
Cephalonia

C ephalonia is the largest of the Ionian Islands but also the least densely populated, with only a third as many people as Corfu. The island escaped mass tourism up until the last decade of the twentieth century, but after the filming of Louis de Bernières' 1994 novel *Captain Corelli's Mandolin*, set in Cephalonia, it became internationally famous as a holiday resort.

Cephalonia is really a sea-girt mountain with its summit at Mount Aenos (1,628m), the highest peak in the Ionian isles. The mountain was once covered with a magnificent forest of cedar-like fir trees known as *Abies cephalonica*, of which more than 1,000 hectares still stand on Aenos and Mount Roudi.

The Cephalonians have always been renowned as seafarers, a tradition that the islanders like to trace back to Homeric times, when 'Odysseus led the high-hearted men of Kephallenia' and the other isles of the Ionian Sea in the great expedition against Troy. Odysseus would have used the dark wood of the straight and tall Cephalonian firs for his twelve ships, which included a contingent from 'Samos', identified as the ancient city of Sami. Sami was one of the four members of the Cephalonian *tetrapolis* mentioned by Thucydides, the others being Krani, Proni and Pali, and he tells us that the latter city contributed 200 men to the Greek allies who defeated the Persians at the Battle of Plataea. In 189 BC Sami held out for four months before surrendering to a Roman army under the consul Marcus Fulvius Nobilior, the only resistance that Rome met in its conquest of the Ionian Islands.

Cephalonians made a significant contribution to the Greek War of Independence, despite the neutrality imposed on the Ionian isles by the British. Colonel Charles Napier, who was British Resident on Cephalonia from 1822 to 1830, offered to abandon his career and fight for the freedom of Greece, proposing that he command an army of 10,000 Greeks, with a nucleus of 500 British soldiers, its officers to include the many Ionian gentlemen who had already volunteered to accompany him. The Greek Committee in London, after seriously considering his offer, eventually decided to equip a fleet under Admiral Cochrane instead.

Napier was very fond of the high-spirited Hellenes, particularly the Cephalonians. As he wrote in a letter home soon after arriving in Cephalonia: 'The merry Greeks are worth all the other nations put together. I like to see them, to hear them; I like their fun; their good humour, their paddy ways, for they are very like Irishmen. All their bad habits are Venetian; their wit, their eloquence, their good humour are their own.' Napier's affection for the Cephalonians was such that he christened one of his daughters Emily Cephalonia, kept two properties in Argostoli after the end of his term as Resident and endowed the islanders with numerous bequests. His most enduring contribution to Cephalonia is the network of roads that he ordered built during his Residency, 216 km in all, as compared to only 32 km of road in all the protectorate in 1824. This project was carried out by his Chief Engineer, Captain John Pitt Kennedy, who also built the quay and harbour works in Argostoli and other structures elsewhere in the island. Napier could not do enough for his beloved Cephalonia, and he wrote in his diary that 'every hour not employed to do her good works appears wasted'.

John Davy, writing in 1842, notes: 'The inhabitants of Cephalonia and Ithaka have shown a more enterprising spirit than any of the other islanders, leading them to engage in adventure and foreign commerce; and it may be added that the Cephalonians have also shown more freedom of will and love of liberty, prompting them to resist oppression and to break into acts of subordination.' The Cephalonians rebelled against British rule in 1848–1849, and after they killed an English officer 21 of the islanders were executed, leaving bitter memories for the remaining years of the protectorate. This insurrection agonised Napier, and when he was off on campaign in India in 1851 he wrote to his old Cephalonian friend Count Metaxas about the sorry state of affairs on the island: 'I always think of my second country, the (to me) dear island of Cephalonia. I have almost cried with vexation to hear all that goes on there. I hear that people have been harshly treated in Cephalonia and I know that there is no need for that for the people are good and noble… Remonstrate, appeal, memorialise the Queen who is good and just. Do all but try the terrible power of an Empire as ours.'

Since *enosis* the islanders have distinguished themselves in the cultural life of Greece, and a local guidebook lists 36 Cephalonians who have made their mark as writers, journalists, educators, scholars, physicians, artists, architects, sculptors, composers, musicians, singers and actors.

The same guidebook also has an essay on the famous Venetian songs of Cephalonia and the other Ionian isles, the *arietta* and the *cantada*, and it also names the 22 different dance steps that are still performed at Cephalonian *paneyeria*. Davy, in his otherwise sober account of life on the Ionian isles, writes:

> The dance is their favourite diversion in Corfu, in which both sexes join, to the wild music of a rustic pipe, and sometimes of the violin. In Zante and Cephalonia the wine-shop is more frequented, and boisterous conviviality practised; in the streets the riotous drunken chorus is common, interrupting the better-conducted serenaders, who, on a fine evening, are frequently to be heard, making very agreeable music, – little parties of young men, singing to the sound of the guitar, which, in the towns, where Italian music is cultivated, is, with the violin, a favourite instrument.

The most famous Cephalonian *cantada* is '*Yialo, Yialo*' ('From Shore to Shore'), and no evening of song in a Greek taverna is complete without it.

> If the sea were only wine and
> the mountains mezedes,
> the ships could be the glasses for
> revellers to drink!
> From shore to shore we go
> And always speak of you
> The sea will take you, bring you back,
> And you'll remember me!

Inter-island ferries land at Sami, a little port town on the eastern side of the island, sheltered from the open sea within a great gulf south-west of Ithaka. Here, as in almost every community on Cephalonia, most of the houses are modern concrete structures of two storeys, for virtually all the earlier buildings were destroyed in the terrible earthquake of 1953. In the town centre there are the remains of a bath of the late Roman period; this is known locally as Rakospito, apparently a corruption of Drakospito, the Dragon's House, long a source of legend in Sami. A fine bronze head of the early third century AD was found here and is now on exhibit in the Argostoli Archaeological Museum.

The ruins of ancient Sami are in the valley between the two hills above the town. The ancient city is described in considerable detail by Leake, who estimated that its defence walls had a perimeter of over 3km, enclosing the 'two summits, an intermediate hollow, and their slope as far as the sea'. Leake identified the northern summit as the citadel of Sami, basing his identification on Livy's account of the Roman siege of Sami in 189 BC.

A secondary road leads north-eastward along the shore towards Akri Dichilia, the promontory that terminates the Gulf of Sami in that direction, with Akri Agiou Andreou on Ithaka just 4km distant. A turn-off to the right before road's end at Dichalia leads up to the old monastery of Ypergias Theotokou Agrilion. Byron and Trelawny and their party spent the night here after their return from a trip to Ithaka, soon after their arrival in Cephalonia in August 1823. During their stay there Byron had an emotional breakdown, brought on by the over-effusive welcome accorded to them by the abbot of the monastery, as Trelawny writes in his *Records of Shelley, Byron and the Author*:

> On coming up to the walls we saw the monks in their grey gowns, ranged along the terrace; they chanted a hymn of glorification and welcome to the great lord [Byron], saying 'Christ has risen to elevate the Cross and trample on the crescent in our beloved Greece'.[...] The Abbot then took from the folds of his ample garments a roll of paper, and commenced intoning through his nasal organ a turgid and interminable eulogium on my 'Lordo Inglese' in a polyglot of divers tongues. Then suddenly Byron broke into a paroxysm of rage and vented his ire in a torrent of Italian execrations on the holy Abbot and all of his brotherhood... Seizing a lamp, he left the room. The consternation of the monks at this explosion of wrath may be imagined. The amazed Abbot remained for sometime motionless, his eyes and mouth wide open... At last he thought he had solved the mystery, and in a low tremulous voice said, significantly putting his finger to his forehead: '*Eccolo, e matto poverto!*' ('Here he is, he is mad, poor thing!')

Sir Harold Nicolson, in *Byron: The Last Journey*, writes of how 'on the following morning Byron was all dejection and penitence'. But the situation was apparently never explained to the poor abbot and his monks, who for the rest of their lives must have wondered about the amazing behaviour of the English lord whom the Greeks had raised to the stature of a national hero.

The area around Sami is noted for its extraordinary geological phenomena, which include caves, chasms and underground lakes. Four of these, the cave lakes of Angalaki, Zervati and Chiridoni, and the Agia Eleousa precipice, are approached by the roads running westward from Sami to the villages of Poulata and Chaliotata. A fifth, the Melisani chasm, is approached by the road leading north-ward along the coast to Agia Evfimia. The roof of this immense cavern has apparently collapsed since antiquity, for two ancient reliefs found here seem to show that it was originally a cave sanctuary. The grotto is some 160m in length, with a lake measuring 60 x 40m, its surface 22m below sea level and having a maximum depth of 13m. One of the reliefs depicts the god Pan surrounded by dancing nymphs, and the other shows three women in a torchlit procession within the cave sanctuary. It is possible that the cave was a shrine of the nymph Melissanthe, after whom the chasm is named.

The road to Agia Evfimia passes the seaside hamlet of Karavomilos. At the edge of Karavomilos a small circular lake of fresh water, which bubbles up from a stream at its centre, flows into the bay of Sami.

The road along the west coast of the bay continues as far as Agia Evfimia, where it cuts across the waist of the island's northern peninsula to join the road along the west coast. Here one might be tempted to stop at Agia Evfimia, a pretty little village set in a picturesque bay. It was once just a simple fishing village, but its sandy beach has now made it a popular summer resort.

The main road from Sami runs across the spine of the island to Argostoli, the capital of Cephalonia. Halfway across Cephalonia the road goes over the Agrapidiases Pass at an altitude of 549m, with the island's highest peaks arrayed on either side; on the right are Mounts Dynati (1,131m) and Evmorfia (1,043m), and on the left Kokkini Rachi (1,078m) and Gioupari (1,125m), with Mount Aenos looming behind the latter peak to the south. Near the pass a road on the left leads via Agios Eleftherios towards Aenos, passing through a forest of *Abies cephalonica* that covers 890 hectares along the ridge leading to the summit. When the Venetians first occupied Cephalonia the whole of Aenos was so densely covered with the dark green growth of this noble fir that they called it Monte Negro, or the Black Mountain. When the Cephalonian nobleman Count Metaxas was presented to Napoleon, the Emperor asked: 'And how is the Black Mountain forest?' The peak is an hour's walk from the end of the road, an easy hike that is rewarded with a spectacular view stretching out across the southern Ionian isles to the coast of western Greece from the Pindus range down to the mountains flanking the Gulf of Patras. The peak is named for Zeus Aenos, an attribute of the King of Gods that probably derives from a mountain deity worshipped on Cephalonia in the late Bronze Age.

Descending from the Agrapidiases Pass, one has a sweeping view of Argostoli and its environs, including its near-neighbour Lixouri. The two towns are separated by 4km at the mouth of the great Argostolian Gulf, which cuts into the western side of the island for a distance of some 15km, with Argostoli to the east and Lixouri to the west.

Argostoli itself is separated from the land to its east by its elongated harbour, whose shallow inner end is known as the Koutavos Lagoon. The town stretches along the inner side of the Lassi peninsula, a long and narrow tongue of land that forms the western horn of Argostoli's harbour. The main road crosses to the town on a causeway and stone bridge 650m long that separate the shallow waters of the lagoon from the much deeper harbour. The causeway and bridge are the earliest extant works of the British protectorate, constructed in 1813 by Colonel Charles De Bosse, who commemorated the completion of the project by erecting the little obelisk at the centre of the crossing; an inscription, removed by the Italians during their occupation of Cephalonia in World War II, recorded its dedication 'To the Glory of the British Nation'.

Argostoli is the largest town on Cephalonia, with a population of some 14,000; it is also the island's principal port. It has been the capital of Cephalonia since 1757, though there is now little evidence of its distinguished past, virtually all its Venetian buildings having been destroyed in the 1953 earthquake, along with its old churches, most of which have been completely rebuilt. Thus Argostoli has completely lost the Italianate aspect that in 1834 led the Rev. Richard Burgess to describe it as 'a little Naples'. Nevertheless, the town still has a very pleasant Mediterranean atmosphere, particularly on summer evenings, as Charles Napier wrote in his book on the Ionian colonies, published in 1833:

> The sounds of music, and of oars, with the songs of
> boatmen, float along its smooth surface in the softness of

a summer's evening with the most pleasing effect. The bright colours in which most southern nations love to dress, increase the liveliness of the scene; and added to the wildness of the overhanging mountains, with their changing evening tints, create a picture in which masses of rocks, water and people, are so grouped as to produce a beauty of scenery that this harbour has no claims to at any other time of day.

There are two museums of interest in Argostoli: the Archaeological Museum, on Odos Rokou Vergoti, and the Korgialeneion Historical and Folk Art Museum, on Odoas Ilia Zervou.

The Archaeological Museum has exhibits from sites all over the island, from the prehistoric era up to Roman times. The oldest objects are principally late Mycenaean pottery sherds, along with bronze weapons that would have been used at the time of the Trojan War. Other objects of interest are the bronze head discovered in the Roman bath at Sami, and a collection of coins from the four principal cities of ancient Cephalonia, ranging in date from the classical period down to the Byzantine era. The most notable exhibits, all found in Mycenaean cemeteries and dating from the twelfth century BC, are: a Mycenaean kylix, or conical footed cup, from Lakkithra; a bronze fibula, in the form of figure-of-eight loops, from Diakata; a large two-handled crater, or wine bowl, from Diakata; and a gold necklace in pairs of spirals, from Lakkithra.

The Korgialenion Historical and Folk Art Museum is housed on the ground floor of the Korgialenion Library. The museum and library were founded in 1924 by Marios Korgialenios and rebuilt after the 1953 earthquake. The purpose of the rebuilt museum is to preserve the memory of the history and social life of Cephalonia before the 1953 earthquake, which otherwise would have severed many of the island's links with its past. The museum contains the historical records of Cephalonia for the years 1531–1900, along with a collection of Charles Napier's papers. The folklore section of the museum has a charming collection of local folk arts and crafts, as well as icons and woodcarvings from Cephalonian churches destroyed in the 1953 earthquake. Other exhibits include historical documents, portraits, oil paintings, watercolours, lithographs, plans and drawings of churches and fortresses, memorabilia of prominent Cephalonians, porcelain, silverware, copperware, embroidery, rural implements and utensils. The library has a special collection of drawings of women's costumes from the sixteenth to nineteenth centuries. The museum has a collection of some 3,000 photographs, including some that show Argostoli as it was before and immediately after the 1953 earthquake – a sad reminder of what the town has lost for ever.

One interesting excursion from Argostoli is to drive around the Koutavos Lagoon to see the ruins of ancient Krani, which are on the acropolis-like hill at the south-eastern end of the bay. Leake took this trip on the second day after his arrival in Argostoli, writing a description of the site that is still useful in understanding its topography.

> The walls of the Cranii are among the best extant specimens of the military architecture of the Greeks, and a curious example of their attention to strength of position in preference to other conveniences, for nothing can be more rugged and forbidding than the greater part of the site. The enclosure, which was of a quadrilateral form, and little, if at all, less than three miles [nearly 5km] in circumference, followed the crests of several summits, surrounding an elevated hollow which falls to the south-eastern extremity of the Gulf of Argostoli. This extremity served for an harbour to the city, and may perhaps have been so narrowed by moles from either shore as to have formed a closed port... Not a vestige of any foundations, either constructed or excavated, is to be seen among the rugged rocks within the enclosure, a remark which I have had occasion to apply to several other ancient sites of great extent, and of the same rocky kind, and which seems to show that the chief intent of these extensive enclosures was to secure the inhabitants, cattle, and property, of the whole district in moments of danger, and that they were very partially occupied in times of tranquility. The mode of

warfare of the Greeks, and the tenor of their history, support this opinion.

Two other excursions from Argostoli are known as the *piccolo yiro* and the *gran yiro*, the small and grand tours. The first of these goes clockwise around the Lassi peninsula to see the two sights at its northern promontory: the sea mill, known in Greek as the *katavothres*, and the lighthouse, or *fener*. The underground salt river that powers the sea mill was discovered in 1835 by an English resident named Stevens, who heard it roaring beneath his house. This led him to build a corn mill at the sea race where it disappeared into the bowels of the earth, and his example was followed by a Greek neighbour who built a second mill. Both mills were destroyed in the 1953 earthquake, but a replica of one of them has been rebuilt as part of a seaside rock garden. The course of the underground river was a mystery until the early 1960s, when a group of geologists from the University of Graz traced it with large masses of yellow dye; the coloured water finally emerged 16km to the east in the Melissani chasm, after having passed under the mountainous spine of the island, and after a brief aeration there it flowed underground once again before finally emerging in a seaside pool on the east coast at Karavomilo.

The lighthouse, which is dedicated to Agioi Theodoroi, is on the tip of the promontory looking across to Lixouri. This is another of Napier's works, a Doric rotunda designed and built by Captain Kennedy, one of several neoclassical structures that he erected in Argostoli. The lighthouse was destroyed in the 1953 earthquake, but it was rebuilt to its original design and from its original stones. It is a pretty sight, particularly on a sunset promenade from Argostoli, and there is nothing else like it on the Greek islands.

Beyond the lighthouse, the *piccolo yiro* goes on for 3km through olive groves and a colonnade of pines as far as the crossroads near Lassi, the nearest beach to town, after which it heads back across the base of the peninsula into Argostoli.

The *gran yiro* is a much larger loop going in the opposite direction through the countryside south-east of Argostoli, the beautiful region known as the Livado. The turning point on this route is the crossroads at Travliata, 8km from Argostoli; there a turn-off winds for some 800m up to Agios Giorgios, an old village at the foot of an acropolis hill ringed by the imposing ruins of a medieval fortress. This is the Castle of St George, which was the capital of Cephalonia for nearly 1,000 years.

The castle, known in Greek as Palaio Frourion, or the Old Fortress, dates back to the medieval Byzantine period, when Agios Giorgios was the capital of the Byzantine theme, or province, of Cephalonia, which included all the islands in the Ionian Sea. During the Latin period this great stronghold was held in turn by the Byzantines, the Normans, the Counts Palatine of Cephalonia, the Genoese, the Latin princes of Achaia, the Angevins, the Tocco dynasty, the Venetians, the Turks and then again by the Venetians. The Turks were finally driven out of Cephalonia in 1500, when the Castle of St George was recaptured by a combined force of Venetians and Spaniards under the command of the Gran Capitano Gonzalo Fernandez de Cordova, the Conqueror of Granada. The castle was then completely rebuilt and Agios Giorgios once again became the capital of Cephalonia, its population reaching a peak of 15,000 as the island prospered under Venetian rule. But then Agios Giorgios was levelled by a severe earthquake in 1757, after which the town was abandoned in favour of Argostoli, which thereafter served as the capital. After the downfall of Venice in 1797 the castle passed in turn to the French, the Russians and the French again, and then in 1809 it was taken by the British, at the beginning of their occupation of the Ionian Islands. The fortress was garrisoned by British troops up to the end of the protectorate, after which it was abandoned.

The Castle of St George is one of the most impressive and best-preserved fortresses on the Greek islands. The eight-sided fortress has a periphery of some 600m and its massive walls range from 10 to 15m in height, the most powerful of its bastions being the one above the village of Agios Giorgios, rising to a height of 25m above the level of the beetling hill. Inside the citadel one can still see the remains of both military and civilian buildings, some of the latter bearing the coats of arms of the noble families who dwelt here during the Latin period. There are also the remains of the Roman Catholic Cathedral of St Nicholas, within which were buried two bishops and several rulers of the Palatine County of Cephalonia. There is another Venetian church in the village of Agios Giorgios itself, and among its icons there are five works by Andreas Carantinos (ca 1660–1740), Cephalonia's most renowned post-Byzantine artist.

The next stop on the *gran yiro* is Peratata, just to the south-east of Travliata. Outside the village is the old monastic church of Agios Andreas, one of the few Cephalonian monuments of the Venetian period to survive the 1953 earthquake. The earthquake shook loose some of the whitewashed plaster on the walls of the church, revealing beautiful wall paintings of the seventeenth century. These have since been restored and transferred to canvas, preserving Cephalonia's most precious heritage of post-Byzantine art. The church also preserves a relic of St Andrew the Apostle, the sole of his right foot, which tradition holds was brought to Cephalonia in the first decade of the sixteenth century by an Epirote nobleman. The church now serves as a museum of Byzantine icons and ecclesiastical treasures.

The *gran yiro* now goes on to Metaxata, passing en route a dirt road on the right that in 500m brings one to the Mazarakata archaeological site. The sixteen chamber tombs here were excavated in 1909, along with late Mycenaean pottery that has dated the site to the twelfth century BC.

The main route comes to a crossroads at Metaxata, once the seat of the Latin archbishops of Cephalonia, a pretty village of red-roofed white houses overlooking the Livado. Byron stayed here for the last four months of 1823, living in a house that he rented from Count Delladecima, his chief adviser among the Greeks of Cephalonia. The house has now vanished, destroyed in the earthquake of 1953, but a marble plaque set into a garden wall commemorates his stay, which ended in late December with his departure for Mesolongi. As Sir Harold Nicolson writes:

The emissaries of the various Greek parties flocked to Metaxata, attracted like vultures by the savour of Byron's fabled wealth... Byron would receive these conflicting missions impartially... And at times, when they arrived together, he would confront them the one with the other; and Count Delladecima would act as interpreter, summarising, in his prolific way, the voluble insults which they would hurtle at each other across the little room; forgetting at moments to interpret, and launching out, upon his own, into a torrent of argument and invective.

But Byron managed to find periods of peace and quiet in Metaxata, as he wrote in his journal at the time: 'Standing at the window of my apartment in this beautiful village, the calm though cool serenity of a beautiful and transparent moonlight, showing the Islands, the Mountains, the Sea, with a distant outline of the Morea traced between the double Azure of the waves and skies, has quieted me enough to be able to write.'

The return leg of the *gran yiro* can be made along either of the two roads that head back to Argostoli from Metaxata. Many prefer the seaward route, passing the airport, for it brings one past the beaches at Platis Yialos and Makris Yialos, which are among the best places to swim in the Ionian Sea.

A somewhat longer itinerary that links up with the *gran yiro* leads back along the Argostoli–Sami road for some 8km; then a signpost on the right directs one to the Monastery of Agios Gerasimos, which is 4km further along in the Omalo vale, the 'valley of the forty wells'.

Agios Gerasimos is the patron saint of Cephalonia, and his monastery is visited by pilgrims from all over Greece, particularly on 15 August, which is the anniversary of his death, and also on 20 October, his feast day. Gerasimos was born in 1509 to a noble Byzantine family, the Notaras, who had left Constantinople at the time of the Turkish conquest and resettled in the Peloponnesos. Gerasimos became a monk on Mount Athos in his early twenties and then spent the next three decades in the Holy Land, Crete and

Zakynthos before settling down on Cephalonia in 1560. He first lived as a hermit in a cave near Argostoli, and then moved to the Omalo valley, where he rebuilt a ruined Byzantine church and then founded the monastery that now bears his name. Gerasimos died in 1579 and was canonised in 1622, by which time he was already a renowned miracle-worker. The saint's speciality was the curing of insanity, which the monks achieved by rites of exorcism using his relics, carried in procession from his tomb in the monastery on his two feast days. But apparently this miracle-working was abused and corrupted life in the monastery, as Ansted reports in his description of the Omalo valley, referring to the British Resident at the time of his visit, the Baron d'Everton.

> The whole of the western face of the Black Mountain, from the valley of San Gerasimo to the summit, is interesting. In the valley is the convent, also dedicated to San Gerasimo, and not long ago the scene of events scandalous enough to all concerned. Miracles – more especially miraculous cures of maniacs and persons supposed to suffer from demonical possession – were here so common, that the place became in the highest degree attractive. Lazy scoundrels, simulating madness, were allowed to come and feed for awhile at the expense of the establishment, and when tired of this kind of life, they would pretend to become cured by the inter-position of the saint. Women also took up their abode in the principal apartments, and there separated from their husbands and friends, received some favoured suitor, either lay or clerical. At length the affair became notorious, and the Resident thought it necessary to interfere. He paid a visit one day unexpectedly, performed a series of unexpected miracles on the sham maniacs, and made a clearance of the whole establishment. It is now respectable enough.

The monastery has a small chapel in addition to its large and recently redecorated *katholikon*, where the sarcophagus of St Gerasimos is enshrined. On the saint's feast days his sarcophagus is carried out of the *katholikon* in a procession and placed under a giant *platanos* that Gerasimos himself planted, and it remains there while the *paneyeri* is celebrated with music and dancing, after which it is carried back to the church.

The road to the monastery continues on as a rough track through the Omalo valley, passing the villages of Troianata and Mitakata before linking up with the *gran yiro* at Travliata, under the shadow of the Castle of St George, where one has a choice of several routes back to Argostoli.

A much longer excursion from Argostoli takes one around the south-eastern end of the island to Nea Skala and Poros. The first part of the excursion follows the same route as the *gran yiro* as far as Peratata, continuing from there around the south-eastern coast of the island, with the long massif of Mount Aenos looming above the left side of the road the whole way along.

A short way beyond Peratata we make a detour to the right on a road signposted for Pesada. At Pesada a secondary road leads seaward to the abandoned church of the Estavromenos, the Crucified Christ. The church was originally the *katholikon* of a convent dedicated to the Holy Cross, abandoned in the past century after the death of the last resident nun.

Continuing along the main road, at Vlachata there is a turn-off on the right for the beautiful beach at Lourdata. Five kilometres beyond that another turn-off on the right leads to the ruins of the old monastery of Sision, destroyed in the 1953 earthquake, with only a small chapel now standing on the site. The name is a corruption of Assisi, stemming from its original dedication to St Francis of Assisi, who according to local tradition was the founder of the monastery. Originally built by the Venetians in the thirteenth century, it was taken over by the Greek Orthodox Church in the sixteenth century, at which time it was dedicated to the Panagia Sisia. The most precious icon of the church is now preserved in the Korgialenion Museum; this is an icon of Our Lady of Akathistos, painted by the Cretan artist Stefanos Tsangarolas in 1700.

Beyond the turn-off to Sision the road comes to a fork, with the road on the left continuing on around Mount Aenos and the one on the right going down towards the south-eastern coast at Katelio and Nea Skala, passing through the pretty coastal region known as Eleios.

The present village of Nea Skala dates from after the 1953 earthquake, when the villagers abandoned their ruined houses in Old Skala, whose skeletal remains can be seen some 4km up a steep road through the olive groves. It is possible that Nea Skala occupies the site of the port of the ancient city upon whose ruins Old Skala was built. The only antiquities in the new town are two Roman mosaic pavements dating from the second century AD.

The left fork bends around the south-easternmost spur of Mount Aenos at Markopoulo, which local tradition claims to be the birthplace of Marco Polo's ancestors, though there is not a shred of evidence to support this. Markopoulo is famous for the extraordinary phenomenon that occurs here every year on 15 August, the feast of the Assumption of the Blessed Virgin. On that day large numbers of a species of small and harmless snake suddenly appear in the village church of the Panagia Lagouvarda, where they crawl up on to the *iconostasis* and drape themselves around a sacred icon of the Virgin, allowing themselves to be fondled by the villagers, who believe that the serpents have healing powers and bring good luck with them. A local legend says that in 1705 the convent of the Panagia Longouvarda was attacked by Turkish corsairs, and when the nuns prayed to the Virgin for deliverance she turned them into snakes and in that way drove the pirates away. Now the snakes reappear on the Virgin's feast day, or whenever the village is threatened by a catastrophe – or so they say.

The arrival of the snakes is vividly described by the Cephalonian folklorist Dr Dimitrios Loucatos, who first observed it at the age of 15, when he came to the church of the Panagia to sing in the choir with his father; as he writes:

> I was happy for days at the prospect of finally going to the famous village of Markopoulo in Eleios, which was, according to local legend, Marco Polo's native place and whence the snakes came out ... We entered the church to find it all lit up and full of people. The emotion shown by

the womenfolk who were inside the church made me forget about the question of the snakes for a few minutes; then suddenly they reminded me of it themselves. Two, three, five, seven...snakes wriggled up and down the gold-painted reliefs of the chancel-screen, the pillars and the chancel's side doors. I looked at them bewildered for a long time... A church warden came close and showed me a snake he was holding in his hand. It was sizeable enough to have wrapped itself around his arm like a bracelet. He moved it toward me that I might caress it. I mustered some courage and placed my finger on its little head. Its skin was like velvet, its eyes shiny and had a small mark like a cross on its forehead. Every now and then it opened its mouth and poked out a thread-like tongue. I was told that if I looked more carefully I would have seen a small cross at its tip.

Beyond Markopoulo the road turns northward and climbs over the eastern side of Mount Aenos via the villages of Kremmydi and Pastra. At Pastra a side road to the right leads down to the coast at Nea Skala. At Aleimmata there is a side road to the left for Fanies, where there are the ruins of a fifteenth-century church that retains fragments of its original wall paintings. The turn-off continues on to a crossroads at Asprogerakas, where the left fork leads back to the main road at Agios Giorgios; from there it winds down to Poros along the spectacular Vale of Arakli, or Heracles, while the right fork provides an alternative route to Poros via Annitata.

The latter route brings one within walking distance of the site of ancient Proni, also called Pronos. This city, one of the four that made up the Cephalonian *tetrapolis*, represented on its coins the club of Heracles. According to their tradition, the Vale of Arakli was created when Heracles struck the mountainside with his club when he accompanied Amphitryon on his expedition against the Teleboans. The ruins of Proni are near the small 'bottomless' lake of Abathon, one of the many *katavothres* discovered on the island by Dr Davy, as Ansted reminds us in his description of the site.

A short distance from the lake are the remains of the ancient city of Pronos, little visited, but showing some fine

Cyclopean walls. Pronos was the fourth of the ancient walled cities of Cephalonia, and according to Polybius, must have been the smallest. It is situated amongst beautiful wooded scenery, and in a rich profusion of orchards, villages and vineyards. The valley above Pronos, and leading to it, is described by Dr. Davy as not unlike Roslin, combining beauty with a certain wildness and grandeur, walled in by mural precipices luxuriantly wooded. The views of Ithaca and Greece are very charming. Not far from Pronos a colony of Maltese was founded by Sir Charles Napier, but it does not seem to have led to any important results.

Continuing along the main road from Pastra, near Agios Giorgios there are the ruins of an ancient monastery of Agios Nikolaos, where the nuns from the convent of Moni Atrou, north of Poros, took refuge when the Turks raided Cephalonia in 1598. Agia Eirene and Tzanata are pretty villages in the Vale of Arakli, and after passing the latter the road turns abruptly eastward to pass through the spectacular Poros Gap, and then 4km further along it ends at Poros.

Poros is an attractive little port town now serviced by a car-ferry from Killini in the north-west Peloponnesos. There is also an occasional boat service from Poros to Nea Skala. Halfway between Poros and Nea Skala the boat passes Akri Kapros, where in times past local mariners made libations to the god of the cape and his sacred fish as they sailed by, also throwing sweet cakes into the sea, a practice first mentioned by Pliny.

South of Cape Kapros there is a seaside chapel of Agios Giorgios, which is built on and from the ruins of a sixth-century BC Doric temple of Apollo, of which three columns have been reused in the church and a capital preserved in the Argostoli museum. This is one of many instances in which a church of St George stands on the site of a temple of Apollo, indicating that the Christian saint, who is almost certainly apocryphal, is a reincarnation of the pagan god. The feast day of St George, which is usually celebrated on 23 April, was on the old calendar held around the day of the spring equinox, which in antiquity was the time of Apollo's festival, for he was the reincarnation of a Bronze Age sun god.

A secondary road leads northward from Poros to Moni Panagia Atrou, an ancient convent 500m high on the seaward slope of Mount Atros. Our Lady of Atros is the oldest monastery on the island, the earliest mention of it being in the 'Records of the Latin Bishopric of Cephalonia', dated 1264.

Returning from Poros, one can take a secondary road at Tzanata that leads north-westward to Sami, passing on the right Mount Atros and Kokkini Rachi and on the left first Mount Aenos and then Mount Gioupari. At Agios Nikolaos, the first village on this route, one can hike eastward to Lake Avythos, known locally as Akoli, which is at an altitude of 300m between Mount Atros and Kokkini Rachi. This is another of the 'bottomless' lakes of Cephalonia, apparently fed by a *katavothres* that supplies water in sufficient power and quantity to drive mills and supply irrigation ditches, as well as being the principal source of the stream that flows down to the sea through the Vale of Arakli.

Another and much shorter excursion from Argostoli takes us across the bridge and then eastward on the Sami road for 3km. We then turn left for Dilinata, a drive of 8km that takes us up under the peak of Mount Evmorfia. Here we find Moni Lamia, an abandoned monastery founded in 1690 to house a miraculous icon, depicting the birth of the Virgin.

Still another excursion from Argostoli takes one to Lixouri and the Paliki peninsula, the long projection of land that forms the western arm of Cephalonia, separated from the adjacent coast of the island by the Argostoli Gulf. A road leads around the gulf, but there is also a car ferry linking Argostoli and Lixouri, a route favoured by most travellers since it gives one more time to explore the Paliki peninsula.

Most travellers have little praise for Lixouri, the second largest town on Cephalonia, a typical description being that of Leake, who at least credited it with being healthier than Argostoli.

> The town of Lixuri is more irregular than that of Argostoli,
> the streets dirtier, the houses of the rich more mean, and

the poorer cottages more numerous. A muddy rivulet crossed by two small bridges, traverses the middle of the town. It is reckoned more populous than Argostoli, and the situation more healthy, which may easily be imagined as it is well ventilated, and has none of the shallow water and marshy ground which are at the head of the Bay of Argostoli: the inhabitants are for the most part strangers.

The 1953 earthquake destroyed all the town's churches, which have been rebuilt in concrete with their original chancel screens still adorned with precious old icons of the Venetian period. Only one building of the Venetian period has survived, the mansion originally owned by the Iakovatos family. This now houses the State Library and the Iakovatos Museum. The library has some 20,000 volumes, the oldest being a tenth-century manuscript bible and a collection of the 'Works of Hippocrates' dated 1595; the museum has an important collection of Cephalonian art, the most notable being an icon by Michael Damaskinos.

On the waterfront there is a statue of Andreas Laskaratos (1811–1901), whose satirical writings led to his excommunication by the Greek Orthodox Church and a four-month incarceration by the British in Napier's model prison. Known in his time as 'the Voltaire of Greece', his most famous work is *The Mysteries of Cephalonia*, a satirical attack upon Ionian morals, a book which is today much praised but seldom read.

Lixouri is renowned for its town band, the second oldest in Greece, surpassed in age only by the band of Corfu town. The town, along with Argostoli, is also famous for its Christmas carols, which in Greece are sung on New Year's Day, the festival of Agios Vasillios, the Greek Father Christmas. Elias Tsitselis reminisces about this caroling in an article published in an Argostoli newspaper in 1904:

> We older folks recall the old-time special singers and rhyme-makers who would carol throughout the night about our well-known Agios Vasillios, which contained many lines praising the members of the household and wishing them the fulfillment of their hopes, ending with the request

of a gift, either in money, sweets or singing birds. The sweet harmony of these songs and praises as they are sung by groups of grown-ups accompanied by musical instruments, especially in Argostoli and Lixouri, is one of the most unforgettable sounds. I dare say that their proper rendition has evolved into a local symphonic music, very characteristic of Cephalonia (even if carols from Argostoli and Lixouri differ). It has added to the simple popular tune an eptanissian polyphonic and harmonic finish. And one enjoys it the most when one hears it fill the streets and neighbourhoods from the time the lights go on for the Eve, to the early morning of New Year's Day.

The Paliki peninsula takes its name from the ancient city of Pali, whose ruins are some 1,500m north of Lixouri between the coast road and the sea. This seems to have been originally a colony of Corinth, probably founded about the same time as Kerkyra, ca 733 BC. There is little left of the ancient city, known locally as Palaeocastro, which seems to have been long used as a quarry by the people of Lixouri, and so it is rarely visited. Leake seems to have been the first to identify the site of Pali (or Pale, as he spells it), which he numbered first among the four cities that made up the *tetrapolis* of ancient Cephalonia.

An interesting excursion on the Paliki peninsula is to the Monastery of the Panagia Kipourion, which is on the west coast of the peninsula, accessible by a secondary road via the village of Ghavrata. On the last stretch of this road one passes the deserted Moni Tafios, or Tafion, abandoned in 1744 in favour of the Kipourion monastery. (The name is a very ancient one, stemming from the people referred to by Homer as the Taphoi or Teleboae.) Kipourion is one of the very few monuments on Cephalonia that survived the 1953 earthquake, but it has recently been spoiled in a tasteless restoration carried out by its resident monks. The monastery still possesses two sixteenth-century icons from the Tafion, and in its little museum there is a seventh-century *iconostasis* and other treasures, including manuscript bibles that probably date back to Byzantine times.

The main road south from Lixouri is asphalted only as far as Mantzavinata, whose village church has some fine post-Byzantine wall paintings. From there a dirt road leads south to the coast at Kounopetra, the famous 'Moving Stone', which is described in the local Cephalonian guidebook:

> Kounopetra is a big rock in Paliki, sticking out of the sea. It is located off the coast south of Lixouri, beyond the village of Manzavinata. Once upon a time it was an internationally unique phenomenon, due to its ceaseless rhythmic movement. There is even a story that some British warships tied chains round it and hauled at it in an attempt to shift it, but without success. However, the earthquakes of 1953 managed, apart from destroying everything standing in Cephalonia, to stabilise the rock's bed, and now it does not move.

On the return drive, one might turn off to the right at Mantzavinata on a road signposted for Lepada. Behind the red sandy beach at Lepada there is a ruined monastery dedicated to Agia Paraskevi. The monastery was founded in 1668 around a cave sanctuary of Agia Paraskevi. St Paraskevi's shrines are always in caves, indicating that her veneration is the survival of an ancient cult of the underworld.

Another asphalted road runs north-west from Lixouri as far as Kontogenada, a village near the neck of the Paliki peninsula. The village churches have a number of important post-Byzantine icons, and in the vicinity Mycenaean tombs have been excavated.

The main road runs north from Lixouri along the eastern shore of the Argostoli Gulf. At the head of the gulf there is a crossroads, with the road to the left leading north to the isolated port hamlet of Agios Spyridon, while the one on the right curves around to join the main road going north from Argostoli at Kardakata. The latter road then heads across the neck of the Paliki peninsula, after which it goes all the way up the western coast of the island, along one stretch running more than 300m above the Gulf of Myrtos, a huge indentation of the sea that cuts into the north-western coast of the island.

The road comes to another crossroads at Siniori, with the right fork cutting across the waist of the island to Agia Evfimia and then to Sami, while the one on the left returns to the western coast at the northern end of the Gulf of Myrtos.

Here we make a detour along the road to Agia Evfimia, and just before Potamianata we turn right on a secondary road signposted for Makriotika and Drakopoulata. A short way beyond Makriotika we turn right on a road that leads to Moni Theotokou Themata, an eleventh-century monastery set in a forest on the slope of Mount Dynati, the second highest peak on the island (1,131m). Pilgrims come here to pray to the miraculous icon of the Virgin Themata, whose ability to answer requests is attested by the many ex-votos that have been fastened to her portrait.

Returning to the crossroads at Siniori, we now drive north for six to seven kilometres before taking a turn-off to the left for Assos. The village is about a 3km drive along a serpentine road leading down to the sea, with ever-widening views of one of the great wonders of the Ionian isles, the sea-girt peninsular fortress of Assos.

The picturesque village of Assos, completely rebuilt after the 1953 earthquake, nestles around the sheltered cove formed by the fortified peninsula, to which it is connected by a very narrow natural causeway. Assos is Venetian in foundation, and for a few years beginning in 1593 it was the administrative capital of northern Cephalonia. The peninsular fortress was built by the Venetians in 1593–1595 as the citadel of Assos, serving as a place of refuge for the people of the surrounding area at times of enemy attack. Leake believed that Assos was one of the subsidiary fortress towns of the ancient Cephalonian *tetrapolis*, basing his theory on the survival of 'several Hellenic names still existing', and on 'the evidence of a piece of Hellenic wall in the modern castle'. But subsequent studies have failed to discover any ancient remains at Assos, and the present fortress seems entirely Venetian in its construction. A path winds up the peninsular hill to the gateway of the fortress, much of whose circuit of walls is still standing, along with the ruins of the Venetian governor's mansion, the barracks of the garrison and a chapel of San Marco. The view from the peak of the peninsula is magnificent, particularly to the south, where a long line of silver-white cliffs extends along the periphery of the Gulf of Myrtos, with occasional stretches of pink strand beneath them in scimitar-shaped coves – a panorama that Edward Lear described as 'one of the sublimest scenes in the Seven Islands'.

Eight kilometres beyond the Assos turn-off the main road comes to a crossroads at Enosis, where a secondary road to the right leads southward through the mountains to Agia Evfimia. Here one might make a 5km detour to the village of Vari. From Vari it is a short walk to the chapel of the Panagia Kouyanna, the only surviving Byzantine church on Cephalonia, which still has faded remnants of its original wall paintings.

The main road continues northward as far as Antipata, the ancient Erisou, which takes its name from Erissos, the northernmost peninsula of Cephalonia. At Erisou the road curves around the northern end of the island to Fiskardo, a little port facing the northwestern cape of Ithaka, about 3km distant across the Ithaki Strait. This is the prettiest village in Cephalonia, undamaged by the 1953 earthquake, the old houses mirrored in its lagoon-like harbour, giving it an enchanting Venetian atmosphere.

The village takes its name from the Norman conqueror Robert Guiscard, who died in a ship offshore here in 1085, during his last campaign against the Byzantine Empire. He was born in Normandy in 1016 as Robert de Hauteville, the sixth son of a minor baron of Viking descent, and when he was 30 he joined his elder half-brothers in their campaigns to conquer the decaying Byzantine exarchate in southern Italy. Within a quarter of a century he had carved out a duchy for himself in Apulia, Calabria and Sicily, capped by his conquest of Bari in 1071, the last remaining Byzantine possession in Italy. Guiscard, whose name means 'the Wise' or 'Cunning', or perhaps more accurately 'the Weasel', then conceived his grandiose scheme of conquering the Byzantine Empire and setting himself up on the imperial throne in Constantinople. He began this campaign a decade later when he took Kerkyra in his first invasion of Greece, in which his son Bohemund penetrated as far as Larissa in Thessaly before being turned back. Guiscard had in the meanwhile captured Rome and given over control of the imperial city to the Pope, leaving him ready to launch another invasion of Greece. He led his forces across the Adriatic again in 1084, recapturing Kerkyra after three naval battles with the Byzantines and their Venetian allies. Guiscard then sailed on to attack Cephalonia, where he died of the plague off the northernmost port of the island, the ancient Panormos, which thereafter was called Fiskardo in his memory.

The identification of Fiskardo as Panormos was made by Leake, based both on his own observations and his reading of ancient sources, as he writes:

> The port of Viskardho is evidently the Panormus, which an epigram of Antipater of Thessalonica describes as being opposite to Ithaca, and which Artemidorus, by attributing to it a distance of twelve stades from that island, shows to have been in this the narrowest strait. The convenience of this harbour, at the part of the entrance of the channels of Ithaca and Leucate [Lefkas], has in all ages rendered it valuable. On a former journey I observed there remains of Roman ruins near the shore, and there would seem, from the ancient authorities which I have cited, to have been a temple of Apollo on the point which shelters the northern side of the port, corresponding to a similar temple on the summit of Leucate. In the time of Strabo, Cephallenia was inhabited by the ex-consul Caius Antonius Nepos, uncle of Marcus Antonius, when he was exiled from Italy. The whole island obeyed him as if it had been his private property, and he projected the building of a new city, but being recalled from banishment, and dying soon afterwards, his intention was never executed. Pale, Pronus, and Crania were then small, and Same a mere ruin.

The only ancient monuments in Fiskardo are a Venetian *pyrgos* and the ruins of a sixth-century basilica, both of which are on the peninsula that forms the northern arm of the harbour, with the village itself built on the southerly and smaller peninsula that forms the other arm of the cove. Local tradition has it that the Normans set out to build a church on this peninsula in 1084 when they thought to bury Robert Guiscard here, but then they decided to bring his body back to Italy for burial in the family tombs of the Hautevilles at Venosa. It is possible that some of the Normans may have settled in and around Fiskardo or left their descendants here, the latter being a suggestion made by Arthur Foss in his excellent book on the Ionian Islands, published in 1969; as he writes, referring to the wife of his friend Christo, a caique master and cafe owner in Fiskardo:

> In looks she and her two daughters seemed French rather than Greek – and Norman-French at that with their fair chestnut hair, blue eyes and pink and white cheeks covered with a pale golden bloom from sun and wind. While we do not know whether any Normans actually settled in Phiscardo, we do know that they never hesitated to attach themselves to the local girls.

The Greek archaeologist George Kawadias has discovered prehistoric stone tools on the northern peninsula at Fiskardo, most of them built into the kitchen gardens of the villagers. He dates these implements to the Palaeolithic period, which would make this one of the earliest inhabited sites on the Greek isles. And so one is reminded once again of the immemorial quality of human life on islands such as Cephalonia, which inspired one of the poems in Waller Rodwell Wright's *Horae Ionicae*.

> Stern Cephalonia braves the
> beating storm and ever restless waves;
> in awful state erects her rugged brow, where mountain
> plants in wild profusion grow.
>
> Same, that long the Roman power defied, In
> ruin'd state o'erhangs the western tide.
> On the eastern shore

We marked the cliffs where distant Cranea stood,
or nearer, Proni overlook'd the flood.

Cephalonia: population 39,527; area 689 sq. km; highest peak: Mt Aenos (1,628m); airport: at Argostoli, connections to Athens; ferries: connections with Astakos, Killini and Patras in Greece, as well as with Ithaka and Zakynthos, and also with the Italian ports of Ancona, Bari, Brindisi and Venice.

ZAKYNTHOS

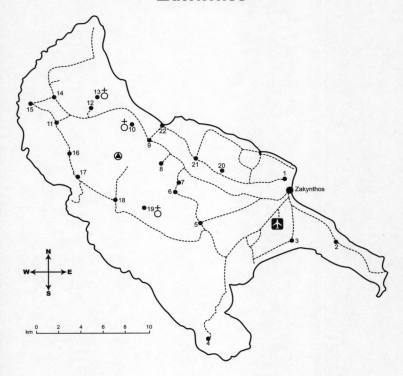

1 Bokhali
2 Xirocastello
3 Kalamaki
4 Keri
5 Machairado
6 Agia Marina
7 Skoulikado
8 Kalithea
9 Katastari
10 Agios Ioannis Prodromos monastery
11 Anafonitria
12 Orthonies

13 Panagia Spiliotissa monastery
14 Volimes
15 Agios Giorgios Krimnon monastery
16 Maries
17 Exo Chora
18 Agios Leon
19 Iperagathou monastery
20 Kalipado
21 Gerakari
22 Alikanas
⏺ Mt Vrachionas
✈ Airfield

nine
Zakynthos

Zakynthos is the southernmost of the six isles of the Eptanisa that lie in the Ionian Sea. Its principal town and port, which also bears the name Zakynthos, is about 18km from the north-western promontory of the Peloponnesos. Ferries cross from Zakynthos town to Killini on the Peloponnesian cape in about 90 minutes, less than half the time of the less frequent service to Argostoli on the inter-island boats. But a ferry line is now operating from a landing near Peratata on southern Cephalonia, plying between there and a little port just below Akri Skinari, the northernmost cape of Zakynthos, cutting the time of the inter-island journey in half, and this is the route that we chose in our most recent journey through the Ionian Islands.

Homer refers to the island as 'wooded Zakynthos', and though much of its ancient forest has vanished it still has woods of Aleppo pine and stone pine and colonnades of columnar cypress trees, as well as the 'leaf-trembling' olive groves that grace all landscapes in the Ionian Sea. Here as on the other Ionian isles the profusion and antiquity of the olive groves are part of the Venetian heritage, along with Italianate architecture and music and even the bloodlines of the island, which was largely resettled by Italian colonists after Venice recaptured Zante from the Turks in 1483. But Zakynthos is Greek, profoundly Greek, for all foreign influences became deeply rooted in the soil of Greece, as did the olive groves and vineyards planted during the days of the Serenissima.

The Venetians also encouraged the growing of currants, the 'raisins of Corinth', increasing their production on Zante forty-fold over the course of three decades in the sixteenth century, with most of the crop exported to satisfy (i.e. 'rot') the sweet tooth of England. Jacob Swan, who visited Zante with George Wheler in 1675, called it 'a terrestrial paradise', and an 'island of gold'. Wheler remarked that the insatiable English demand for currants was for long a mystery to the islanders: 'The Zantiots have not long known what we do with them; but have been persuaded that we use them only to Dye Cloth with; and are yet strangers to the luxury of Christmas Pies, Plumpotage, Cake and Puddings, etc.' He also praised the fertility and pleasantness of the island, attributing its richness to the development of the currant trade by the Venetians.

> Zante is but a little island... But to make amends it is one of the most fruitful and pleasant places I ever saw... It hath been called... the Golden Island; which it well deserves, because of the fruitfulness and pleasantness of its soil and abode. But now it more truly merits that name from the Venetians, who draw so much gold, by the Currant trade, from hence and Cephalonia, as beareth the ordinary charge of their Armada at sea.

The currant trade made Zante town one of the busiest ports in the Greek islands during the latter part of the Venetian period, its bustle and prosperity contrasting dramatically with the torpor of those parts of the eastern Mediterranean that were stagnating under Turkish rule. Richard Chandler noted this contrast when he arrived in the port of Zante in 1765, on his homeward voyage after two years of travel studying the ruins of the ancient Greek cities of Asia Minor.

> A capacious harbour filled, besides other vessels, with large ships and other galleys, a flourishing city with steeples and noble edifices, the sound of bells, the dress and manners of Italy, were all articles to which we had been long disused.

The transition from misery and desolation was as striking as it had been sudden.

Zante continued to be a prosperous port town throughout the period of the British protectorate, and its handsome Italianate buildings led travellers to refer to it as the 'Venice of the Ionian Sea'. Ansted describes the town as it appeared in 1863, 90 years before the earthquake that destroyed virtually all the island's monuments:

> It is small and not very sheltered, but wonderfully picturesque. It lies at the foot of a steep hill, which is crowned with the castle, and broken off in the most singular manner by a chasm, said to have been produced by an earthquake; but of which the fracture is constantly kept fresh and clean by the rain. It stretches far away on each side, having an appearance of greater magnitude even than Corfu, and far exceeding in style and variety of its public buildings any of the island capitals. There is a mole and small harbour, and near the landing-place a large square. The streets are numerous, wide, decently paved, and full of shops; they are covered with arcades, as in Italy, and built in tolerably regular style. The Strada Marina is very extensive; but it is really handsome in its noble quay, its wide road, and its beautiful churches. The market place is handsome and well-filled; the people cheerful and lively, and crowding the streets. Zante contrasts favourably with all the other cities of the Ionian Islands. It is more uniform, and has more characteristic features than Corfu, and if we except the Palace, it is quite equal to that city in public buildings. Not being enclosed or fortified, it has expanded more naturally than Corfu, and has not the poor suburbs of the metropolis. There are in it many fine old Venetian houses still inhabited by the families in whose possession they have been for centuries, and these give it an air of solidity and respectability that is not felt elsewhere.

Ansted also remarks on the high spirits and amiableness of the Zantiots:

> The character of the Zantiots is and always has been, somewhat different from that of the other Ionians. The

people are singularly lively, and quick-tempered, and are excitable, even compared with other inhabitants of the Mediterranean shores and islands. Crimes of violence are more common among them than elsewhere in the islands; but all classes are agreeable in their manners, possessing many useful and amiable qualities.

Like the Cephalonians, the Zantiots have distinguished themselves in the political and cultural life of Greece from Venetian times to the present day, and a local guidebook lists more than 50 who have made their mark in the arts and letters, scholarship and music. The most famous writers are Dionysios Solomos (1798–1857), author of the 'Hymn to Liberty', the first verses of which were set to music and became the national anthem of Greece; the poet and playwright Andreas Calvos (1792–1863); and the poet Ugo Foscolo (1778–1867), born in Zakynthos to a Greek mother and Italian father, and renowned as one of the great men of letters in both Italy and Greece. In addition to the native Zantiots, a number of distinguished Cretan artists moved to Zakynthos after Crete was conquered by the Turks, and many of their works adorn the island's churches or are preserved in the town's museums.

The island is also renowned for its folk dances, of which 15 different types are listed in the local guidebook, all of them still performed at *paneyeria*. The most important *paneyeria* are held on 24 August and 17 December, the two festivals of Agios Dionysios, the patron saint of Zakynthos. At those and other *paneyeria* there are processions in which the marchers dress in medieval costumes and mummers perform folk plays called *omilies*, a custom introduced from Venice in 1571. The *cantadas* of Zakynthos rival those of Cephalonia in their popularity at tavernas throughout Greece. One Zakynthian favourite is *I Xanthoula*, 'The Little Blonde Girl', one of the first poems that Solomos wrote in Greek, composed on his return to Zante in 1822 after his education in Italy.

> I saw the little blonde girl,
> I saw her late yesterday;

She boarded the small boat
To go to a foreign land...

I don't cry for the little boat
With the white sails,
I only cry for the little blonde girl
Who goes to the distant land.

The beautiful churches and fine old Venetian houses mentioned by Ansted were virtually all destroyed in the 1953 earthquake. Nevertheless, many of the churches of the island have been reconstructed and still preserve their treasures of post-Byzantine art. The important icons and other treasures of some of the churches that were utterly destroyed are housed in the Byzantine Museum. The museum is in Plateia Solomou, the seaside square at the ferry landing, where a statue of Dionysios Solomos stands in the centre of a pleasant park.

The museum collections include: works in wood and wood-carving (sixteenth to nineteenth centuries); wall paintings (twelfth to thirteenth and seventeenth to eighteenth centuries); icons of the fifteenth to sixteenth centuries from the Cretan-Ionian school; sculptural works of the Hellenistic, early Christian, Byzantine and post-Byzantine periods; and utilitarian implements and vessels. There is also a scale model of the town of Zakynthos during the period 1930–1950, completed in 1986 by the artist Yianni Manesi.

One exhibit of particular interest is a painting 60 centimetres (cm) in height and 7.6m long completed by Ioannis Korais in 1756 for the church of Agios Haralambos in Zakynthos town. This depicts the procession of the saint's relics on his feast day, representing among the marchers all the various levels of Zantiot life in the last half-century of Venetian rule, including the *nobili* (the nobility), the *civili* (those of the middle class and the professions) and the *populari* (the artisans and common people). The *populari* were reduced to the level of serfs during the Venetian period, and in 1628 they rose up in the first people's rebellion in modern Greek history, which was crushed within four years by the governor of

Zante, the *Provveditore*. The last Venetian *Provveditore* surrendered the town and the island to the French on 14 July 1797, whereupon the *populari* of Zante gathered together for a triumphant celebration in the Plateia San Marco, where they burned the *Libro d'Oro* and destroyed the coats of arms of the hated *nobili*.

Other important works in the museum are: the gilded carved wooden *iconostasis* from the church of St Dimitrios of Kola, by an unknown artist, dated by an inscription to 1690; an eighteenth-century ceiling panel from the church of the Faneromene in Zakynthos town, depicting the 'Birth of the Virgin Theotokos', by Nikolaos Doxaras; an eighteenth-century painting from the church of the Faneromene depicting the 'Prophet David', by Nikolaos Doxaras; a wall painting from the sanctuary apse of the church of the Saviour in the Kastro of Zakynthos, depicting 'SS Cosmas and Damian flanking their mother St Theodote', by an unknown artist, end of the twelfth century or the beginning of the thirteenth; a sanctuary door from the church of the Panagia Gavalousa, showing 'The Apostles Peter and Paul', artist unknown, second half of the sixteenth century; an icon of the 'Panagia Amolyntos' from the church of the Faneromene, by Emanuel Tzane Bounialis, dated 1641; an icon of 'St Anna holding the Virgin and Christ', from the church of Agios Nikolaos sto Molo in Zakynthos town, an anonymous work of the fifteenth century; and a painting of 'The Descent from the Cross', from the church of St Andreas of the Gardens, by Nikolaos Kantounes.

The oldest surviving church in the town, Agios Nikolaos sto Molo, stands on the seaward end of the square by the ferry landing. The church was built in 1483 on an islet that was connected to the shore by a short mole, hence the name. An oil lamp in the church belfry served the port as a lighthouse up until recent times, when the present area of Plateia Solomou was filled in and made into a park. The church was rebuilt in 1560 by the fishermen's guild, and it was reconstructed once again after being severely damaged in the earthquake of 1953.

The avenue at the far right-hand corner of Plateia Solomou leads to Plateia Agiou Markou, the oldest square in Zakynthos town.

The square takes its name from the Church of San Marco, the Roman Catholic cathedral, ruined in the 1953 earthquake and since rebuilt. The square is also the site of the Museum of Dionysios Solomos and Eminent Zakynthians. The tombs of Dionysios Solomos and Andreas Calvos are in the courtyard of the museum, and in the rooms above there is an exhibition of their manuscripts and memorabilia along with those of Ugo Foscolo. The museum has a library with books and documents on the history and culture of Zakynthos, as well as a large collection of photographs, period furniture, and archaeological and folk art collections. Among the exhibits are the coats of arms of the 41 noble families of Zante listed in the *Libro d'Oro*.

There is still another museum, devoted to Grigorios Xenopoulos (1867–1951), the Zakynthian novelist and playwright. The museum houses a collection of his manuscripts, memorabilia and personal effects, as well as period furnishings and decor.

Odos Mitropoleos leads in from Plateia Agiou Marko to the Greek Orthodox cathedral, which was also destroyed in the 1953 earthquake and is currently being rebuilt. A block or so to the north of the cathedral is Kyria ton Angelon, the church of Our Lady of the Angels, founded in 1687 by the hairdresser's guild of Zante and rebuilt after the earthquake of 1953. One of the icons in the church is by Panagiotis Doxaras (1662–1700), a founder of the Zakynthos School of painting.

There are two other important churches at the south end of town. The most prominent of these is the church of Agios Dionysios, whose campanile stands as a landmark on the quay where the southern breakwater of Zakynthos town curves out to shelter the harbour. The church was built in 1708 and is richly decorated with wall paintings, as well as icons by Nikolaos Koutouzis and Nikolaos Doxaras.

Agios Dionysios was born in Zante in 1547 to the noble Sigouros family, who were of Norman descent, and after a distinguished career as a churchman he ended his days in monastic retirement on the Strofades isles, a tiny group some 55km south of Zakynthos, where he died and was buried in 1622. When the Strofades were raided by the Turks in 1717 two monks brought his remains to Zante, whereby then he had already become the patron saint of the island through his reputation as a healer and miracle-worker. His body is now enshrined in a silver casket in the church dedicated to his memory in Zakynthos town, a modern structure rebuilt after the 1953 earthquake, replacing two earlier predecessors on the same site. Like Agios Spyridon, St Dionysios is always on the move, and so his slippers too have to be renewed every year.

The other church of interest at the south end of the town is that of the Faneromeni, which was founded in 1659 to house a sacred icon of the Virgin that miraculously floated to the shores of Zakynthos late in the Byzantine period. The present church was built in 1659 and superbly reconstructed after the 1953 catastrophe. Among its icons there are works by the Cretan painters Ilias Moskos and Victoras, whose major work here is his 'Beheading of St John the Baptist'. Other paintings that originally hung in the church are now in the town museum, including works by Nikolaos Doxaras and Nikolaos Koutouzis.

There are two unusual burial grounds on the northern outskirts of the town. One of these is the British cemetery, the last resting place of members of a community that began in Elizabethan times with the Levant Company and continued through the half-century of the protectorate. George Wheler writes that the English in Zante 'had a little factory consisting of a Consul and five or six Merchants... They have neither church, nor chapel, nor pastor, so that it seems to the people of this country that they live without religion and die without hope, which is a great scandal for their neighbours...'

The other burial ground is that of the Sephardic Jews, who established themselves on Zante in the fourteenth century, flourishing here until their virtual extermination by the Germans during World War II.

A road leads up from Plateia Agiou Marko to Psiloma, a wooded hill above the town to the north-west. Here one finds the historic little chapel of Agios Giorgios ton Philikon, where the patriots of Zakynthos gathered secretly in 1819 and again in 1821 to swear their allegiance to the cause of Greek independence and the *enosis* of their island with the rest of Greece. Andreas Calvos was originally buried here, alongside his second wife Charlotte, and seeing the site of his grave one recalls the first verse of his paean to Zante, translated by Richard Stoneman:

> O beloved homeland,
> loveliest of islands,
> Zante, you have given me
> breath, and given Apollo's
> golden gifts.

The road continues past the church to Lopho Strani, where a monument commemorates Dionysios Solomos, who here wrote his 'Hymn to Liberty' in a place where he loved to walk and think. A turn-off from this road leads to Bokhali, a pretty suburban hamlet embowered in flowers, with the village church of the Panagia Chrysopigis noted for a sacred Byzantine icon of the Virgin and another fine icon by Nikolaos Kantounis.

Bokhali is an extremely pleasant place to spend a summer evening, for its setting in a pine grove high above the sea makes it much cooler than the often sweltering town below, whose lights can be seen twinkling as if an extension of the celestial sphere between the midnight blues of the night sky and the sea. There are a number of excellent tavernas around the village square, and these are the places to go for authentic Zantiot music and dancing, with virtually all the customers taking their turn to circle around the floor, the most distinctive dances being the Zakynthian *syrtos*, which is paced more slowly than elsewhere in Greece, and the *stavrotos*, the *volimiatikos*, the *panourgia*, the *manfrena*, the *gaitani*, the *galariotikos*, the *ringotos*, the *tsakistos*, the *nyphiatikos*, the *panorios*, the *levantinikos* and the *yiaryitos*. The *yiaryitos* was brought to Zakynthos by refugees from Crete, and it is believed to be a survival of the ancient *yerano*, or crane dance, which Plutarch describes in his *Life of Theseus*. There he writes that Theseus and his companions stopped off at the sacred isle of Delos on their way home from Crete, and that in celebration they did 'a dance that is still performed by the inhabitants of Delos, miming the twists and turns of the Labyrinth and danced in regular time with complicated variations. This sort of dance is called the Crane...'

There is also a chapel of Profitis Ilias in the vicinity of Bokhali, and this seems to be where an apocryphal tradition once placed Cicero's tomb, as George Wheler writes:

> The church of St Helias lies above the Town, on the right hand of the way leading to the Citadel. It is a pretty pleasant place, set round with Orange-trees; and is besides remarkable for the fame of Cicero's Tomb, which, (as some have written), hath been found there, and his wife Terentia Antonia; wherof now there remains nothing but the bottom of an Urn of Porphyry. Nor could we learn what became of the rest; there being none at Zante so curious concerning the antiquity of their Country, as at Corfu.

One can continue uphill to the Kastro, the site of the ancient acropolis of Zakynthos. Excavations on the hill in the 1920s led the archaeologist Sylvia Benton to conclude that this was the site of ancient Zakynthos, the only important city on the island in antiquity. According to legend, this city was named for the hero Zakynthos, a son of Dardanos, the founder of Troy, with another version of the myth suggesting that the founder was an Arcadian from the city of Psophis in the Peloponnesos, a tradition referred to by Pausanias and other ancient sources. Local tradition in antiquity credited Zakynthos with being the founder of the city of Sagentum in Spain, and Theocritus in one of his *Idylls* mentions that the Zakynthians founded Croton in southern Italy:

> I sing the praises of Croton – O beautiful town of Zakynthos! –
> where the shrine of Lacinia faces the dawn, and where the boxer
> Aigon all alone devoured eighty loaves.

The numerous earthquakes that Zakynthos has endured have destroyed most of the walls of the Kastro, half of it having gone in a great subsidence of the cliff during the tremor of 1514. The original fortifications probably enclosed all of the ancient city of Zakynthos, with the structure being rebuilt in Byzantine and Venetian times and buildings within it erected even during the British protectorate, but today all is in ruins, with the most impressive remains being those of the main gate to the castle and its northern ramparts.

A road at the southern end of town leads out along the north-easternmost peninsula of the island, passing to the north of one of the two Zakynthian peaks known as Skopos, meaning 'Lookout'. (The other one forms the south-easternmost cape of the island.) Just beyond the church of Agios Haralambos the road passes on its left the church of Agia Ekaterini, built in 1664 as a *metochion*, or dependency, of the famous monastery of St Catherine on Mount Sinai. The original *iconostasis* of the church is still in place, restored after the 1953 earthquake, and it is hung with several works by Michael Damaskinos.

Some 4.5km from town the road passes Argasi, a seaside village that has now become a popular summer resort. Nearby is the ruined Domenigini Pyrgos, the tower from which Kolokotronis set out in 1821 at the beginning of the Greek War of Independence. Three and one half kilometres further along the road passes Xirocastello, a village on the northern spur of Mount Skopos. After rounding Mount Skopos the road passes through the scattered parts of Vassilikos, the easternmost village on Zakynthos, after which the route comes to an end at Porto Roma, an idyllic little cove at the tip of the peninsula.

On the return journey from Vassilikos to Zakynthos town one might stop at Xirocastello, from where there are paths leading up Mount Skopos. It is a half-hour walk up to the peak of the mountain (492m), where there is a monastery dedicated to the Panagia Skopiotissa. The monastic church was built ca 1400 from the ruins of a temple of Artemis. This is the only church on the

Ionian isles that is administered by the Patriarchate of Constantinople rather than from Athens. It has a number of remarkable icons, the most renowned of which is a miracle-working portrait of the Virgin that was apparently brought to Zakynthos from Constantinople after the fall of Byzantium in 1453.

The view from the summit of Mount Skopos is superb, and in its essentials it is the same as the prospect that Ansted describes in the last years of the British protectorate:

> The view from Scopes in clear weather must certainly be very fine, including the whole of the lower island of Zante, reaching to Cephalonia and the islands adjacent, and also including the greater part of the Morea. Looking down on the town of Zante and its castle hill behind, and carrying the eye along the cliff to Acroteria, the whole of the bay of Zante is displayed; and beyond this first low range are the other low hills of the east of the island, crowned with small villages or isolated buildings. These strike the eye, and contrast with the garden-like appearance of the plain and hill sides, thus adding much to the beauty. Most of the houses being whitewashed, they are very prominent, even at the distance of many miles.

Another road at the south end of Zakynthos town cuts across the eastern end of the island to Keri, a village under the other Mount Skopos. At the beginning of the road there is a turn-off on the left for Kalamaki, the largest beach resort on Zakynthos, and then after Ambelokipi a road leads off to the left for Laganas, another popular seaside village, where the rare breed of turtles known as *caretta caretta* can be seen on the beach. At Laganas there is a boat service in summer out to the islets of Agios Sostis, Pelouzo and Marathonissi, where there is a sea cave large enough for a caique to enter. Continuing along the Keri road, one can see off to the left the old Venetian villa known as Sarakina, built in the eighteenth century as the country seat of the noble Lunzi family; the mansion has recently been restored and is now a country inn, where performances of Zantiot music and dances are given during the summer months. Ansted stayed at Sarakina as a guest of Count Lunzi during his tour of Zante, remarking on the old-fashioned Ionian hospitality that he received there:

> I was taken in his own carriage by my kind friend, the Count Nicolo Lunzi, across a series of ploughed fields and through narrow lanes, scarcely wide enough to allow our conveyance to pass. Arrived at the house, we found that friendly reception that I have nowhere seen more charmingly illustrated than in the Ionian islands. It is indeed worth a visit to the islands to be thrown into a society so primitive, and exercising so unreservedly the ancient rites of hospitality on the largest scale.

As the road approaches the southern Mount Skopos peninsula it passes on its left Limni Keriou, a swampy lagoon that is the site of bituminous springs mentioned by Herodotus, and which up until recent years were still used by local fishermen for the tar with which they caulk their caiques.

The road finally makes its way around the western side of Mount Skopos to Keri, a pretty village noted for its panoramic views, particularly at sunset. The village church, dedicated to the Panagia Keriotissa, dates from the seventeenth century; it is adorned with a baroque *iconostasis*, with a sacred icon of the Virgin encased in silver and framed in gold. A path leads from the village to the lighthouse on Akri Keri, the southernmost beacon in the Greek isles of the Ionian Sea.

Nearby is the hamlet of Ambelo, where Davy was told about a spectacular exploit that he relates in his book on the Ionian isles and Malta, writing of it in the chapter entitled 'Notice of a Journey Through the Mountainous District of Zante in 1824'.

> We were led to a spot on the cliff called Diglidani's Leap. About five or six feet [just under 2m] from the margin of the cliff, and about twelve feet [4m] below, a mass of crumbling rock projects upwards, terminating almost in a point. The exploit which has given this spot celebrity amongst the country people, was performed about 120

years by a native whose name it bears, – a man of extraordinary activity, strength, and daring. By way of display, the story goes, he jumped on the pinnacle mentioned, alighting like a bird, and there not being sufficient space to turn, he leapt back backwards. The height of the cliff here is between two and three hundred feet [60 and 90m]; the detached mass, however, when the extraordinary feat was performed, it is said, was on a level with the boundary margin. His descendants still reside in his native village, and possess the tar-springs in the adjoining valley, which were originally granted to him for some service of difficulty which he performed for the Venetian government...

A path leads from Keri up to the summit of the southern Mount Skopos, 423m above sea level. From here on a clear day one can just barely see the Strophades Islands, a pair of islets some 55km to the south-south-east. These are the most remote of the western Greek isles, with caiques sailing down to them from Zakynthos only a few times a year. But it was the remoteness of the Strophades that attracted St Dionysios there to spend his last years in solitary retirement within the monastery of the Transfiguration, founded in the thirteenth century. This fortified *pyrgos*-monastery can still be seen on the largest of the two islands, its once numerous community now reduced to a handful of monks. The body and other relics of the saint were preserved there by the monks up until 1716, when an attack by Turkish corsairs forced them to bring his remains to Zante, where they were enshrined in the church that is dedicated to his memory. The monks are the sole inhabitants of the island other than the lighthouse keeper, whose beacon is the only one between Cape Keri and Sapienza, the tiny islet off Methoni in the south-westernmost peninsula of the Peloponnesos.

Mythology has it that the Strophades were home to the Harpies, or Body-snatchers, winged genie who, along with Iris, were the daughters of Thaumas (a primordial sea divinity) and Electra (the Oceanid, one of the daughters of Oceanus and Tethys). Hesiod and most other sources name only two of the Harpies, Aello (who is also called Nicothoe) and Ocypete, but a third, Celaeno, is sometimes mentioned as well. As Hesiod writes in his *Theogony*: 'And Thaumas wed Electra the daughter of deep-flowing Ocean, and she bare him swift Iris and the long-haired Harpies Aello (Storm-swift) and Ocypetes (Swift-flier), who on their swift wings keep pace with the blasts of the winds and the birds, for quick as time they dart along.' The Harpies are depicted in Greek vase paintings and funerary sculptures as winged maidens who carry off the souls of the dead, as on the Harpy Tomb from Xanthus that is now in the British Museum. The names of the Harpies suggest that they are the mythopoeic personifications of shearwaters, the oceanic birds that skim endlessly over the surface of the sea, for the Strophades have always been one of their nesting places, and in both Greek and Turkish folklore they are believed to be the souls of the dead in flight to the netherworld.

The main road to the interior of the island leaves Zakynthos town from the end of Odos Agiou Lazarou. This takes one out into the great plain that make up all of eastern Zakynthos except for its north-western peninsula.

About 10km along the road comes to a junction at Machairado, a beautiful little town below the eastern side of Oros Vrachionis, the mountain range that forms the spine of the island. The town's landmark is the very striking belfry of the church of Agia Mavra, whose peal of bells can be heard for kilometres around. The principal adornment of the church, which has been splendidly restored after the 1953 earthquake is an icon of Agia Mavra, the Dark Lady, dating from ca 1600; her miraculous image is bedecked with necklaces presented to her by her devotees, who celebrate her *paneyeri* here on 3 May. (One of the necklaces was a gift of Queen Olga of Greece.) The church also has some remarkable icons and wall paintings by renowned Zakynthian artists.

The other villages that cluster around the junction also have interesting churches dating from the Venetian period; these include the Panagia Eleftherotria, on the road to Lagopodon; Ipapandi, on the road to Melinado; and in Melinado itself Agios Dimitrios, which is built on the ruins of a temple of Artemis, of which some Ionic columns and their bases remain.

At Bougiato, the next village north of Melinado, the church of Agios Ioannis is built on the ruins of an early Christian basilica. Next come Langadakia, Fiolitis and Agioi Pantes, after which there is a turn-off on the left for Agia Marina. The latter village is named for the Venetian church of Agia Marina, noted for its baroque *iconostasis*, considered to be the finest on Zakynthos.

The main road then goes on to Drakas and Skoulikado, one of the most picturesque villages on the island, clustering around the church of Agios Nikolaos. The road then makes a great S-bend to pass through the village of Agios Dimitrios, after which it runs generally westward, with successive turn-offs on the left for the villages of Kallithea and Pigadakia. Kallithea has the Vertzagio Folk Museum, consisting of a reconstituted Zakythian house – kitchen, dining room and bedroom – with traditional furniture, decor and utensils, as well as a stone grinding wheel used to press grapes and olives to make wine and oil.

The road then comes to Katastari, the main crossroads at the north-western corner of the plain, set among vineyards and olive groves at the north-eastern foot of Mount Vrachionas (756m), the highest peak on Zakynthos. A path leads westward from the village to the monastery of Agios Ioannis of Langadas.

The main road at the Katastari crossroads goes on to the north-west, passing on its left some 3.5km from the village a path that leads up in five minutes to the monastery of Agios Ioannis Prodromos, founded just before the fall of Constantinople in 1453. The impressive entrance portal bears the date 1666, and close by are the ruins of a sixteenth-century *pyrgos*. The most notable painting in the monastic church is an icon of St John the Baptist by Theodore Poulakis.

The road then veers westward to cross Mount Vrachionas on its way to Anafonitria and other mountain villages in the northern end of the island. Halfway across the island there is a turn-off on the right that leads in 800m to the village of Orthonies, from where a

path leads northward to the abandoned and half-ruined monastery
of the Panagia Spiliotissa, Our Lady of the Cave. The monastery
was founded in 1548 by the monk Ioannis Kopsidas, who left a large
library of rare books and ancient manuscripts. Davy and his party
rode here on horseback after spending the night in Katastari, as
he writes:

> On the following morning, after breakfast, we continued
> our journey, and in about three hours, after a rather
> laborious ascent through a rugged pass, at the foot of which
> the marl foundation of the plain is succeeded by mountain
> limestone, we arrived at the monastery of Speliotissa,
> situated in a hollow of the mountains, and distant, it is
> reckoned, from Catastari about nine and a-half miles
> [15km]. The contrast between the luxuriant plain we had
> just before left, and the surrounding hills was striking:
> the vegetation was scanty and stunted, and confined
> chiefly to the fissures of the rocks of grey limestone; the
> arbutus was the common shrub; the myrtle did not reach
> so high; heath and wild thyme were abundant. Excepting
> a small space of ground in which the monastery stood,
> then in stubble and in possession of a large flock of goats,
> not a single spot bearing marks of cultivation was visible.
> The monastery is a pretty extensive building, in the form
> of a hollow square, within which is a neat chapel, containing
> a picture of the Virgin Mary, said to have been found in
> an adjoining cave, and in honour of which the edifice was
> erected. The establishment supports a priest and thirteen
> calloyers, or lay brothers, the main occupation of the latter
> of whom is to till the ground and look after the flocks.
> Here we rested and took some refreshment during the heat
> of the day, and experienced much civility from the inmates,
> one of whose duties is to receive strangers, for which an
> allowance is made by the government, – a humane and
> very necessary measure, in a wild and thinly populated
> country, without inns or rest-houses. Before taking leave,
> the Papa brought me a patient, a little boy, a relative of his
> own – labouring under chronic disease of the abdominal
> viscera, the consequence of fever contracted in the plain,

who on coming to me, prettily kissed my hand, according
to the graceful usage of the country.

At Orthonies a secondary road leads back to the coast at Koroni.
Along the coast north of Koroni there is a sea cave with a famous
therapeutic spring known as Xingia, whose ash-coloured water turns
the sea white for some 500m from the shore. About a kilometre
from the cave there is another medicinal spring called Heli, whose
water is used as a cathartic and as a cure for rheumatism – at least,
according to the locals.

Continuing beyond the Orthonies turn-off, we turn right at the
next crossroads, where a road winds through the mountains to
Volimes and other villages in the northern end of the island.

Volimes is the most distinctive of the mountain villages of
Zakynthos. The village church of Agia Paraskevi dates from the
seventeenth century and has been well restored since the 1953
earthquake, incorporating many of its original baroque architectural
elements in the façade of its new structure, with a remarkable
belfry. The beautiful icons and painted woodwork of the church
make it a treasury of post-Byzantine Zakynthian art. The village has
a cheese dairy and a school for weavers, both of which are open to
the public, and virtually every house on the main street displays
home-made carpets and embroideries for sale. But aside from
tourism, particularly the traffic passing to and from the ferry near
Cape Skinari, life in the village seems to go on as in the past,
following the same immemorial cycle that Davy observed when
he passed this way.

> The year round, their occupations are nearly as follow: – In
> October, after the rains, they plough; in November, sow; in
> December and January, they gather the olives and make
> oil; in February, they turn over the soil in the vineyards;
> and in March, they do the same round the olive-trees; in
> April they cut hay; in May and June, their different kinds
> of corn; in July, they level the ground around the vines;
> in August they gather and dry their currants; and in
> September, they gather their grapes and make wine. When

there are no olives (of which they expect a crop only every
alternate year) in January and February, they make lime,
an article with which the mountains supply the town and
plain. Besides these their principal occupations, there are
many minor ones. The women are even more busily
employed than the men, and as variously: spinning, weaving,
and knitting may be considered almost as their amusements
and recreations, after the more important and laborious
labours of the day. They spin both cotton and worsted
thread; and weave hair-cloth for bags, cotton cloth for dress
and household purposes, and some carpeting, of which I
saw two or three pretty samples in the form of rugs.

Davy was very taken by the country people that he met in these
remote hill villages; as he writes, describing them in loving detail
at the end of his description of the Zakynthian mountains.

I shall conclude the journal of this little excursion, which
was of uninterrupted gratification and amusement, with
a few observations on the inhabitants of the villages
we visited. Generally they were better looking than the
inhabitants of the town and plain, and decidedly fairer;
very many of them indeed have light-blue and hazel
eyes, and light hair. We saw several women possessed of
considerable beauty, and not a few with good clear
complexions, and some colour. The dress of the men was
very similar to that used by the same class in town. The
covering of the head is a small skull-cap, the prevailing
colour of which is brown. The hair is allowed to flow over
the shoulders (at least of the young men), and shaved
about the temples. The growth of hair over the upper lip is
encouraged, but not beneath, nor is the whisker tolerated:
they pride themselves in their mustaches, and would
consider it a very great indignity to be deprived of them.
When our Greek interpreter asked the old Stelleano [who
claimed to be 110] if he would cut them off, he replied
with some briskness, drawing his hand across his throat,
that he should cut that first... The most peculiar part of the
womens' dress is a white scarf, worn so as to envelope the
head and cover the shoulders, for which sometimes a

handkerchief is substituted, simply wrapped round the head. Their gown is long, with long sleeves, tight around the waist, and high, concealing the bosom. When formally dressed, they wear stockings and shoes, and very large shoe-buckles. On ordinary occasions, they commonly go barefooted, at least around the house. They are under little restraint, appear to be quite at liberty to show themselves, and in their manners very much resemble women of the same class in England.

Two roads lead from Volimes to the northern end of the island, forming a loop. The road on the left leads to the hamlet of Korythi, the northernmost community on the island. The northern end of the loop is just beyond Korythi, and from there a secondary road leads to Akri Skinari, where there is a lighthouse on the northernmost promontory of the island, a landmark for mariners since the days of Odysseus. The promontory now serves as a landing place for a ferry service from Cephalonia. A short way to the south-east of the lighthouse is the famous Kyanoun Spileo, known in English as the blue cave, the largest and most beautiful sea cave on the island, its main entrance 6m wide and 3.5m high.

The road south from Volimes comes to a junction with the cross-island road, where we turn right to come to Anafonitria, the village named for the famous monastery of Anafonitrias, which is approached via the side road leading south to the village of Plemonari and the Bay of Agios Ioannis. The monastery was founded in the early fifteenth century by the Tocco family, soon after they severed their feudal ties to the Angevins and became independent rulers of Zante, Cephalonia and Ithaka. The fame of Anafonitrias is due to its association with St Dionysios Sigouros, who ended his career as abbot of the monastery before going off to die on the Strophades isles.

Another secondary road leads north-west from Anafonitria to Volimes, passing on its left the sixteenth-century monastery of Agios Giorgios Krimnon, St George of the Precipice, supposedly on the site of a Byzantine monastery. According to John Davy, writing in 1824: 'The ancient monastery, of which there are no traces remaining, excepting eighteen cisterns, is said to have been founded seven hundred years ago, – four hundred before the present building, which was erected by the Spaniards, and by them fortified by a tower.' Davy then goes on to describe a nearby grotto, known as Spilia tou Gerasimou; according to local tradition, this once sheltered Agios Gerasimos, the patron saint of Cephalonia, who lived here for five years in the mid-sixteenth century.

> Observing a little arched-way in a small valley running down towards the sea, we descended to examine it; it proved to be a small cavern in the limestone rock, luxuriantly shaded with wild myrtle, rosemary, and arbutus; above which was another cave of larger dimensions, partly lighted by a perforation in its roof. Here we were assured that Saint Jerasimo took refuge when he was ill-treated and pelted with stones by the inhabitants of Plemonario, a neighbouring village, and that from hence he crossed over to Cephalonia, of which island he became the tutelary saint... The tradition is, that the saint of Cephalonia, in consequence of the treatment which he received here, pronounced a malediction on the place, owing to which a great part of the population was soon swept off by disease, and the village never after flourished. Now it is thought to be reviving; but it still has a cursed appearance, and looks sufficiently miserable.

On their way to the monastery of Agios Giorgios, Davy and his party fell in with a group of hunters from one of the villages on Mount Vrachionas. As Davy writes, catching the atmosphere of life in the remote mountains of Zakynthos in his time:

> We met a party of villagers, who, with their dogs and guns, had been out shooting; they had killed a hare, which the Capo, who was of the party, very civilly sent us as a present. The liberty which these mountaineers enjoy, must give a great charm to the kind of life which they follow, and attach them strongly to their native place. Almost all are on an equality; they must live quite independent and free; and their general air and manner betokened it. They have no

game laws, – no great landed proprietors, – no gentlemen; they are all cultivators and labourers, plowing their own fields, tending their own flocks; and he must become richest who is most industrious, and who has most children to assist him. Descending gradually, the turn of a hill brought us suddenly in sight of a pretty extensive grove of firs, which, being of a lively green, made a very agreeable appearance: they seemed to be growing wild, and resembled the Scotch fir. The air was strongly perfumed by the resin which exuded from them, and the smell was more like that of myrhh than of turpentine. Crossing this grove, we arrived at the monastery of St George, where we found excellent quarters.

The main road south-east from Anafonitria comes to its next crossroads at Maries. Local tradition has it that the village is named for Mary Magdalene, who is supposed to have passed through Zakynthos on her way to Rome, bringing with her, they say, the message of Christ's love. The village church, the Mariesotissa, is named in her memory, the only such dedication that I know of in Greece. Maries itself is still much as Davy describes it, 'a very pretty and considerable village, situated toward the head of a fine valley, – a great part of it cultivated, either covered with vineyards or spotted with olive trees, the cypress and fir intermixed. Even in the village, the cypress was common; and in graceful clumps amongst neat white-washed houses, in company with the vine and fig-tree, imparted peculiar beauty to the spot, the sense of which, perhaps, was heightened by the wild and rocky barrier of hill on each side.'

The next village along the main road is Exo Chora, one of the few villages on Zakynthos whose traditional stone houses survived the 1953 earthquake. The seventeenth-century village church of Agios Nikolaos has an unusually beautiful *iconostasis*.

A short way beyond Exo Chora a road leads to the pretty coastal hamlet of Cambi, where Greek archaeologists have unearthed Mycenaean tombs and vases, one of the few prehistoric sites discovered on the island.

The main road south-east from Exo Chora comes next to a crossroads at Agios Leon, which is still, as Davy describes it, 'rather a pretty village'. The left fork at the crossroads leads up to Loucha and Gyri, the highest villages in Zakynthos, the latter being 550m above sea level. Near Gyri there is an enormous cavern known as Megale Spilio.

The main road from Agios Leon heads eastward along the southern flank of Oros Vrachionas towards Agios Nikolaos. About halfway between the two villages we see off to the left the monastery of Iperagathou, founded in 1608 by Kostis Parthenios; in 1679 this became a *metochion* of St Catherine's monastery on Mount Sinai.

The village of Agios Nikolaos looks out over the Zakynthian plain from the southern tier of Mount Vrachionas. The village church has a very unusual belfry, which commands a sweeping view of the plain below. Just outside the village is the convent of Eleftherotria, a quite recent foundation.

A road leads south from Agios Nikolaos to the village of Agalas, from where a path leads down to the coast and the marine cave known as Spilia Damianou.

The main road east from Agios Nikolaos crosses Oros Vrachionas and then heads north to come to Lagopodo and Machairado, from where one can can drive back to Zakynthos town, completing a circuit of the island's mountainous interior.

We now make a tour of the villages in the great plain in the north central region of the island, the most fertile part of Zakynthos. Davy and his party rode through this plain on horseback during his exploration of the island in 1824, when the British were just beginning to build the first roads on the island, as he writes:

> Crossing the beautiful plain, we stopped for the night at the village of Catastari, close to the bay of the same name, and almost skirting the mountain barrier. It has been before mentioned, that scattered solitary houses, with a few exceptions, are very uncommon in these islands, and that the natives residing in this country live chiefly in the villages. The most remarkable exception to this is in the plain of Zante; and it owes much of its peculiar beauty to the villas and farm-houses dotting its surface, each

commonly white-washed – in the midst of trees – the cypress and orange the most conspicuous, and frequently enclosed by a fence of aloes. At that time a macadamised road was only just commenced; the island was without a carriage road; we met mules, in rapid succession, coming towards the town, laden with bags of new currants, each led by an attendant. On our way we called at the villas of several of the proprietors, most of whom we found at home, superintending the gathering of their valuable crop; at one of them we were received by the lady of the house, in the absence of her husband; she was young and handsome – indeed the reputed belle of Zante, and withall a countess. She was at the door of the house when we arrived with some female servants, her infant in her arms, and so plainly attired, as to be hardly distinguishable in her dress.

Leaving town by the Bochali road, we come first to Gaitani, a pretty village surrounded by grape arbors. The village church of the Pantocrator contains the tomb of Agios Iosif of Samakos (1440–1511).

The road then passes between the villages of Vanapato and Sarakinado before coming to Kalipado. The village of Kalipado was founded soon after Venice regained Zante from the Turks in 1482. The Knights Hospitallers of St John established themselves here while they were still in possession of Rhodes, which they lost to the Turks in 1522. The village church of Agios Ioannis, originally the private chapel of the noble Voultsou family, has a remarkable though damaged series of paintings by Nikolaos Koutouzis (1741–1813).

The road continues westward to the Gerakari, a constellation of three villages. At Ano Gerakari, the uppermost of the three villages, a path leads up to the hilltop chapel of Agios Nikolaos, from which there is a splendid view of the Zakynthian plain and its farmland, orchards, vineyards and pastures. Edward Lear writes of this abundant landscape in his *Views of the Ionian Islands*:

The old nursery rhyme: 'If all the world were apple-pie/And all the trees were bread and cheese' supposes a sort of Food-landscape hardly more remarkable than that presented by this vast green plain, which may be, in truth, called one unbroken continuance of future currant dumplings and plum puddings.

After passing the Gerakari villages the road curves down to the coast at Alikanas, a popular beach resort. After pausing there one can return by an alternative route, which goes inland to Alonia, Ano Gerakia and Meso Gerakia before curving back to the coast, after which it passes the seaside resorts of Planos and Tzilibi on its way back to Zakynthos town.

As we sailed away from Zakynthos, wondering when we would see it again, I recalled Ugo Foskolo's ode 'To Zante', in the translation by Edgar Allan Poe, who never saw the Ionian isles except in his romantic imagination.

> Fair Isle, that from the fairest of all flowers,
> Thy gentlest of all gentle names dost take!
> How many memories of what radiant hours
> At sight of thee and thine once awake!
> How many scenes of what departed bliss!
> How many thoughts of what entombed hopes!
> How many visions of a maiden that is
> No more, – no more upon thy verdant slopes!
> No more! alas, that magical, sad sound
> Transforming all! Thy charms shall please no more,
> Thy memory no more! Accursed ground
> Henceforth I hold thy flower-enamelled shore,
> O hyacinthine isle! O purple Zante!
> 'Isola d'oro! Fior di Levante!'

Zakynthos (Zante): population 38,680; area 435 sq. km; highest peak: Mount Vrachionas (756m); airport: connections with Athens; ferries: connections to Astakos, Killini, Patras and Cephalonia, as well as to the Italian ports of Ancona, Bari, Brindisi and Venice.

KYTHERA

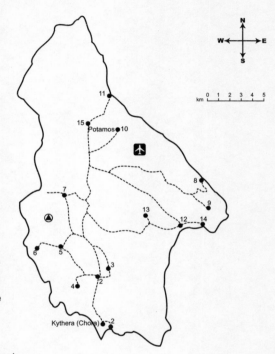

1 Kythera (Chora)
2 Kapsali
3 Livadi
4 Kato Livadi
5 Kantouni
6 Pourko
7 Kalokerines
8 Myrtidia monastery
9 Mylopotamos
10 Mylopotamos cave
11 Areoi
12 Dokana
13 Aroniadika
14 Diakofti
15 Agios Giorgios church
16 Frilingianika
17 Palaeochora (Agios Giorgios)
18 Potamos
19 Agios Prokopius
20 Agia Pelagia
21 Fratsia
22 Kastri
23 Palaeopolis
24 Avlemonas
⦿ Mt Mermigaris
✈ Airport

ten
Kythera

Kythera is only nominally one of the Ionian Islands, for it is far, far away from the Ionian Sea off the south-easternmost promontory of the Peloponnesos – Cape Malea – with Cape Matapan, the ancient Taenarian promontory of the Mani peninsula, off to its west. Its companion isle – Antikythera – is more remote, lying halfway between Kythera and the north-western capes of Crete.

Strabo considered that Kythera and Antikythera marked part of the maritime boundary between the Cretan and Sicilian Seas, forming stepping stones as they do between Crete and the Peloponnesos. Kythera is historically linked with the other six isles of the Eptanisa because of an administrative decision made by Venice in 1669, and they remained part of the Ionian Islands until *enosis* in 1864. When it became part of Greece, Kythera was still known by its Latin name – Cerigo – while Antikythera was called Cerigotto, and only in the past century have they reacquired their classical names.

The earliest references to Kythera are in the *Odyssey* and the *Iliad*. In both epics Homer refers to the island as 'sacred Kythera' because of its famous shrine of Artemis Kytheria, the 'sweet garlanded' goddess of love. The archaic poet Alcman of Sparta writes of his love for a devotee of her cult in one of his lyric poems:

Again sweet love, by Kytheria led,
Hath all my soul possest;
Again delicious rapture shed
In torrents o'er my breast.
Now Megalostrata the fair,
Of all the virgin train
Most blessed – with her yellow floating hair –
Hath brought me to the Muses' holy fane,
To flourish there.

The earliest account of Aphrodite's birth is in Hesiod's *Theogony*, where the poet describes how Uranus, god of the sky, was castrated by his son Cronus 'wily and most terrible, who hated his lusty father'. Cronus then threw his father's severed genitals into the sea, where they gave birth to Aphrodite.

> And when first he had cut off the genitals with the adamant and cast them from the land on the swelling sea, they were carried off for a long time on the deep. And white foam arose from the immortal flesh and in it a maiden grew. First she was brought to holy Kythera, and then from there she was brought to sea-girt Cyprus. And she emerged a dread and beautiful goddess and grass grew under her slender feet. Gods and men called her Aphrodite, and the foam-born goddess because she grew amid the foam, and Kytheria of the beautiful crown because she came to Kythera, and Cyprogenes because she arose in Cyprus washed by the waves.

Herodotus writes that the earliest sanctuary of the goddess was at Askalon in Syria, where she was worshipped as Aphrodite Urania, the Heavenly One, with her cult being brought from there to Cyprus and Kythera by the Phoenicians. She was undoubtedly worshipped in Mesopotamia in earlier times as a fertility goddess and a celestial deity, the latter cult perpetuated in the name of the planet Venus, the Greek Aphrodite. According to Pausanias, 'The Assyrians were the first of the human race to worship the Heavenly One; then the people of Paphyos on Cyprus, and of Phoenician Askalon, and the people of Kythera, who learnt her worship from the Phoenicians.'

According to Aristotle, in prehistoric times the island was known as Porphyrousa, from its abundant beds of murex (*purpura haemastoma*), the mollusc shell that was so popular in antiquity for making purple dye. Large beds of the porphyry-coloured shell have been found on the east coast of Kythera at Kastri, on a cove of Avelemonas Bay known as Agios Nikolaos; the Phoenicians may have had a trading colony there, for Xenophon writes that the port was originally called Phoenicus.

Thucydides, in describing the fighting during the seventh year of the Peloponnesian War, 425/424 BC, writes of the Athenian amphibious landing on Spartan Kythera, noting that the port, then called Skandeia, was used by 'merchant ships from Egypt and Libya and also served as a protection to Laconia from attack by pirates from the sea ...'.

> Here the Athenian expeditionary force put in to land. With ten ships and 2,000 hoplites from Miletos they captured the city of Skandeia, on the sea; with the rest of their force they made a landing on the part of the island that faces Malea and moved forward against the city of Cythera, where they found all the inhabitants drawn up ready to meet them. Battle was joined, and for some time the people of Cythera stood firm, but finally they were routed and took refuge in the upper city. Afterwards they came to terms with Nicias and the other commanders, agreeing to submit themselves to the discretion of Athens so long as their lives were guaranteed... After the surrender the Athenians occupied the town of Skandeia on the harbour and put a garrison into Cythera itself.

Schliemann was the first to make an archaeological exploration of the island, and in 1888 he thought, mistakenly, that he had discovered the ruins of the famous temple of Aphrodite at Palaeopolis, a site some distance inland from Kastri. Sylvia Benton of the British School began excavating Kastri in 1932, unearthing the remains of a Minoan trading colony dating from ca 2000–1550 BC. Subsequent researches by her and other archaeologists at the British School shows that the Minoan colony at Kastri traded with places as far away as Pylos, Troy and Egypt. Excavations elsewhere on the island have unearthed Mycenaean remains, indicating that here, as in Crete, the Achaians from the Peloponnesos seized power from the Minoans in the late Bronze Age. The island is not referred to in the Homeric Catalogue of Ships, but elsewhere in the *Iliad* there is mention of two heroes from Kythera: Lykophron and Amphidamas. The island is also mentioned in Book IX of the *Odyssey*, in which Odysseus tells Alkinoos of his storm-tossed passage through these seas early on in his long homeward journey from Troy.

> And now I would have come home unscathed to the land
> of my fathers,
> but as I turned the hook of Malea, the sea and current
> and the North Wind beat me off course, and drove me on
> past Kythera.

The strait between Kythera and Cape Malea has been feared by Greek mariners since antiquity, for until the opening of the Corinth Canal ships sailing between the Ionian and Aegean Seas had to pass this way to round the Peloponnesos, many of them never to return. An old Greek proverb, first quoted by Strabo, says: 'When you round Cape Malea, forget your home.'

The strait narrows to just over 9km between the northernmost tip of Kythera and Elafonissi, an islet off the peninsula just west of Cape Malea. Anciently this was known as Onugnatos, or Donkey's Jaw, and originally it must have been connected to the mainland, for Strabo describes it as 'a low-lying peninsula'. The nearest port on the mainland is Neapoli, where ferries cross to Agia Pelagia and Diakofti, the northernmost of the three ports on the island. The other island port is on the south coast at Kapsali, which is the harbour of Chora, Kythera's capital. The crossing from Neapoli to Agia Pelagia is about 4km eastward from the narrowest point of the strait, between Elafonissi and Akri Spathi, the Kytheran cape known in antiquity as Platania, the Plane Trees. Pausanias writes that in his day the crossing was made 'from the cape on the mainland known as the Donkey's Jaw to the cape on the island called the

Plane Trees, a distance of five miles [8km] sailing. The people of Kythera have the port of Skandeia on the coast, but the city of Kythera itself is about a mile and a quarter [2km] inland from Skandeia. The sanctuary of the Heavenly Goddess is most sacred and the most ancient of all the sanctuaries in Greece.'

These passages from Thucydides and Pausanias have led most authorities to identify Kastri as the site of Skandeia and Palaeopolis as that of the ancient city of Kythera, capital of the island in classical times. But Leake, the first European to make a detailed study of the island, held that Chora, then known as Cerigo, stands on the site of the ancient capital, and that Kapsali is to be identified with Skandeia, though he admitted that his theory 'cannot be reconciled with the historians'.

Leake came to the island quite by accident in 1804, when he was a passenger aboard the brig *Mentor*, the British warship that was transporting the first shipment of the Elgin Marbles from Athens to England; as he writes in his journal on a later visit to the island: 'We anchor this evening at Kapsali, in Cerigo, after having encountered off the Taenarian promontory some stormy weather, which threatened to send us to the coast of Africa. It was in consequence of an adverse gale in the same place and at the same season that I had the misfortune... to be shipwrecked at Avlemona in this island.' After this introduction, Leake reviews the conflicting evidence for the identification of the various ancient sites on Kythera, beginning with a plausible etymology of the island's Latin name.

The obscurity of the history of Greece during the middle ages, renders it impossible to trace the modern appellation of this island to its origin. It is almost the only instance of a Sclavonic name in the Greek islands. Tzerigo was perhaps a Servian chieftain, who obtained possession of Cythera when the... barbarians of Sclavonic race settled in the Peloponnesos in such numbers that a name of Sclavonic origin has ever since remained. Tzerikos, in Italian Cerigo, contains about 50 villages and 7000 inhabitants; in the town [Chora] there are scarcely 1000...The situation so much resembles that of the generality of ancient sites in the islands of the Aegean, and the harbour ... was so important by its position on the line of maritime communications between the eastern and western coasts of Greece, that one cannot but presume that the modern site was occupied by some ancient town or fortress; but there is some difficulty as to the name...At Paleopoli, about three miles [5km] inland from the port of Avlemona, are the ruined walls of an ancient town, and as its situation is not far from the Cape of Cythera opposite to the promontory of Laconia, which is still named Malea, it seems evidently to have been the upper Cythera intended by Thucydides, in which case it cannot but follow that Avlemona was the site of maritime Cythera. From Xenophon we learn that the lower town was also called Phoenicus... Every circumstance, therefore, in the transactions related by the historians favours the supposition that Paleopoli was the site of upper Cythera, and Avlemona that of Phoenicus or the lower town; and that Scandeia stood at the modern town of Cerigo. Pausanias, however, is directly opposed to this conclusion; for he describes Scandeia as the harbour of the city which contained the temple of Venus...which leads directly to the conclusion that Cythera was at the modern town; that Scandeia was at Kapsali, and that it was the same place as the lower Cythera...

The Slav invaders mentioned by Leake were eventually absorbed through conversion to Christianity, a process that occurred during the medieval Byzantine period in mainland Greece and on some offshore islands such as Kythera. There are a dozen churches and monasteries on the island dating from the Byzantine period, here as elsewhere showing how the Greek Orthodox Church kept Hellenic culture alive during the barbarian invasions that took place in the Dark Ages following the collapse of classical Graeco-Roman civilisation. Then in later Byzantine times the island was laid waste by the repeated attacks of pirates and foreign conquerors, so that at times it must have been virtually uninhabited.

After the fall of Constantinople to the Latins of the Fourth Crusade in 1204, Kythera was one of the places that fell to the lot of Venice, and in 1207 the Serenissima gave the island over to Marco Venieri, who set himself up there as the 'Marquess of Cerigo'. The Venieri were a noble Venetian family who traced their descent back to Julius Caesar and through him to the goddess Venus, the mother of Aeneas, thus giving them some poetic licence for ruling over the island where Aphrodite first emerged from the foam of the sea. But for all practical circumstances the island was controlled by the Monemvasian family of Eudaemonoyanidis until 1263, when the two families were united by marriage and the island given to the Venieri as a dowry. By 1248 the largest Byzantine-Venetian settlement was at Agios Dimitrios, a site known today as Palaeochora, south-east of Agia Pelagia.

Four brothers of the Venieri family divided up the island between themselves in 1309, creating 24 feudal fiefs; but these did not include Palaeochora and Kapsali, which continued to be governed as communes, probably because both of them were already fortified and independent. In 1363, after the Venieri had been involved in a rebellion on Crete, the Serenissima assumed direct control of Cerigo and the following year they sent their own *Castellan*, or Commander of the Castle. Administratively, Cerigo was placed under the direction of the governor of Crete, but after the fall of Candia in 1669 the island was ruled from Corfu by the *Provveditore Generale del Levante*. Thus Kythera became one of the Ionian Islands, an arrangement that continued throughout the Venetian period and on down to the end of the British protectorate. The Venieri were given back 13 of their 24 fiefdoms in 1393, and they continued to maintain their feudal rights on the island until the end of the eighteenth century; nevertheless, during this period the island was actually governed by the Venetian *Provveditore*, the *Castellans* of the fortified towns, and the aristocracy of Greek and Venetian nobles, most notably the Venieri.

The Byzantine citadel in Chora was rebuilt by the Venetians in 1502, but they appeared to have neglected the fortifications at

Palaeochora, which in 1537 fell to the Turkish pirate-admiral Barbarossa, who carried off 7,000 captives to be sold in the Istanbul slave market. Thereafter Palaeochora was abandoned and the capital was moved to Chora, where it remains today. After Barbarossa's raid Cerigo was repopulated by Greeks fleeing from Turkish-occupied regions in the Peloponnesos, and then after the fall of Candia in 1669 large numbers of Cretan refugees resettled there. But this influx was countered by the death and destruction wrought by earthquakes, epidemics and pirate raids, so that by the end of the Venetian period the population was actually less than it had been at the beginning of the seventeenth century. The Turks captured the island again in 1714, but at the Peace of Passarowitz four years later they were forced to restore Cerigo to Venice. At that time the Venetian governor again became subordinate to the *Provveditore Generale del Levante* on Corfu, so that Cerigo and Cerigotto once more became part of the Ionian Islands, remaining as such until *enosis* was achieved in 1864.

By the beginning of the nineteenth century the people of Kythera began moving abroad in search of work and better living conditions, a wave of emigration that subsequently spread all over Greece, particularly in the poorer areas of the country. As Leake remarked of Kythera: 'As in Zakytho and Kefalonia, many of the men obtain subsistence abroad as agricultural labourers, not in general like the natives of those islands, on the neighbouring continent, but in Asia Minor, where they cultivate the Turkish lands... By these means they often bring back a few purses to their native island, and are enabled to buy some land there.' But few of the Kytheraens who left returned permanently, and today there are far more of them living in Australia than in Kythera itself. This diaspora is lamented in a category of folk poems called *xeniteias*, or songs of exile, one of the best-known throughout Greece being '*Stin Afstralia Makria*', or 'Far Away in Australia'. But when Kytheraens gather 'down under' they sing a threnody called '*Tsirigotikos Diplos*', or 'Couplets from Cerigo'.

Cerigo, lovely island
I'm here perforce abroad
and when I hear your name
my eyes are filled with tears.

There below Cape Malea
this side of Crete,
lovely Cerigo
gave birth to Aphrodite.

The sun when first he rises
bathes your flanks in gold,
The moon, too, looking down
sees all your charms,

Swift running sea
and cooling wind,
Take me a thousand greetings
to give them down there.

The first European traveller known to have visited Cerigo was
Cyriacus of Ancona, who in 1437 explored Palaeopolis and made a
drawing of the ruined temple of Aphrodite. By that time a legend
had developed that Helen of Troy had been living in Cerigo with
Menelaus when she was raped by Paris and taken to Troy. The
English traveller Sir Richard Guylforde repeats this tale in his
garbled account of the island and its mythology, published in 1511.

> Upon tewsdaye ayenst nyght we passed by the yle called
> Cerigo/ whiche yle was sometyme called Citheria where
> Helena the Grekysshe Queene was borne/ but she was
> ravysshed by Paris in ye next yle by/ called Cicerigo Doynge
> sacryfyce in the Temple/ for the whiche Rape followed the
> distruccion of Troye/ as ye famouse Storye thereof sheweth/
> known in every tonge.../And the sayde yle Cerigo is
> directly ayenst the poynt of Capo Maleo in Morea/ and in
> the same eyle was Venus borne...

The ruins of the temple were last seen in 1551 by Nicholas
Daulphinios, the French court chamberlain and geographer.

Daulphinios reported that while in Cerigo he saw the ruins of Aphrodite's temple 'on a high mountain'; two Ionic columns were still standing along with a great portal surmounted by 'a statue of a woman of monstrous size clothed in Greek fashion', presumably Aphrodite. Below the temple an islander showed him the supposed ruins of the 'Castle of Menelaos', though he failed to see the 'Baths of Helen' pointed out to later travellers. George Wheler and his party visited the island in 1675, by which time the 'Baths of Helen' were on the itinerary for foreign sightseers; as he writes:

> Cerigo hath the Morea North of it; and was anciently called Cithera; famous for being the native country of Venus and Helena. So that we are to frame an Idea of this place from the fame of these Beauties, we might imagine it as one of the most charming places of the World. But, on the contrary, the greatest part of it is a barren, rocky and Mountainous Soil, ill peopled, and can brag of no plenty, neither Corn, Wine or Oyl; which undoubtedly made Venus change her own country for Cyprus; and Helena so willing to be stollen and carried into the pleasant plains of the continent. What beauties it now produceth, I am ignorant of; for I remember not that I saw a woman there.

Wheler's ship then entered Avlemonas Bay to take on fresh water at Agios Nikolaos, the cove known to the Venetians as Porto San Nikola, where a local guided them to the ruins.

> We found ancient ruins near this place, which we took to be the ruins of Menelaus his City, in old times the King of this Isle. They are almost level with the ground. Among the ruins are some Grottos cut out of the Rock, which one of the Island pretending to be an Antiquary, assured us was anciently the Baths of Helena, affirming that her Palace was not three or four miles [5 or 6km] thence in the Hills. We took this Antiquary for our guide, and we went to see what we could find of it. But all we discovered were two Pillars standing upright, but without Chapitars [capitals], and the Bases so deep in the ground, that we could not judge what order they were... I rather believe it to have been some

ancient Temple than a Palace. They now call this place
Paleo-Castro, or Old Castle.

The French writer Fenelon used the *Odyssey* as the model for his
Telemaque, published in 1699, which chronicles the wanderings of
Telemachos in search of his lost father, describing his stay in Kythera
as a pastoral idyll. Fenelon set the scene for romantic paintings of
this remote and supposedly enchanted isle, the most famous being
Watteau's 'Voyage to Kythera'. But some who travelled there were
soon disappointed, as was Francis Pouqueville, whose *Travels in the
Morea* was published in 1813.

> Cerigo is well known to be the ancient Cythera. Here, by a
> strange caprice of imagination, altars were built to the gay
> laughter-loving goddess in the midst of a most wild and
> desolate country. The view from the rocks, though some
> cultivated fields are to be seen here, is sufficient to
> disenchant the ideas of poets and lovers who visit the
> island to indulge in the recollections of antiquity. Instead of
> Celadons they will see rough peasants; instead of Venus
> and the Graces, half wild Greek women; and instead of
> beautiful lawns enamelled with flowers, naked and rugged
> rocks or valleys overgrown with brushwood.

Travellers approaching Kythera from Athens usually land at
Kapsali, which is on a small cove separated from a larger bay by
a peninsular headland, the typical topography of ancient Greek
harbours. (The airport is south of Paleochora.) The only Venetian
structures that remain in Kapsali are some eighteenth-century
warehouses and the seventeenth-century lazaretto, where those
arriving from plague-ridden countries were quarantined before
being allowed to land on the island. William Lithgow stopped
here on his way to Crete in 1609, and in his *Rare and Painful
Peregrinations*, published 23 years later in London, he recounts a
scandalous incident that occurred while his ship lay in port.

> In the time of my abode, at the village of Kapsalo (being a
> haven for small barkes, and situate below the Castle), the
> Captaine of that same Fortress kild a Seminary Priest,

whom he had found in the night with his whore in a
Brothel-house; for the which sacrilegious murther, the
Governour of the ile deposed the Captaine, and banished
him, causing a boate to be prepared to bring him to Crete.
O! if all the priests which doe commit incest, adultry, and
fornication (Yea, and worse, *Il peccato carnale contra natura*)
were thus handled and similarly rewarded; what a sea of
sodomiticall irreligious blood would overflow the halfe
of Europe...

A winding road some 2.5km long winds up from Kapsali to
Chora. Although Chora is the capital of Kythera it is only the third
largest community on the island, surpassed in population by both
Agia Pelagia and the inland village of Potamos, both of them in
the north of the island. The tiered white houses of Chora make it
seem more like a Cycladic village than one in the Ionian isles,
perched high on its peninsular rock above the port of Kapsali,
clustering around the ruins of its Venetian fortress, the Kastro.
Leake's description of Chora still catches the dramatic quality of
the scene.

> The town of Cerigo stands on a narrow ridge 500 yards
> [450m] in length, terminating at the south-eastern end in a
> precipitous rock, crowned with a castle which is accessible
> only on the side towards the town, by a steep and winding
> path, but is commanded by a conical height at the opposite
> end of the ridge. The town is enfiladed by a battery of three
> guns in the castle, which was erected by the French when
> they took possession of the Venetian islands.

There was a fortified town on this site in Byzantine times. But
when the first Venetian *Provveditore*, Quirini, came to Cerigo in 1503
he had orders to rebuild the Kastro completely; his accomplishment
is recorded in a still extant inscription beneath a relief of the
winged lion of San Marco. The fortress had a length of 200m and a
width of 80m, and in most cases the height of the walls was 25m.
The northern and western sides were the most heavily fortified,
while on the other sides the precipitous cliff provided a natural

fortress, though additional walls were built above the rock face of the precipice. During the sixteenth century the town consisted of two quarters, with the one within the walls known as Kastro and the one outside the citadel called the Vourgo. The main entrance to the citadel is at the north-west, while there is a secondary portal that connects Kastro to Vourgo on the northern side of the fortress. The final line of defence was a walled section to the east. The outer fortifications at Vourgo are formed by the external walls of the houses and churches and by sections of curtain wall between the towers, the ruins of which can be seen today on the lower slopes of the rock on that side.

The Kastro quarter was built on a level area at the top of the rock within the citadel. This was once the centre of the town, containing the offices and residences of the Venetian officials, the barracks of the fortress garrison, the mansions of the local nobility, the marketplace and several churches. All that remains within the Kastro today are the *Castellan's* residence, the barracks and four churches, with another half-dozen chapels clustered below the precipitous northern side of the fortress in the Vourgo.

Some of the old Venetian mansions in the Chora can be identified by the inscriptions and coats of arms above their doorways, including those of the Kassimatis and Darmaros families. One distinguishing feature of the houses is their chimneys, some of which rest on carved stone corbels and project high above the roof with a prismatic top. The church of the Estavromenos, which originally belonged to the Darmaros family, is now the metropolitan church, the seat of the bishop of Kythera. It is distinguished by its remarkable *iconostasis*. The church of Agioi Pantes, near the west wall of the Venetian Kastro, also has a notable *iconostasis*, with many beautiful icons. Another place of particular interest in Chora is the museum, which has exhibits found in archaeological sites around the island, including objects from both the Minoan and Mycenaean eras.

The main road from Chora north divides into two branches at Livadi, where one of Kythera's Byzantine churches is located near the crossroads. This is Agios Andreas, which was originally constructed as a basilica in the ninth century and rebuilt several times, most recently in 1628, with some segments of its twelfth-century wall paintings still visible. Another early church in the vicinity of Livadi is the Panagia of Konteletou, built in 1551, with some of its original wall paintings still visible. The village also has some well-preserved country houses, the most notable of which is the Kalligeros mansion.

Off to the east at the crossroads one can see the Kantouni Bridge, an impressive span 110m long carried on 12 high arches. This was built in 1826 by John MacPhail, the British Resident on Cerigo, part of a projected roadway to Avlemonas that was never completed.

A secondary road from Livadi leads to its satellite village of Kato Livadi. Here the Byzantine Museum of Kythera is housed in the post-Byzantine church of the Analypsis. The museum has a precious collection of icons and wall paintings from abandoned churches on the island, rescued by the Greek Department of Archaeology. The exhibition includes examples of artistic styles from the early Christian era through the late post-Byzantine period. There are also fragments of an early Christian floor mosaic from the ruins of the church of Agios Ioannis at Potamos.

The road to the west at the Livadi crossroads winds around through the villages in the south-west quarter of the island, rejoining the other branch above Dokana. Some 5km beyond Livadi on this road there is a turn-off to the left for Pourko, from which it is a five-minute walk to the church of Agios Dimitrios, dated by an inscription to the eleventh century, with wall paintings ranging in date from the twelfth century to the fourteenth. Archaeological excavations have revealed a Mycenaean settlement near the church, and objects discovered there are now in the Chora museum.

A somewhat longer walk from Pourko leads to Moni Agia Elesa, a convent founded in Venetian times and rebuilt in 1871, with a view from its grounds south-east to Chora and the southern capes of Kythera. The *paneyeri* of Agia Elesa, who is believed to have been martyred on this site in 375, is celebrated here on 1 August, with celebrants spending the eve of the feast in the convent.

The road through the south-west part of the island comes to a crossroads at Kalokerines, where a turn-off to the left leads out to the Myrtidia monastery on the west coast of the island. Local tradition dates the founding of this monastery to the thirteenth century, though the present structure dates only to 1841. The monastery was built to house an icon of the Virgin that a shepherd boy found on the branches of a myrtle tree on the west shore of the island, and thus it was originally called Myrtidiotissa, Our Lady of the Mytles, known locally as Myrtidia. (The seas of Greece must have been filled with such icons at the time, for there are chapels of the Myrtidiotissa on many of the Greek isles, and the story is always the same.) The *paneyeri* of the Myrtidia is celebrated on 7 October, when the sacred icon is carried in a procession led by the bishop of Kythera. This has been the most important festival of Kythera since late Byzantine times, and William Miller, in *The Latins in the Levant*, suggests that the Myrtidiotissa is a survival of the ancient cult of Aphrodite Kytheria, for on that day all the islanders flock here to celebrate 'the festival of their patron saint, Our Lady of the Myrtle Bough, whose image borne by the waves to the island and found in a myrtle tree represents the Christian version of Aphrodite rising from the sea'.

The main south-west road continues on to Mylopotamos, a very pretty constellation of three villages – Kato Hora, Limionas and Agia Sophia – on the northern side of Mermigaris, the highest peak on Kythera (507m). Mylopotamos means the 'River mill', stemming from the mills that were once powered by the stream that still supplies water to the village fountain, pouring from the mouth of a stone lion into a basin and washing trough below the *plateia*. These mills were operating in full force when Davy passed through what he described as the 'beautiful glen of Mylopotamos, deriving its name from the stream which flows through it, and to the mills which the stream works'. He describes the glen in more detail in a lyrical footnote:

> The most picturesque part of the glen exhibits extraordinary
> luxuriance of vegetation, depending on the perennial supply

of water. The platanus, the chestnut, the myrtle, the tutsan, etc. overshadow the stream, and indeed the glen, forming a dense shade and a cool retreat, very delightful in the sultry days of summer. The small stream is conducted by an artificial channel, and in a short space turns twenty-five little mills for grinding corn, of a very primitive and simple structure.

There are two churches on the village square, Agios Haralambos and Agios Sozon, the latter decorated with frescoes of the late seventeenth century. Just beyond Agios Sozon the road divides into two branches, with the one on the right leading out to the monastery of the Panagia Orfani and the left to Kato Chora, the 'Lower Town', a Byzantine village fortified by the Venetians. There are a number of post-Byzantine churches in the village, most notably Agios Athanasios, Panagia Mesosporitissa and Agios Ioannis Prodromos, but unfortunately all three of these are closed to the public. In the *plateia* one is confronted with a totally unexpected building, a Lancastrian school erected by MacPhail in 1825, a charming little structure with Gothic windows. The street to the left of the school leads to the gateway of a little citadel. The gate of the citadel has a relief of the lion of St Mark and the date 1566, and within its ruined walls there are seven chapels dating from the sixteenth and seventeenth centuries. This is one of several fortified communities built by the Venetians in the sixteenth century, after Barbarossa's raid had destroyed the island capital at Palaeochora.

A path leads from Kato Chora to the Mylopotamos cave, one of the most famous caverns in Greece, better known locally as the cavern of Agia Sophia. The latter name stems from a small chapel at the mouth of the cave dedicated to Agia Sophia. The so-called 'tourist trail' extends for more than 500m into the cave, which is a labyrinth with innumerable chambers and corridors covering an area of some 2,000sq. m. The various chambers have been given extravagantly romantic names, such as the 'apartments of Aphrodite', 'Aphrodite's boudoir', the 'chamber of the lions', the 'chamber of the bats' and 'swan lake'. The cavern was visited by Davy in the company of Sir Frederick Adam, for whom the locals illuminated its depths, putting on a spectacular show.

> [The cave of] St Sophia, is a very remarkable one, and possesses singular beauty, which it chiefly owes to the enormous stalactites and stalagmites with which it abounds, formed of clear-coloured marble, descending from the roof, – sometimes resembling columns, others altars, others buildings in ruins, and many resembling animals: the mimic forms, in all kinds, and of the most fantastic shapes. I saw this cavern to great advantage, when it was illuminated in a rude manner, on the occasion of the Lord High Commissioner, Sir Frederick Adam, paying it a visit. The lurid light of the fires of brushwood, the wild action and appearance of the natives, running to and from with their firebrands, added much to the picturesque effect. Considering the vast size of some of the stalactital columns, many feet in circumference, and their highly crystalline prismatic structure...one cannot reflect on their formation without a feeling of marvel, as regards the length of time their growth must have required, especially as there is only an inconsiderable dropping of water from the roof. The approach to this cave is hardly less remarkable than the cavern itself, and it is worthy of the attention of the traveller. It is a glen of savage wildness, without any traces of culture, and only the slightest of vegetation; a chasm between two rugged heights, of black limestone, perhaps 600 feet [180m] high.

Davy does not mention the cave sanctuary of Agia Sophia in the outer chamber of the cavern; the present structure dates to 1785, but part of its original structure of the thirteenth century survives, along with some very well-preserved frescoes. Archaeological evidence indicates that this may have been a cave sanctuary in Minoan times, perhaps sacred to Eleitis, the Cretan fertility goddess, whose cult would have been replaced by that of Aphrodite in the archaic period.

Another road from the *plateia* in Mylopotamos passes the church of Agios Haralambos, and after a bit more than a kilometre comes to the village of Areoi. From there it is a five-minute walk to the church of Agios Petros, which dates from the late twelfth or early thirteenth century, with some of its original wall paintings still visible. Around the church there are the remains of prehistoric structures. Another Byzantine church near Mylopotamos is Agios Nikolaos, which is in the hamlet of Meligkates.

The road from Mylopotamos continues beyond Areoi to a fork above Dokana, where it joins the main highway to the north. The highway comes to another fork at Aroniadika, where a side road to the right leads eastward via Frilingianika to the airport and then on to the convent of Agia Moni, passing under the southern slopes of Mount Digenis, the second highest peak on the island (490m). The convent was founded in 1840 and dedicated to the Virgin Mary, standing on a hilltop with a stunning view of the north-east coast of the island and across the sea to the Peloponnesos.

A secondary road leads off to the right at the approaches to the convent and takes one to Diakofti, a seaside hamlet on the north-east coast that is now becoming a popular summer resort, served by ferries and hydrofoils.

Along the approach to Diakofti a rough road leads off to the right and heads up towards the peak of Mount Agios Giorgios. The road soon degenerates into a track and one must do the final ascent on foot, a half-hour walk.

On the peak there are two of the oldest chapels on the island, one of them dedicated to Agios Giorgios and the other to the Virgin. The original church of Agios Giorgios is dated to the sixth century, but all that remains of this early structure in the present building is an architectural fragment above a window and some areas of a mosaic floor. The chapel of the Virgin also dates in its origin to the sixth century, and it is thought to have been a baptistry or martyrium of the original church of Agios Giorgios. Near the church there are the remains of a Minoan sanctuary, discovered in 1992.

We now return to the main north–south highway at Aroniadika, passing once again through Frilingianika, where there is a Byzantine church dedicated to Agios Blasios. Continuing north, about a kilometre beyond Aroniadika there is an unmarked turn-off to the right that in 4km leads to Palaeochora, originally known as Agios Giorgios, the ruined and abandoned medieval capital of the island.

According to Leake, Palaeochora was 'Upper Kythera', one of the three cities on the island mentioned by Thucydides. During the Byzantine period the town came to be known as Agios Giorgios, whose Kastro is believed to have been built in the twelfth century by the Eudaemonoyanidis, Byzantine lords who ruled Monemvasia and also, for a time, Kythera, after the island had been recaptured from the Venetians in 1278 by Admiral Likarios, commander of the imperial fleet under the Emperor Michael VIII Palaeologos. The position of this fortified Byzantine town is described by the Greek scholar Dimitrios Zaghlanakis.

> The town was built above and beside a deep and precipitous ravine on the north-east coast of Kythera, one kilometre in a straight line from the shore. It is a rocky area surrounded by the ravine, which can be crossed by a neck on the south-west side. The ravine has steep, reddish-coloured rocks, frightening to the gaze, rearing up perpendicularly and split from top to bottom by terrible tectonic earthquakes.

Zaghlanakis then goes on to write of how the original Eudaemonoyanidis lord who built this fortress exacted the feudal *droit du seigneur*, forcing young brides to spend the night with him on their wedding day. A young nobleman named Venieri objected to this and was sentenced to death by Eudaemonoyanidis, who ordered him to be thrown from the ramparts of the Kastro of Agios Giorgios. But at the final moment Venieri grabbed Eudaemonoyanidis by the hand and pulled him over the precipice as he jumped, with the two of them dashed to death on the rocks below, or so the story goes.

Agios Giorgios reached the peak of its fortunes in the early sixteenth century, when its inhabitants included many wealthy Byzantine noble families who had moved there from Turkish-occupied areas in the Peloponnesos. Local tradition has it that there were 72 noble families living in Palaeochora at the time, each of them with their own chapel. But this all came to a sudden and

violent end in 1537, when Barbarossa attacked the island with a fleet
of 3,000 vessels, on his way back to Istanbul after his attack on
Corfu. Palaeochora was taken by storm, and when the Turkish
troops burst into the town many of the women threw themselves to
death from the ramparts, some of them with their children in their
arms, as evidenced by the shattered skeletons found among the
rocks below late in the Venetian period. Some managed to escape
and took refuge in the nearby cave known as Kharkomatou, but
the Turks discovered their hiding place and slaughtered them.
Barbarossa then made a clean sweep of the island, carrying off all
those who had not been killed by his troops, sailing away with 7,000
captives to be sold as slaves in Istanbul. Although Kythera was
eventually repopulated, Agios Giorgios was abandoned and the
capital of the island was shifted to Chora. Agios Giorgios then came
to be called Palaeochora, the Old City, and the islanders avoided its
blood-stained ruins, for the horror of what had happened there
gave it a sinister reputation, the haunt of ghosts and vampires, who
were referred to locally as 'Paliachoritis'.

The remains of a dozen churches can be seen among the ruins of
Palaeochora, most of them with wall paintings of the fourteenth
and fifteenth centuries. The best-preserved of the churches in
Palaeochora itself are those of Agios Antonios, the Panagia and
Agia Varvara. About a kilometre or so away one finds the ruined
church of Agios Theodoros, which dates from the late twelfth or
early thirteenth century. The church is named for Osios Theodoros,
Holy Theodore, whose skull is preserved there in an ornate reliquary
shaped like a bishop's mitre. According to the *Life of Agios
Theodoros*, Theodore moved to Kythera from Monemvasia during
the reign of Romanus II (reigned 959–963), seeking a life of solitude
on the island. When he arrived he found Kythera completely
deserted, for the island had been abandoned after a series of raids
by Arab corsairs during the previous century, and it was not
repopulated until after 963, when Nicephorus Phocas, the 'Pale
Death of the Saracens', recaptured Crete. Theodore lived alone for
several years in the interior of Kythera, building a church dedicated

to SS Sergius and Bacchus, where he lived for the rest of his days. After his death his undecomposed body was found by two hunters who had crossed over from the Peloponnesos, and when news of this reached the Duke of Sparta he ordered that a church be built in Theodore's memory – the present chapel of Agios Theodoros.

The main road north from Aroniadika comes to a crossroads at Potamos, the largest village on the island, where the local church of Agios Nikon dates from the Byzantine period. The road to the left continues on to the northern end of the island, ending at Plateia Ammos, a beach just to the south-east of Akri Spathi, passing the solitary church of Agia Anastasia halfway along on the right, and at the end the little seaside chapel of Agios Prokopios.

The road to the right at the Potamos crossroads passes within sight of another of MacPhail's constructions, a seven-arched bridge built in 1825. The road comes to an end at Agia Pelagia, the second largest village on Kythera and the island's largest port.

An interesting excursion from Chora takes one out to the south-east coast of the island at Avlemonas, stopping en route at the site of Palaeopolis. The route takes one north from Livadi to Fratsia, where a turn-off to the right is signposted for Kastri. Some 5km out of Fratsia the road passes on the left a chapel of Agios Vasilios, and a short distance beyond that one sees an unmarked path leading off to the left towards Palaeokastro, the hill on which the ancient city of Palaeopolis is located.

A walk of about 20 minutes takes one to the church of Agios Kosmas, which is thought to date from the eleventh century. The church is built with ancient architectural members including four columns and six half-columns, all unfluted, and four Doric capitals. These have been identified as parts of a small archaic temple of the sixth century BC, which probably stood elsewhere on the Palaeokastro hill. Schliemann thought that the columns and capitals were from the temple of Aphrodite, which he believed stood on the site where Agios Kosmas was built, but archaeologists at the British School disagree, suggesting a possible site about midway between the church and the chapel of Agios Giorgios on the summit of the hill of that same name, which rises to the north of Avlemonas Bay. In any event, this was the temple that Herodotus says was founded by the Phoenicians, and which, according to Pausanias, was the earliest of the Greek sanctuaries dedicated to the goddess of love. West of Agios Kosmas there is a well-preserved stretch of the defence wall of the archaic city, dated to the late seventh or early sixth century BC. The lower town of Palaeopolis is thought to have been on the south-west slope of the hill.

The road comes down to the shore of Avlemonas Bay at Kastri, a low ridge just beyond the torrent bed of the river Palaeopolis. This is the site of Skandeia, Kythera's principal port in classical times. An archaeological excavation by the British School has revealed that Kastri was the site of a Minoan trading colony from ca 2000 to 1550 BC. This would also have been the place known variously as Porphryousa or Phoenicus, as evidenced by the beds of murex shells found around Avlemonas Bay.

The road continues around the bay from Kastri to Avlemonas, a tiny fishing village in a sheltered cove under Mount Agios Giorgios, with the ruins of a small sixteenth-century Venetian fort guarding the entrance to the haven. In times past this was known as Agios Nikolaos, so-called from a seaside chapel dedicated to the patron saint of mariners. During the eighteenth and nineteenth centuries Agios Nikolaos was the principal port of the island, and it was here in 1802 that the brig *Mentor* put in after being damaged by a storm off Cape Malea, sinking offshore with most of the Elgin Marbles; these were eventually recovered by sponge divers and finally shipped off to England, arriving in 1805.

Gerard de Nerval stopped here in 1851, recording his impressions of disappointment in *Voyage en Orient*, for this barren and virtually uninhabited shore of Kythera bore no resemblance to the enchanted isle of Fenelon and Watteau; as he writes, in the translation by Richard Stoneman:

> One must admit that Cythera has kept none of its beauties except its rocks of porphyry, as gloomy to look at as ordinary sandstone rocks. Not a tree on the coast we

followed, not a rose, alas! not a shell along this shore where
the Nereids once chose a conch for Aphrodite. I searched
for the shepherds and shepherdesses of Watteau, their ships
adorned with garlands made fast to flowery shores; I dreamt
of those crazy bands of pilgrims of love in cloaks of
variegated satin...and I saw only a gentleman shooting
at woodcock and pigeon, and blond and dreamy Scottish
soldiers, seeking on the horizon, perhaps, the fogs of their
own country... As we skirted the coast, before putting in at
San Nicolo, I observed a small monument, vaguely outlined
against the azure of the sky, which, atop its rock, seemed to
be the statue, yet standing, of some protecting dynasty...
But as we came closer, we distinguished clearly the object
which signalled this coastline to attentive voyagers. It was
a gibbet, a gibbet with three branches, one of which alone
was adorned. The first real gibbet I had ever seen, and
it was given to me to see it on the soil of Cythera, an
English possession!

These lines inspired Charles Baudelaire's *Voyage à Cythère*,
published in 1851, and superbly translated by Robert Lowell. The
first three stanzas set the scene.

> My heart, a seagull rocketed and spun
> about the rigging, dipping joyfully;
> our slow prow rocking under cloudless sky
> was like an angel drunk with the live sun.
> What's that out there? Those leagues of hovering sand?
> 'It's Cythera famous in the songs,
> the gay old dogs' El Dorado, it belongs
> to legend. Look closely. It's a poor land.'
> Island of secret orgies none profess,
> the august shade of Aphrodite plays
> like clouds of incense over your blue bays,
> and weighs the heart with love and weariness.

***

Antikythera, the Latin Cerigotto, is one of the loneliest and most
remote of the Greek isles, lying in the seldom travelled seas between

Kythera and the north-western capes of Crete. During the summer months there is a twice-weekly ferry service to Kythera, Crete and the Piraeus, but in the winter service is less frequent and during bad weather the island is often cut off from the rest of the world for days on end.

Potamos, the island's only village, nestles in its deeply indented bay at the northern end of the island. Most of the island's population of some 120 souls lives there, although a few have farm dwellings and summer houses elsewhere on the island. Potamos is near the site of Aigilia, the principal city of ancient Antikythera, whose fragmentary defence walls can be see on the Palaeokastro headland, about 1.5km north-east of the town. Palaeokastro was also the site of the medieval town, which throughout the Venetian period was ruled by the Viari, a noble family from Venice who took possession of Cerigotto soon after the Latin conquest of Constantinople.

Remote as it is, Antikythera must have been a stopping point for ancient mariners sailing between Crete and the Peloponnesos or those passing between the Aegean and Sicilian Seas. Dramatic evidence of this was discovered in 1900, when a sponge boat from Symi anchored in Potamos Bay to escape from a storm. A diver from the boat went down to look for sponges and found a wrecked ship of the Roman period on the sea bottom, its cargo including a consignment of statuary, including an almost perfectly preserved bronze figure of a young man, now exhibited in the National Archaeological Museum in Athens. Now known as the Ephebe of Antikythera, the statue represents a nude and well-muscled youth, his right arm raised with the fingers curled around as if holding a spherical object, now lost. It has been suggested that the youth is Paris, son of King Priam of Troy, and that he is offering the apple of Eros to Aphrodite in the contest of beauty that was held on Mount Ida in the Troad, judging her the winner over Hera and Athena. If so, this would be the famous statue of Paris made by the renowned sculptor and painter Euphranor, who worked in Athens in the mid-fourth century BC. The ship on which it was found has been dated to the first or second century BC, perhaps a merchant vessel taking works of art from Athens to Rome, wrecked here on this most remote of the Ionian isles. As Waller Rodwell Wright wrote of Antikythera in *Horae Ionicae*:

> Forsaken isle, around thy barren shore
> Wild tempests howl and wintry surges roll!

Kythera (Cerigo): population 3,000; area (not including Antikythera) 277 sq. km; highest peak: Mount Mermigaris (507m); airport: connection to Athens ferries: connections from Diakofti and Kapsali to Neapoli and Gythio in the Peloponnesos, and Kastelli in Crete; in summer there is a hydrofoil service from Diakofti to Piraeus, via Monemvasia, Kyparissi, Leonidi, Porto Heli, Spetse and Hydra.

Appendix 1:
Chronology

(all early dates are approximate)

Palaeolithic period (70,000–40,000 BC): First inhabitants on Corfu, as evidenced by finds in cave on Agios Mattheos.

Mesolithic period (10,000–6000 BC): Flint works on beaches of Cephalonia and Zakynthos.

Neolithic period (6000–3000 BC): Settlement on Corfu (late seventh millennium BC) at Sidari.

Bronze Age (3000–1150 BC): Settlements on Corfu at Kephali, Aphionas and Ermones. Influx of settlers from Asia Minor on all of the other islands. Trading colony established on Kythera by Minoans from Crete (2000–1550 BC). First Greek-speaking people arrive during the Mycenaean period (1500–1150 BC).

Dark Ages (1150–750 BC): Phoenician trading station on Kythera.

Archaic period (750–490 BC): Corinthians found colonies on Kerkyra (733 BC) and Lefkas (625 BC).

Classical period (490–336 BC): Lefkas contributes contingent to Greek fleet that defeated the Persians at Salamis (480 BC). Lefkadians and Cephalonians fight alongside Greek allies in victory over Persians at Plataea (479 BC). Civil war in Kerkyra during fourth year of the Peloponnesian War (427 BC).

Hellenistic Period (336–146 BC): Alexander the Great becomes ruler of Greece (336 BC). After death of Alexander in 323 BC Ionian Islands become part of Macedonia. Kerkyra captured by Queen Teuta of the Illyrians (229 BC). Romans defeat Illyrians and Kerkyra becomes a

Roman colony. Other Ionian Islands fall to Romans during their war with Philip V of Macedon (reigned 200–188 BC).

Roman period (146 BC – AD 330): Ionian Islands became part of the Roman province of Macedonia in 146 BC.

Byzantine period (330–1207): Constantine the Great shifts capital of the Roman Empire to Constantinople (330). Ionian Islands become province of Byzantine Empire. Christianity comes to the Ionian Islands (fourth century). Islands left undefended against corsair raids. Normans capture Kerkyra (1081). Norman Admiral Margaritone takes possession of Ithaka, Cephalonia and Zakynthos (Zante) (1187). On death of Margaritone in 1194 his possessions pass to Matthew Orsini, founder of County Palatine of Cephalonia. Latin knights of Fourth Crusade and Venetians capture Constantinople (1204). Latins divide up the possessions of the Byzantine Empire, with the Greek islands given to Venice.

Venetian period (1207–1797): Venetians take Kerkyra (1207), which in 1214 is recaptured by Byzantines. Other Latin rulers control the various Ionian isles before Venice re-establishes its control, taking Kythera (Cerigo) (1309), Kerkyra (Corfu) (1386), Zakynthos (Zante) (1482), Cephalonia (1500), Lefkas (Santa Maura) (1502) and Ithaka (1503). Constantinople falls to the Ottoman Turks in 1453, ending the Byzantine Empire. Turkish attacks on the Ionian Islands, some of which were under Ottoman occupation for a time: Lefkas (1479–1502, 1503–1684, 1716–1797), Ithaka (1479–1503), Cephalonia (1479–1481, 1485–1500), Zakynthos (1479–1481), Kythera (1714–1718). Venice falls to Napoleon in 1797, ending Venetian rule on the Ionian Islands.

Modern period: Ionian Islands held by the French Republic (1797–1799), Russia (1798–1807) and the French Empire (1807–1814), before being taken by the British in the years 1809–1814. British protectorate of the Ionian Islands (1815–1864). Founding of Greek Kingdom (1833). Ionian Islands become part of Greece (1864). Ionian Islands occupied by Italians and Germans in World War II (1941–1945).

Appendix 2: Festivals (*Paneyeria*)

1 January: Agios Vassilios

6 January: Epiphany

7 January: Agios Ioannis Prodromos (St John the Baptist)

18 January: Agios Athanasios

30 January: Treis Ierarchai (the Three Fathers: SS Basil, Gregory and John Chrysostomos)

1 February: Agios Tryphon

2 February: Ipapantis (Candelmas)

3 February: Agios Spyridon

10 February: Agios Haralambos

11 February: Agia Theodora

25 March: Evangelismos Theotokou (Annunciation of the Virgin Mother of God)

23 April: Agios Giorgios

3 May: Agia Mavra

8 May: Agioi Anargyroi (SS Cosmas and Damianos); Agios Ioannis Theologos; Agios Arsenios

12 May: Agios Theodoros of Kythera

20 May: Agios Thalaleos

21 May: Agioi Constantinos and Eleni

15 June: Agia Triada (the Holy Trinity)

23 June: Agios Ioannis Theologos

24 June: Birthday of St John the Baptist

29 June: Agioi Petros and Pavlos

30 June: Agioi Apostoloi (the Holy Apostles)

7 July: Agia Kyriaki

17 July: Agia Marina

20 July: Agios Profitis Ilias

15 July: Agia Anna

26 July: Agia Paraskevi

27 July: Agios Pandelimon

1 August: Agia Elesa

6 August: Metamorphosis tou Sotiros (Metamorphosis of the Saviour)

9 August: Agios Mattheos

15 August: Koimisis tis Theotokou (Dormition of the Virgin Mother of God)

16 August: Agios Gerassimos

25 August: Agios Dionysios

27 August: Agios Phanourios

29 August: Beheading of St John the Baptist

1 September: Agios Simeon

8 September: Gennesis tis Theotokou (Birth of the Virgin Mother of God)

14 September: Exaltation of the Cross

16 September: Agia Efimia

25 September: Agioi Anargyroi; Agios Ioannis Theologos

20 October: Agios Gerassimos

26 October: Agios Artemios; Agios Dimitrios

8 November: Taxiarchoi (the Archangels Michael and Gabriel)

11 November: Agios Menas

21 November: Isodia tis Theotokou (Presentation of the Virgin)

25 November: Agia Ekaterini

30 November: Agios Andreas

4 December: Agia Barbara

6 December: Agios Nikolaos

12 December: Agios Spyridon

17 December: Agios Dionysios

21 December: Isodia tis Panagia

25 December: Christmas

26 December: Agios Stephanos Protomartyr

Apokreas (Carnival): the three weeks before Lent

Cheese Week: the last week of Carnival

Kathara Deftera (Clean Monday): the first day of Lent

Agioi Theodoroi: the first Saturday in Lent

Panagia Zoodochos Pigi (Our Lady of the Life-giving Spring): the Friday
    after Easter
Analypsis (Ascension): 40 days after Easter
Pentecost (Whit Sunday): the seventh Sunday after Easter
Agia Triada (the Holy Trinity): the seventh Monday after Easter

Appendix 3:
Bibliography

Aeschylus, *Plays and Fragments*, tran. Herbert Weir Smyth, 2 vols, Cambridge, Mass., 1959–1963

Alevizos, Susan, and Ted Alevizos, *Folk Songs of Greece*, New York, 1968

Ansted, D. T., *The Ionian Islands in the year 1863*, London, 1863

Apollonius Rhodius, *Argonautica (The Voyage of Argo)*, translated by E. V. Rieu, Harmondsworth, 1959

Burn, A. R., *The Pelican History of Greece*, Harmondsworth, 1966

Byron, George Gordon (Lord), *The Works of Lord Byron, Letters and Journals*, vol. VI, London, 1901

Byron, George Gordon, *Childe Harold's Pilgrimage*, ed. Samul C. Chew, Cambridge, ca. 1936

Cavafy, Constantin, *The Poems*, translated by John Mavrogordato, London, 1951

Chandler, Richard, *Travels in Greece*, Oxford, 1776

Chesterton, G.K., *Essay, Stories, Plays and Other Writings*, ed. Raymond T. Bond, Garden City, Long Island, 1960

Davy, J., *Notes and Observations on the Ionian Islands and Malta*, London, 1842

Durrell, Gerald, *My Family and Other Animals*, London, 1956

Durrell, Lawrence, *Prospero's Cell*, London, 1945

Finlay, G., *The History of Greece under Ottoman and Venetian Domination*, London, 1856

Foss, Arthur, *The Ionian Islands*, London, 1969

Gell, W., *The Geography and Antiquities of Ithaca*, London, 1807

Hammond, N. G. L., *A History of Greece to 322 BC*, Oxford, 1965

Haslip, Joan, *The Lonely Empress: A Biography of Elizabeth of Austria*, 1965

Herodotus, *The Histories*, translated by Aubrey de Selincourt, Harmondsworth, 1972

Hesiod, *Theogony*, translated by Dorothea Wender, Harmondsworth, 1973

Homer, *The Iliad*, translated by Richmond Lattimore, Chicago, 1951

Homer, *The Odyssey*, translated by Richmond Lattimore, New York, 1965

Jervis, H. J.-W., *History of the Islands of Corfu and the Republic of the Ionian Islands*, London, 1852

Kendrick, T. T. C., *The Ionian Islands: Manners and Customs; Sketches of Ancient History*, London, 1822

Kirkwall, Viscount, *Four Years on the Ionian Islands. Their Political and Social Condition, with a History of the British Protectorate*, vol. II, London, 1864

Lane, Frederic C., *Venice: A Maritime Republic*, Baltimore, 1973

Lattimore, Richmond, *Greek Lyrics*, 2nd edition, London, 1960

Leake, William Martin, *Travels in Northern Greece*, vol. III, 1835

Lear, Edward, *Letters of Edward Lear*, ed. Lady Strachey, London, 1907

Lithgow, William, *The Rare Adventures and Painefull Peregrinations*, London, 1632

MacPherson, Donald, *Melodies from the Gaelic*, London, 1824

Megas, George A., *Greek Calendar Customs*, Athens, 1963

Meinardus, Otto F. A., *The Saints of Greece*, Athens, 1970

Miller, William, *The Latins in the Levant: A History of Frankish Greece (1204–1261)*, London, 1908

Milton, John, *Milton's Ode on the Morning of Christ's Nativity*, Cambridge, 1931

Moore, Thomas, *The Poetical Works*, ed. A.D. Godley, London, ca. 1900

Napier, Charles James, *The Colonies: treating of their value generally – of the Ionian Islands in particular…*, London, 1833

Napier, W. P. F., *The Life and Opinions of Charles James Napier*, vol. 1, London, 1857

Nicolson, Harold, *Byron: The Last Journey*, London, 1924

Ostrogorsky, George, *A History of the Byzantine State*, translated by Joan Hussey, Oxford, 1956

Pausanias, *Guide to Greece*, 2 vols, translated by Peter Levi, Harmondsworth, 1971

Petrides, Theodore, and Elfeida Petrides, *Folk Dances of the Greeks*, New York, 1961

Petris, Tassos N., *Cephalonia, History, Art, Folklore, Routes*, Athens, 1985
    Zakynthos, History, Art, Folklore, Routes, Athens, no date

Petrocheilou, Anna, *The Greek Caves*, Athens, 1984

Philippides, Dimitri, *Greek Traditional Architecture*, vol. I, Athens, 1983

Plutarch, *Moralia*, 'Why the Oracles Fail to Give Answers', translated by
    R. Midgley, London, 1870

Pouqueville, Francis, *Travels in the Morea…*, London, 1813

Pratt, Michael, *Britain's Greek Empire; Reflections on the History of the
    Ionian Islands from the Fall of Byzantium*, London, 1978

Pym, Hilary, *Songs of Greece*, London, 1968

Rochford, Noel, *Landscapes of Corfu*, London, 1987

Sands, Martin, J. S., *Paxos Walking and Wild Flowers*, Walton-on-
    Thames, 1980

Schliemann, Heinrich, *Ithaque, la Peloponnese et Troie*, Paris, 1869

Sitwell, Sacheverell, *Great Palaces*, Feltham, 1969

Stoneman, Richard, *A Literary Companion to Travel in Greece*,
    Harmondsworth, 1984

Strabo, *The Geography*, translated by H. L. Jones, vols III, V, London,
    1924, 1928

Tataki, A. B., *Corfu, History – Monuments – Museums*, Athens, 1980

Theocritus, *The Idylls of Theocritus*, translated by Thelma Sargent, New
    York and London, 1982

Thucydides, *History of the Peloponnesian War*, translated by Rex Warner,
    Harmondsworth, 1954

Trelawny, E. J., *Records of Shelley, Byron and the Author*, London, 1857–1878

Wheeler, William, *The Letters of Private Wheeler*, London, 1962

Wheler, George, *Journey*, London, 1682

Woodhouse, C. M., *Modern Greece: A Short History*, 4th edition,
    London, 1986

Wright, Waller Rodwell, *Horae Ionicae*, London, 1809

Young, Martin, *Corfu and the other Ionian Islands*, London, 1981

Appendix 4: Glossary

acropolis: the fortified upper part of a Greek city
Agia: female saint or 'Holy'
agiasma: holy well or spring
Agios (pl. Agioi): male saint or 'Holy'
agora: marketplace; the civic centre of an ancient Greek city
akri: cape or peninsula
apano: up, upper
ashlar: hewn or squared stone
bema: the part of a Greek church containing the altar
capital: the uppermost member of a column
Chora: the principal town of an island
chorio: village
ciborium: a canopy, usually supported on four columns, covering an altar
demarcheion: town hall
Doric: an order of ancient Greek architecture
ex-voto: a votive offering
heroon: shrine of a deified hero
icon: religious picture
iconostasis: screen on which icons are placed in a Greek church
Ionic: order of ancient Greek architecture
kafenion: coffee house
kastro: a castle, fortress or fortified town
katholikon: central church of a monastery
kato: below, lower
metochion: possession of a monastery

mezedes: hors d'oeuvre

Minoan: civilisation that developed in Crete during the Bronze Age, named
    for the legendary King Minos

moni: monastery or convent

Mycenaean: civilisation that developed in Greece during the late Bronze
    Age, named for the city of Mycenae

narthex: the vestibule of a Greek church

necropolis: the cemetery of an ancient Greek city

nisiotika tragoudia: songs of the Greek islands

nisos (pl. nisoi): island

odos: street

Panagia: the Virgin Mary

paneyeri (pl. paneyeria): religious festival

paralia: waterfront promenade

pigi: spring or well

platanos: plane tree

plateia: town square

portico: an arcaded walkway

pyrgos (pl. pyrgoi): watchtower, fortified monastery or mansion

stoa: colonnaded walkway

vouno: mountain

Index

Adam, Sir Frederick 17, 36, 61, 69, 83, 223
Aeschylus 10
Alcman of Sparta 207–208
Alexander the Great 11, 233
Alexius I Comnenus, Emperor 72
Ali Pasha of Tebelen 55, 89, 112, 113
Ansted, D.T. 56, 90, 106, 109–110, 121, 122–123, 162, 165–166, 181–182, 190, 191
Antikythera (Cerigotto) 207, 214, 229–231
Antipaxos 95–96
Antony, Mark 90
Aphrodite 207–208, 213
Aristotle 209

Barbarossa, Admiral 214, 226
Baudelaire, Charles 229
Benton, Sylvia 210–211
Beyazit II, Sultan 105, 106

Bohemund, Count 72
Bounialis, Emanuel Tzane 34, 41, 42, 43, 45, 59, 184
Britain, British 15, 16, 17, 18, 31, 32, 34, 35, 36, 37, 90, 91, 105, 150–151, 234
Byron, Lord 119, 131–132, 134, 152, 153, 161

Caesar, Julius 213
Calvos, Andreas 182, 185, 187
Capodistrias, Count John 3, 16, 17, 18, 36, 40, 49, 56, 112, 113
Carantinos, Andreas 160
Cavafy, Constantin 127, 145–146
Cephalonia 1, 3, 7, 8, 9, 11, 12, 13, 17, 149–175, 233, 234
Chandler, Richard 180–181
Charles of Anjou, King 13
Chesterton, G.K. 128
Chronis, Ioannis 45, 46

Cicero 72, 288
Cleopatra 90
Comnena, Princess Maria
    103, 111
Constantine the Great,
    Emperor 12, 234
Corfu (Kerkyra) 1, 10, 11, 12,
    13, 14, 16, 17, 18, 27–53,
    55–65, 67–86, 233, 234
Corfu Town 18, 27–53
Cyriacus of Ancona 215

Damaskinos, Michael 33, 41,
    43, 59, 62, 189
Dandolo, Doge Enrico 13
Daulphinios, Nicholas 215–
    216
Davy, John 95, 96, 97, 150,
    151, 191–192, 195, 196,
    197, 198, 199, 200, 201,
    202, 221–222, 222–223
Dionysios, Agios (Saint) 180,
    185–186, 192, 198
Dörpfeld, Wilhelm 113–114,
    118
Doxaras, Nikolaos 185, 186
Douglas, Sir Howard 57
Durrell, Gerald 85
Durrell, Lawrence 27, 52, 68,
    71, 76–77

Echinades 9, 127–128
Eudaemonoyanidis dynasty
    213, 225
Elizabeth of Austria, Empress
    84

Fenelon 217, 228
Foscolo, Ugo 182, 185, 203
Foss, Arthur 174
France, French 15, 16, 18, 31,
    234

Gedik Ahmet Pasha 104
Gell, Sir William 131, 132, 138
George I, King of Hellenes 18
Gerasimos, Agios (Saint)
    161–163, 199
Germans 18, 38, 45, 234
Gladstone, William 90–91
Guilford, Lord 36–37
Guiscard, Robert 12, 72,
    172–173
Guylforde, Sir Richard 215

Haralambos, Agios (Saint)
    94
Hearn, Lefcadio 107
Herodotus 129, 208, 228
Hesiod 10, 192, 208
Homer 3, 9, 22, 28, 63, 74, 75,
    76, 80, 85, 112, 114, 115,
    129–130, 132, 134, 135,
    137, 138–139, 141, 143,
    145, 149, 179

Ithaka (Ithaki) 1, 7, 8, 9, 11,
    13, 74, 75, 76, 127–146,
    234

Jason 10, 65
Jervis, H.J.-W. 52, 64–65
Jews 51–53, 105, 106

John VIII Palaeologos,
Emperor 50
Judas Iscariot 52–53

Kanoni peninsula 32, 55–65
Kara Mustafa Pasha 30
Kennedy Onassis, Jacqueline
114
Kilich Ali Pasha 78, 128
Kirkwall, Viscount 35, 90
Kolokotronis 189
Koutouzis, Nikolaos 185, 186,
202
Kythera (Cerigo) 1, 3, 7, 8, 10,
11, 13, 31, 207–231, 233,
234

Lane-Poole, Stanley 103
Lear, Edward 23, 35, 36, 40,
41, 47, 62, 63–64, 79, 86,
202–203
Leake, William Martin 106,
110, 129, 130–131,
135–136, 142, 143, 152,
156, 157–158, 167–168,
173, 211, 212, 214, 218,
225
Lefkas (Leucadia, Lefkada,
Santa Maura) 1, 7, 13, 15,
31, 103–123, 233, 234
Lithgow, William 217–218
Lombardos, Emanuel 33
Lowell, Robert 229

MacPhail, John 220, 221
MacPherson, Donald 142

Maitland, Sir Thomas 16, 17,
32, 34, 36, 37
Margaritone, Admiral 12, 234
Mary Magdalene 200
Medea 10, 65
Megas, George 93, 116–117
Mehmet II, Sultan 14
Miller, William 104
Milton, John 98
Moore, Thomas 119
Morosini, Doge Francesco
46, 104, 108, 121

Napier, Sir Charles 17, 37, 61,
150, 151, 155, 156
Napoleon 15, 154, 234
Nero, Emperor 72
Nerval, Gerard de 228–229
Nicholson, Sir Harold
160–161
Nicholson, Nigel 32
Nur Banu, Sultana 70–71

Odysseus 2, 3, 9, 28, 63, 74–
75, 80, 112, 114, 129–130,
131, 132, 133, 134, 135,
137, 138, 139, 141, 143,
145, 149
Onassis, Aristotle 92, 114
Orsini, John I 103, 110, 111
Orsini, Matthew 12, 234
Othoni, 27–28

Palaeologos, Catherine 60
Palaeologos, Empress Helena
104, 122

Palaeologos, Tsarina Sophia
    60, 104
Palaeologos, Thomas 60,
    104
Palamas, Kostis 2
Pausanias 209, 210, 211,
    228
Paxos (Paxoi) 1, 3, 7, 89–99
Philip V of Macedon, King
    12
Philip, Prince, the Duke of
    Edinburgh 61
Poulakis, Theodore 34, 56, 73,
    80
Pouqueville, Francis 217
Plutarch 97–99, 187–188

Robert of Taranto, Count
    13
Russians 15, 16, 18, 55, 67,
    112

Sappho 118, 119
Schliemann, Heinrich
    133, 137, 138–139, 209,
    227
Schulenburg, Count Matthias
    von der 30, 31, 37, 50,
    105
Seaton, Lord 18
Sikelianos, Angelos 107
Solomos, Dionysios 3, 39,
    182–183, 185, 187
Sphrantzes, George 59–60
Spyridon, Agios (Saint) 18,
    31, 37, 43–44

Storks, Sir Henry 18, 38
Strabo 118, 119, 129, 130

Theocritus 188
Theodora, Agia (Saint)
    43
Theodore, Osios (Holy)
    226–227
Theotoki, Baron 34–35
Thucydides 11, 83, 129, 209,
    211
Tiberius, Emperor 72
Tocco dynasty 13, 103, 104
Trelawny, E. J. 132, 152, 153
Turks 14, 15, 30, 31, 55, 67,
    73, 78, 104, 106, 130, 179,
    214, 234

Valaoritis, Aristotelis 107,
    108–109, 114
Venice, Venetians 13, 14, 15,
    30, 38, 46, 50, 51, 60, 72,
    73, 77–78, 104, 130, 159,
    179, 183–184, 213, 214,
    234
Venieri, Marco 213
Venieri dynasty 213
Victoria, Queen 18
Vido 67
Virgil 28–29

Watteau 217, 228
Wheeler, Private William
    34–35
Wheler, George 106, 180,
    188, 216–217